Charles Fort's
WILD TALENTS

This edition published by John Brown Publishing Ltd.
The New Boathouse, 136-142 Bramley Road, London W10 6SR

Distributed in Canada and the United States of America by
the INFO Research Library,
Box 220, Wolfe Island, Ontario, K0H 2Y0, Canada

Enquiries should be sent to *Fortean Times* magazine at
PO Box 2409, London NW5 4NP, UK

British Library Cataloguing in Publication Data available.
ISBN 1-870870-298

Printed in Great Britain by
Redwood Books, Trowbridge, Wilts.

WILD TALENTS

Charles Hoy Fort

Revised by X

Introduction by Michel Meurger

John Brown Publishing
London 1998

A NOTE ON THIS EDITION

This is the first wholly new edition of *Wild Talents* for 66 years. It is also, as far as known, the first paperback edition since that published by Ace Books (N.Y., 1972). While that edition reprinted the text from the collected edition of Fort's works (Henry Holt & Co., N.Y., 1941; reprinted Dover Publications, Inc., 1974), which was edited by Tiffany Thayer for his Fortean Society and contains many of his own interventions, the text of this Fortean Times edition, if so it may be called, is based on the first edition, published in hardback by Claude H. Kendall of New York in 1932.

Special thanks must go to the Canadian scholar of Fort's works, Mr X, whose contribution to this edition makes it a landmark in Fortean publishing. He has devoted years to the rediscovery of Fort's source material and has applied his considerable experience to the preparation of this text, restoring lines that were missing or corrupt, correcting typographical and other errors and standardising the chaotic citation of references. I have added an index.

While there has been some correction of factual errors and expansions of Fort's occasionally vague references, these have largely been left to Mr X's work in progress – a definitive and annotated edition for scholars and purists. In this project, Mr X (his legal name) deserves the admiration and thanks of all Forteans.

The cover is a detail from a collage by Max Ernst.

Fort's first three books, *The Book of the Damned, New Lands* and *Lo!* have already been published in this series (1995, 1996 and 1997) in uniform editions.

SM

INTRODUCTION

UNDEVELOPED MAGICIANS

> "I think, therefore I jaunte"
> Alfred Bester: *Tiger! Tiger!*

Wild Talents is Charles Fort's final book. As such, it may be considered as his intellectual testament. Furthermore, one can find a thematic unity in it lacking in preceding works. Indeed, *Wild Talents* is mainly a study about witchcraft. But Fort gives to this word a very specific interpretation, meaning not a fixed set of beliefs, or a cult, but a loose aggregate of psychic powers, including the faculty to project images or objects, to inflict wounds from a distance, or to set a house afire by mental volition. The agents producing such frightening manifestations are no discarnate entities but "undeveloped magicians", mostly youngsters, using their extraordinary abilities as symbolic expressions of long repressed feelings.

It would be dishonest to stigmatize Fort as an advocate of superstition, trying to lay the intellectual foundations of a modern witch hunt. For him, "wild talents" were conceived as primarily neutral, and he even imagines a socially integrated witchcraft of the future.

In different parts of the book, the author ponders on the origin of such powers, interpreting fire agents as "the most valuable members of a savage community". Thus, fire agents and werewolves my be considered as "atavistic persons", both biological relics and "insurances" against times of massive reversions. Fort establishes a crucial distinction between an "external witchcraft" where the agent's mind may affect the bodies of other persons, and an "internal" one, where the agent can affect his own body. Stigmatic girls are classified in this last category. While maintaining a strong conceptual autonomy, *Wild Talents* dovetails harmoniously with other books by Fort. Thus, in *Lo!* (chapter IV) the author had already given a full definition of his concept of "teleportation", and made use of it to tentatively explain many phenomena, including bombardments of stones. He also adds that this talent may be directed towards positive or criminal ends. In the same chapter, Fort offers his suggestion as to the relationship between children and psychic manifestations. In earlier times, such powers were more necessary to help human groups than they are now, "and that, wherein children are atavistic, they may be in rapport with forces that mostly human beings have outgrown".

In both *Lo!* and *Wild Talents* Fort relates the production of psychic phenomena to a capacity for visualizing, helping the agent to project images or objects on a precise place. Fort's speculations need to be understood within the context of the times in which they were written. During the thirties, some concepts, elaborated in the preceding century, were still dominant, such as purported similarities between youngsters and primitives, social survivals equated with vestigial structures in the human body, and psychic phenomena treated as reversions towards a more archaic stage of evolution. One may also find some affinities between Fort's idea of magic visualization and the visual eidetism described by German psychologist Erich Jaensch (1883-1940).

One has also to take account of the influence of the so-called "law of recapitulation" on a wide number of scientific as well as cultural issues. According to German biologist Ernst Haeckel (1834-1919) ontogenesis recapitulated phylogenesis: the individual, in the history of his foetal development, has to pass through the same stages as the whole species. Haeckel was thinking in biological terms. But his model was soon extended to present an evolutionary model for the psychic unfolding of the individual as well. Through the various phases of his mental development, the child was considered to replay the psychical dispositions of his ancestors. Works appeared, stressing alleged mental similarities between babies and monkeys, boys and savages. Sometimes, this development stopped at a specific stage; for instance, the influential criminal anthropologist Cesare Lombroso described the "born criminal" as someone "frozen" in adult life at the infantile or savage stage. The deviant is not only stamped with the psychological stigmata of the primitive; his body is also marked with morphological signs betraying him as a throwback to a simian past. Scientists discovered other atavistic persons lurking in the midst of civilized society. Under Haeckel's influence, Freud saw neurotics as people arrested at the stage of savagery; the founder of psychoanalysis also considered psychic phenomena from the angle of atavism. He speculated that telepathy may represent a vestigial form of a primitive mode of communication, replaced by speech. One can even proceed further along the same lines: since *all* children had to pass through a savage phase, and since for the anthroplogist, savages were assimilated to modern primitives, then the magical thinking ascribed to primitives may be a common attribute of young persons, alongside some remnants of the extraordinary abilities once possessed by our forebears. One can therefore find an explanation for the fact, observed by many psychic researchers, that poltergeist phenomena are often children-centered.

Fort's system of natural witchcraft thus appears as an extension and a radicalized version of the recapitulationist world-view. The author of *Wild*

Talents aims in this direction in a passage of chapter XIII where, after mention of "atavistic persons in society", he alludes to "vestigial organs" in human bodies, meaning the rudimentary tail of some human beings, categorized not only as a "relic" but also as an "insurance" against times of collective reversions, "when back to the furry state we may go". Fort interprets the episode of the gorilla from Long Island as an individual case in the same process of devolution (chapter X). In his seminal work, *The Descent of Man* (1871), Charles Darwin had already set the stage, describing reversion as a natural phenomenon; he linked the descent of man to a "hairy, tailed quadruped". According to him, modern man was liable to reversion towards lower animals. Victorian treatises and periodicals never tired of showing pictures of tailed babies, or tailed and hairy adults, presented as living proofs of the law of reversion. Through the cultural absorption of Darwinism, literature, art and thought became imbued with representations of furry missing links and atavistic throwbacks. In 1932, this whole ideological background helped a reader of *Wild Talents* to relish Fort's caricatures of the loftiest ratiocinations of the recapitulationists. The tongue-in-cheek description of the Long Island citizen unsatisfied with nudism and reverting to the ape-man stage still lingering in his mind, our putative reader might enter the next movie theatre, to see the transformation scene from *Dr Jekyll and Mr Hyde*, where Frederic March turns from a civilized man into a brutish double of the Neanderthal of popular imagery.

Viewed in this context, Fort's book appears as a very personal answer to general questions. Some ideas expressed in *Wild Talents* are supra-individual concepts readapted by the author. Thus, in 1926, French psychic researcher Gustave Geley (1868-1924) had already presented witches as persons gifted with paranormal talents. Still better, one can find in the first novel by the Italian writer Giovanni Papini (1881-1956), some jocular definitions of magic. In *Gog*, published around the same time as *Wild Talents*, Papini's eponymous hero meets Sir James Frazer, and the British scholar declares to him that modern civilization being the "lawful daughter" of magic, intellectuals are no more than "evolved sorcerers". Thinking about the "cultivation" of wild talents, Fort envisions a future world where human telepaths are concentrating upon the running of motors (chap. XXVII). Papini too, imagines the harness of psychic powers in an institute using various mediumistic specializations. Telepaths replace telegraphists and run motors, while ectoplasms are sold as ghostly servants. On a more serious level, many of the phenomena studied by Fort were still discussed among psychic circles around 1930.

The sum of half a century of investigation, the monumental *Encyclopedia of Psychic Science* (1934) by the psychoanalyst Nandor Fodor includes entries on "Lycanthropy" and "Vampire". About "Transportation" (teleportation), Fodor says that "it is a comparatively rare but fairly well authenticated occurence" [1]. Few parapsychologists will today endorse such a statement. We are living in quite a different context, and I am convinced that many readers will subscribe to Lyons and Truzzi's dictum that the validity of psi: "cannot be established or dismissed beyond a reasonable doubt" [2].

Yet, this will hardly bother the true Fortean. Fort himself, as a relativist, was not trying to sell us certainties, or bargain with the gullible over were-wolves' skins and the techno-kits of poltergeist girls. He cannot be portrayed either as a fellow traveller of spiritualists or as one of the founding fathers of parapsychology. He was rather testing his wild talents like a science fiction writer, picking up a theme, granting it a quotient of speculative probability, and studying the consequences of its interaction with the natural world. Hence Fort's influence on science fiction. Take for example Bester's *Tiger! Tiger!* (1956), where a researcher named Charles Fort Jaunte (!) discovers the ability to move oneself from one place to an other by the power of the mind. Bester follows Fort's definitions closely when showing the need for self-preservation as a motive behind "jaunting". In *Wild Talents* (chapter XVI), Fort wrote about teleportation that "a common knowledge may be developed to enormous advantage in commercial and recreational and explorative transportations". In Bester's novel, such hints are worked out.

But it would be too short-sighted to limit Fort's approach to wild talents to exercises in speculation. For him, fire-raising capacities, stone throwing and dowsing are likewise philosophical "exempla", demonstrative tools to help his reader grasp a world of Oneness, where, as in fairy tales, wishes are realized, with hilarious and terrible consequences. A world built for a Fortean Alice, eager to "bridge the gap between the subjective and the objective".

In some aspects, Fort's philosophy seems to present affinities with Para-celsianism; both are primarily systems of "correlative thinking" [3]. Further-more, in the doctrine of the Macrocosm and Microcosm, a cardinal principle of Paracelsianism, universe and mankind constantly interact. Every reader of *Lo!* or *Wild Talents* will easily find parallels in the concept of an "Homo Forteaniensis" linked to the cosmos by a web of complex relations. Again, one can also find striking analogies between the Fortean "wisher" of a "new era" who harnesses psychic energies in a way beneficial to mankind, and the Renaissance magus, controlling sympathies and antipathies.

Yet, the Paracelsian Prospero tried to master the *supernatural* forces while Fort insists on the *natural* character of the talents he wanted to cultivate. Notwithstanding this major difference, the Fortean "transmediumizer" and the Renaissance magus share the same Faustian impulse to operate on all levels of creation.

For a deeply religious man like the British writer Arthur Machen, magic was evil, and trying to give an example of a world fiendishly turned upside down, he referred to a short story by Guy de Maupassant, where items of furniture "move in procession" [4]. In sharp contrast with such fear of the unusual, Fort declared once that the one great ambition of his life would be to say to chairs and tables "Fall in! forward! march!" and have them obey him (*Wild Talents*, chap. XXVII). Here, we have two opposed world-views. According to Machen, man is a tool of demoniac forces, and may achieve salvation only through religion. In Fort's cosmogony instead, man may better his status through knowledge and mastery of natural forces.

Forteanism is deeply optimistic. In an inclusive world there is a place for all: wise men, fools and batteries of poltergeist girls.

Michel Meurger

1 - Nandor Fodor: *Encyclopedia of Psychic Science.* London: Arthurs Press, 1934, p.392.
2 - Arthur Lyons and Marcello Truzzi: *The Blue Sense.* New York: Warner Books, 1991, p.286.
3 - Joseph Needham forged this expression to characterize Chinese organic naturalism. See J. Needham: *Science and Civilisation in China.* Cambridge University Press, 1956, vol.2, p.504.
4 - Arthur Machen: *The White People* (1899). – Guy de Maupassant: *Qui sait?* [Who knows?] (1890).

CHAPTER 1

You know, I can only surmise about this – but John Henry Sanders, of 75 Colville Street, Derby, England, was the proprietor of a fish store, and I think that it was a small business. His wife helped. When I read of helpful wives, I take it that that means that husbands haven't large businesses. If Mrs. Sanders went about, shedding scales in her intercourses, I deduce that theirs wasn't much of a fish business.

Upon the evening of March 4th, 1905, in the Sanders' home, in one of the bedrooms, there was a fire. Nobody was at home, and the firemen had to break in. There was no fireplace in the bedroom. Not a trace of anything by which to explain was found, and the firemen reported: "Origin unknown." They returned to their station and were immediately called back to this house. There was another fire. It was in the housemaid's bedroom. Again – "Origin unknown."

The Sanders, in their fish store, were notified, and they hastened home. Money was missed. Many things were missed. The housemaid, Emma Piggot, was suspected. In her parents' home was found a box, from which the Sanders' took, and identified as theirs, £5, and a loot of such things as a carving set, sugar tongs, table cloths, several handkerchiefs, salt spoons, bottles of scent, curtain hooks, a hair brush, Turkish towels, gloves, a sponge, two watches, a puff box.

The girl was arrested, and in the Derby Borough Police Court, she was charged with arson and larceny. She admitted the thefts, but asserted her innocence of the fires. There was clearly such an appearance of relation between the thefts and the fires, which, if they had burned down the house, would have covered the thefts, that both charges were pressed.

It is not only that there had been thefts, and then fires: so many things had been stolen that – unless the home of the Sanders was a large household – some of these things would have been missed – unless all had been stolen at once. I have no datum for thinking that the Sanders lived upon any such scale as one in which valuables could have been stolen, from time to time, unknown to them. The indications were of one wide grab, and the girl's intention to set the house afire, to cover it.

Emma Piggot's lawyer showed that she had been nowhere near the house, at the time of the first fire; and that, when the second fire broke out, she, in the street, this off-evening of hers, returning, had called the attention of neighbours to smoke coming from a window. The case was too complicated

1

for a police court, and was put off for the summer assizes (*Derby Mercury*, March 8, 15, and 22, 1905).

Derby Mercury (July 19) – trial of the girl resumed. The prosecution maintained that the fires could be explained only as of incendiary origin, and that the girl's motive for setting the house afire was plain, and that she had plundered so recklessly, because she had planned a general destruction, by which anything missing would be accounted for.

Again counsel for the defence showed that the girl could not have started the fires. The charge of arson was dropped. Emma Piggot was sentenced to six months' hard labour, for the thefts.

Upon Dec. 2, 1919, Ambrose Small, of Toronto, Canada, disappeared. He was known to have been in his office, in the Toronto Grand Theater, of which he was the owner, between five and six o'clock, the evening of Dec. 2nd. Nobody saw him leave his office. Nobody – at least nobody whose testimony can be accepted – saw him, this evening, outside the building. There were stories of a woman in the case. But Ambrose Small disappeared and left more than a million dollars behind.

Then John Doughty, Small's secretary, vanished.

Small's safe deposit boxes were opened by Mrs. Small and other trustees of the estate. In the boxes were securities, valued at $1,125,000. An inventory was found. According to it, the sum of $105,000 was missing. There was an investigation, and bonds of the value of $105,000 were found, hidden in the home of Doughty's sister.

All over the world, the disappearance of Ambrose Small was advertised, with offers of reward, in acres of newspaper space. He was in his office. He vanished.

Doughty, too, was sought. He had not only vanished: he had done all that he could to be unfindable. But he was traced to a town in Oregon, where he was living under the name of Cooper. He was taken back to Toronto, where he was indicted, charged with having stolen the bonds, and with having abducted Small, to cover the thefts.

It was the contention of the prosecution that Ambrose Small, wealthy, in good health, and with no known troubles of any importance, had no motive to vanish and to leave $1,125,000 behind, but that his secretary, the embezzler, did have a motive for abducting him. The prosecution did not charge Small had been soundlessly and invisibly picked out of his office, where he was surrounded by assistants. The attempt was to show that he had left his office, even though nobody had seen him go: thinkably he could have been abducted, unwitnessed, in a street. A newsboy testified that he had seen Small, in a nearby street, between 5 and 6 o'clock, evening of Dec. 2nd, but the boy's father contradicted this story. Another newsboy told that, upon this evening, after 6 o'clock, Small had bought a newspaper from him: but, under examination, this boy admitted he was not sure of the date.

It seemed clear that there was relation between the embezzlement and the disappearance, which, were it not for the inventory, would have covered the thefts; but the accusation of abduction failed. Doughty was found guilty of embezzlement and was sentenced to six years' imprisonment in the Kingston Penitentiary.

In the *News of the World* (London; June 6, 1926), there is an account of "strangely intertwined circumstances." In a public place, in the daytime, a man had died. On the footway, outside the Gaiety Theatre, London, Henry Arthur Chappell, the manager of the refreshment department of the Theatre, had been found dead. There was a post-mortem examination by a well-known pathologist, Prof. Piney. The man's skull was fractured. Prof. Piney gave his opinion that, if, because of heart failure, Chappell had fallen backward, the fractured skull might be accounted for; but, he added that, though he had found indications of a slight affection of the heart, it was not such as would be likely to cause fainting.

The indications were that a murder had been committed. The police inquired into the matter and learned that not long before there had been trouble. A girl, Rose Smith, employed at one of the refreshment counters, had been discharged by Chappell. One night she had placed on his doorstep a note telling that she intended to kill herself. Several nights later, she was arrested in Chappell's back garden. She was dressed in a man's clothes and had a knife. Also she carried matches and a bottle of paraffin. Presumably she was bent upon murder and arson, but she was charged with trespassing and was sentenced to two months' hard labour. It was learned that Chappell had died upon the day of this girl's release from prison.

Rose Smith was arrested. Chappell had no other known enemy. Upon the day of this girl's release, he had died.

But the accusation failed. A police inspector testified that, at the time of Chappell's death, Rose Smith had been in the Prisoners' Aid Home.

CHAPTER 2

I am a collector of notes upon subjects that have diversity – such as deviations from concentricity in the lunar crater Copernicus, and a sudden appearance of purple Englishmen – stationary meteor-radiants, and a reported growth of hair on the bald head of a mummy – and "Did the girl swallow the octopus?"

But my liveliest interest is not so much in things, as in relations of things. I have spent much time thinking about the alleged pseudo-relations that are called coincidences. What if some of them should not be coincidences?

Ambrose Small disappeared, and to only one person could be attributed a motive for his disappearance. Only to one person's motives could the fires in the house in Derby be attributed. Only to one person's motives could be attributed the probable murder of Henry Chappell. But, according to the verdicts in all these cases, the meaning of all is of nothing but coincidence between motives and events.

Before I looked into the case of Ambrose Small, I was attracted to it by another seeming coincidence. That there could be any meaning in it seemed so preposterous that, as influenced by much experience, I gave it serious thought. About six years before the disappearance of Ambrose Small, Ambrose Bierce had disappeared. Newspapers all over the world had made much of the mystery of Ambrose Bierce. But what could the disappearance of one Ambrose, in Texas, have to do with the disappearance of another Ambrose, in Canada? Was somebody collecting Ambroses? There was in these questions an appearance of childishness that attracted my respectful attention.

Lloyd's Sunday News (London; June 20, 1920) – that, near the town of Stretton, Leicestershire, had been found the body of a cyclist, Annie Bella Wright. She had been killed by a wound in her head. The correspondent who wrote this story was an illogical fellow, who loaded his story with an unrelated circumstance; or, with a dim suspicion of an unexplained relationship, he noted that in a field, not far from where the body of the girl lay, was found the body of a crow.

In the explanation of *coincidence* there is much of laziness, and helplessness, and response to an instinctive fear that scientific dogma will be endangered. It is a tag, or a label: but of course every tag, or label, fits well enough at times. A while ago, I noted a case of detectives who were searching for a glass-eyed man named Jackson. A Jackson, with a glass eye, was arrested in Boston. But he was not the Jackson they wanted, and pretty soon they got their glass-eyed Jackson, in Philadelphia. I never developed anything out of this item – such as that, if there's a Murphy with a hare lip, in Chicago, there must be another hare-lipped Murphy somewhere else. It would be a comforting idea to optimists, who think that ours is a balanced existence: all that I report is that I haven't confirmed it.

But the body of a girl, and the body of a crow –

And, going over files of newspapers, I came upon this:

The body of a woman, found in the River Dee, near the town of Eccleston (London *Daily Express,* June 12, 1911). And nearby was found the body of another woman. One of these women was a resident of Chester: the other was a visitor from the Isle of Man. They had been unknown to each other. About ten o'clock, morning of June 10th, they had gone out from houses in opposite parts of Chester.

New York American (Oct. 20, 1929) – "Two bodies found in desert mystery." In the Coachella desert, near Indio, California, had been found two dead men, about 100 yards apart. One had been a resident of Coachella, but the other was not identified. "Authorities believed there was no connection between the two deaths."

In the *New York Herald* (Nov. 26, 1911), there is an account of the hanging of three men, for the murder of Sir Edmund Berry Godfrey, on Greenberry Hill, London. The names of the murderers were Green, Berry, and Hill. It does seem that this was only a matter of chance. Still, it may have been no coincidence, but a savage pun mixed with murder. *New York Sun* (Oct. 7, 1930) -- arm of William Lumsden, of Roslyn, Washington, crushed under a tractor. He was the third person, in three generations, in his family, to lose a left arm. This was coincidence, or I shall have to come out, accepting that there may be "curses" on families. But, near the beginning of a book, I don't like to come out so definitely. And we're getting away from our subject, which is *Bodies.*

"Unexplained drownings in Douglas Harbour, Isle of Man." In the London *Daily News* (Aug. 19, 1910), it was said that the bodies of a young man and of a girl had been found in the harbour. They were known as a "young couple," and their drowning would be understandable in terms of a common emotion, were it not that also there was a body of a middle-aged man "not known in any way connected with them."

London *Daily Chronicle* (Sept. 10, 1924) – "Near Saltdean, Sussex, Mr. F. Pender, with two passengers in his sidecar, collided with a post, and all were seriously injured. In a field, by the side of the road, was found the body of a Rodwell shepherd, named Funnell, who had no known relation with the accident."

An occurrence of the 14th of June, 1931, is told of, in the *Home News* (Bronx; June 15). "When Policeman Talbot, of the E. 126th St. station, went into Mt. Morris Park at 10 A.M., yesterday, to awaken a man apparently asleep on a bench near the 124th St. and Madison Ave. gate, he found the man dead. Dr. Patterson, of Harlem Hospital, said that death had probably been caused by heart trouble." *New York Sun* (June 15) – that soon after the finding of this body on the bench, another dead man was found on a bench near by.

I have two stories, which resemble the foregoing stories, but I should like to have them considered together.

In November, 1888, (*St. Louis Globe-Democrat,* Dec. 20, 1888), a resident of Birmingham, Alabama, was murdered, and a local farmer disappeared after selling his produce in the market. In the woods, near Birmingham, was found the body of a stranger. "The Hawes' murder mystery is for a time overlooked, if not forgotten, in this city, and people are now busy with theories of two later mysteries. The body of the man found in the woods near town Monday night still lies unidentified at the undertaking rooms, and this may become a greater mystery than the Hawes crime. No one who has seen the body can remember having seen the man in life, and identification seems impossible. The dead man was evidently a man in good circumstances, if not wealthy, and what he could have been doing at the spot where the body was found is a mystery. Several parties who have seen the body are of the opinion the man was a foreigner. Anyway, he was an entire stranger in this vicinity, and his coming must have been as mysterious as his death."

I noted these circumstances, simply as a mystery. But when a situation repeats, I notice with my livelier interest. This situation is of local murders, and the appearance of the corpse of a stranger, who had not been a tramp.

Philadelphia Public Ledger (Feb. 4, 1892) – murder near Johnstown, Pa. – a man and his wife, named Kring, had been butchered, and their bodies had been burned. Then, in the woods, near Johnstown, the corpse of a stranger was found. The body was well-dressed, but could not be identified. Another body was found – "well-dressed man, who bore no means of identification."

There is a view by which it can be shown, or more or less demonstrated, that there never has been a coincidence. That is, in anything like a final sense. By a coincidence is meant a false appearance, or suggestion, of relations among circumstances. But anybody who accepts that there is an underlying oneness of all things, accepts that there are no utter absences or relations among circumstances –

Or that there are no coincidences, in the sense that there are no real discords in either colours or musical notes –

That any two colours, or sounds, can be harmonised, by intermediately relating them to other colours, or sounds.

And I'd not say that my question, as to what the disappearance of one Ambrose could have to do with the disappearance of another Ambrose, is so senseless. The idea of causing Ambrose Small to disappear may have had origin in somebody's mind, by suggestion from the disappearance of Ambrose Bierce. If in no terms of physical abduction can the disappearance of Ambrose Small be explained, I'll not say that that has any meaning, until the physicists intelligibly define what they mean by physical terms.

CHAPTER 3

In days of yore, when I was an especially bad young one, my punishment was having to go to the store, Saturdays, and work. I had to scrape off labels of other dealers' canned goods and paste on my parent's label. Theoretically, I was so forced to labour to teach me the errors of deceitful ways. A good many brats are brought up, in the straight and narrow, somewhat deviously.

One time I had pyramids of canned goods, containing a variety of fruits and vegetables. But I had used all except peach labels. I pasted peach labels on peach cans and then came to apricots. Well, aren't apricots peaches? And there are plums that are virtually apricots. I went on, either mischievously, or scientifically, pasting the peach labels on cans of plums, cherries, string beans, and succotash. I can't quite define my motive, because to this day it has not been decided whether I am a humorist or a scientist. I think that it was mischief, but, as we go along, there will come a more respectful recognition that also it was scientific procedure.

In the town of Derby, England – see the *Derby Mercury* (May 31, 1905) – there were occurrences that, to the undiscerning, will seem to have nothing to do with either peaches or succotash. In a girls' school, girls screamed and dropped to the floor, unconscious. There are readers who will think over well-known ways of peaches and succotash and won't know what I am writing about. There are others, who will see "symbolism" in it, and will send me appreciations, and I won't know what they're writing about.

In five days, there were forty-five instances of girls, who screamed and dropped unconscious. "The girls were exceedingly weak, and had to be carried home. One child had lost strength so that she could not even sit up." It was thought that some unknown, noxious gas, or vapour, was present: but mice were placed in the schoolrooms, and they were unaffected. Then the scientific explanation was "mass psychology." Having no more data to work on, it seems to me that this explanation is a fitting description. If a girl fainted, and, if, sympathetically, another girl fainted, it is well in accord with our impressions of human nature, which sees, eats, smells, thinks, loves, hates, talks, dresses, reads, and undergoes surgical operations, contagiously, to think of forty-three other girls losing consciousness, in involuntary imitativeness. There are mature persons who may feel superior to such hysteria, but so many of them haven't much consciousness.

In the *Brooklyn Eagle* (Aug. 1, 1894), there is a story of "mass psychology." In this case, too, it seems to me that the description fits – maybe. Considering the way people live, it is natural to them to die imitatively. There was, in July, 1894, a panic in a large vineyard, at Collis, near Fresno, California. Somebody in this vineyard had dropped dead of "heart failure." Somebody else dropped dead. A third victim had dropped and was dying. There wasn't a scientist, with a good and sticky explanation, on the place. It will be thought amusing; but the people in this vineyard believed that something uncanny was occurring, and they fled. "Everybody has left the place, and the authorities are preparing to begin a searching investigation." Anything more upon this subject is not findable. That is the usual experience after an announcement of a "searching investigation."

If something can't be described any other way, it's "mass psychology." In the town of Bradford, England, in a house, in Columbia Street, 1st of March, 1923, there was one of those occasions of the congratulations, hates, malices, and gaieties, and more or less venomous jealousies that combine in the state that is said to be merry, of a wedding party. The babble of this wedding party suddenly turned to delirium. There were screams, and guests dropped to the floor, unconscious. Wedding bells – the gongs of ambulances – four persons were taken to hospitals.

This occurrence was told of in the London newspapers, and, though strange, it seemed that the conventional explanation fitted it.

Yorkshire Evening Argus (Bradford; March 3, 1923) – particulars that make for restiveness against any conventional explanation – people in adjoining houses had been affected by this "mysterious malady." Several names of families, members of which had been overcome, unaccountably, were published – Downing, Blakey, Ingram.

If people, in different houses, and out of contact with one another – or not so circumstanced as to "mass" their psychologies – and all narrowly localised in one small neighbourhood, were similarly affected, it seemed clear that here was a case of common exposure to something that was poisonous, or otherwise injurious. Of course an escape of gas was thought of; but there was no odour of gas. No leakage of gas was found. There was the usual searching investigation that precedes forgetfulness. It was somebody's suggestion that the "mysterious malady" had been caused by fumes from a nearby factory chimney. I think that the wedding party was the central circumstance, but I don't think of a factory chimney, which had never so expressed itself before, suddenly fuming at a wedding party. An *Argus* reporter wrote that the Health Officers had rejected this suggestion, and that he had investigated, and had detected no unusual odour in the neighbourhood.

9

In this occurrence at Bradford, there was no odour of gas. I have noted a case in London, in which there was an odour of gas; nevertheless this case is no less mysterious. In the *Weekly Dispatch* (London; June 12, 1910), it is called "one of the most remarkable and mysterious cases of gas poisoning that have occurred in London in recent years." Early in the morning of June 10th, a woman telephoned to a police station, telling of what she thought was an escape of gas. A policeman went to the house, which was in Neale Street (Holborn). He considered the supposed leakage alarming, and rapped on doors of another floor in the house. There was no response, and he broke down a door, finding the occupants unconscious. In two neighbouring houses, four unconscious persons were found. A circumstance that was considered extraordinary was that between these two houses was one in which nobody was affected, and in which there was no odour of gas. The gas company sent men, who searched for a leak, but in vain. Fumes, as if from an uncommon and easily discoverable escape of gas, had overcome occupants of two houses, but according to the local newspaper, (*Holborn Guardian,* June 17), the gas company, a week later, had been unable to discover its origin.

In December, 1921, there was an occurrence in the village of Zetel, Germany (London *Daily News,* Jan. 2, 1922). This was in the streets of a town. Somebody dropped unconscious: and, whether in an epidemic of fright, accounted for in terms of "mass psychology," or not, other persons dropped unconscious. "So far no light has been thrown on the mystery." It was thought that a "current of some kind" had passed over the village. This resembles the occurrence at El Paso, Texas, June 19, 1929 (*New York Sun,* Dec. 6, 1930). Scores of persons, in the streets, dropped unconscious, and several of them died. Whatever appeared here was called a "deadly miasma." And the linkage goes on to the scores of deaths in a fog, in the Meuse Valley, Belgium, Dec. 5, 1930 – so that one could smoothly and logically start with affairs in a girls' school, and end up with a meteorological discussion (*New York Times,* Dec. 6, 1930; *New York Telegram,* Dec. 6, 1930; *New York Herald Tribune,* Dec. 19, 1930).

Lloyd's Weekly News (London; Jan. 17, 1909) – story from the Caucasian city of Baku. M. Krassilrukoff, and two companions, had gone upon a hunting trip, to Sand Island, in the Caspian Sea. Nothing had been heard from them, and there was an investigation. The searchers came upon the bodies of the three men, with their arms folded over their chests, "as if reverently prepared for the tomb." No marks of injuries; no disarrangement of clothes. "No trace of poison was, however, found, and the physicians could arrive at no other conclusion than that the trio had been in some way stifled. The doctors would, however, not absolutely commit themselves to this view."

The *Observer* (London; Aug. 23, 1925) – "A mysterious tragedy is reported from the Polish Tatra mountains, near the health resort of Zakopane. A party composed of Mr. Kasznica, the Judge of the Supreme Court, his wife, a twelve-year-old son, and a young student of Cracow University, started in fine weather for a short excursion in the neighbouring mountains. Two days later three of them were found dead."

Mrs. Kasznica was alive. She told that all were climbing, and were in good condition, when suffocation came upon them. "A suffocating wind" she thought. One after another they had dropped unconscious. The post-mortem examinations revealed nothing that indicated deaths by suffocation, nor anything else that could be definitely settled upon. "Some newspapers suggest a crime. So far, the case remains a mystery."

There have been cases that have been called mysterious, though they seem explicable enough in known circumstances of human affairs. See a story in the *New York World-Telegram* (March 9, 1931) – on March 9th, about thirty men and women at work in the Howard Clothes Company factory, Nassau Street, Brooklyn – sudden terror and a panic of these people, to get to the street. The place was filled with a pungent, sickening odour. In the street, men and women collapsed, or reeled, and wandered away, in a semi-conscious condition. Several dozen of them were carried into stores, where they were given first-aid treatment, until ambulances arrived.

The phenomena occurred in the second floor of the Cary Building, occupied by the clothing company. Nobody in any other part of the building was affected. All gas fixtures in the factory were intact. No gas bomb was found. Nothing was found out. But, considering many crimes of this period, the suspicion is strong that in some way, as an expression of human hatred, of origin in industrial troubles, a volume of poisonous gas had been discharged into this factory.

And it may be that, in terms of revenges, we are on the track of a general expression, even if we think of a hate that could pursue people far up on a mountain side.

In hosts of minds, today, are impressions that the word "eerie" means nothing except convenience to makers of crossword puzzles. There are gulfs of the unaccountable, but they are bridged by terminology. Four persons were taken from a wedding party to hospitals. Well, if not another case of such jocularity as mixing brickbats with confetti, it was ice cream again, and *ptomaine* poisoning. There is such satisfaction in so explaining, and showing that one knows better than to sound the *p* in *ptomaine,* that probably vast holes of ignorance always will be bridged by very slender pedantries. *Asphyxiation* has seduced hosts of suspicions that would be resolute against such a common explanation as "gas poisoning."

New York Sun (May 22, 1928) – story from the town of Newton, Mass. In this town, a physician was, by telephone, called to the home of William M. Duncan. There was nobody to meet him at the front door, but he got into the house. He called, but nobody answered. There seemed to be nobody at home, but he went through the house. He came to a room, upon the floor of which were lying four bodies. There was no odour of gas, but the doctor worked over the four, as if upon cases of asphyxiation, and they revived and tried to explain. Duncan had gone to his room, and, upon entering it, had dropped, unconscious. Wondering at what was delaying him, his wife had followed, and down she had fallen. One of his sons came next, and, upon entering this room, had fallen to the floor. The other son, by chance, went to this room, and felt something overcoming him. Before losing consciousness, he had staggered to the telephone.

The doctor's explanation was "mass psychology."

It is likely that the readers of the *Sun* were puzzled, until they came to this explanation, and then – "Oh, of course! Mass psychology."

There is a continuity of all things that makes classifications fictions. But all human knowledge depends upon arrangements. Then all books – scientific, theological, philosophical – are only literary. In Scotland, in the month of September, 1903, there was an occurrence that can as reasonably be considered a case of "mass psychology," as can be some of the foregoing instances: but now we are emerging into data that seem to be of physical attacks. There will be more emerging. One can't, unless one be hopelessly, if not brutally, a scientist, or a logician, tie to any classification. The story is told in *Galigani's Daily Messenger* (Paris; Sept. 13, 1903).

In a coal mine, near Coatbridge, Scotland, miners came upon the bodies of three men. There was no coal gas. There was no sign of violence of any kind. Two of these men were dead, but one of them revived. He could tell, enlighteningly, no more than could any other survivor in the stories of this group. He told that his name was Robert Bell, and that, with his two cousins, he had been walking in the mine, when he felt what he described as a "shock." No disturbance had been felt by anyone else in the mine. Though other parts of this mine were lighted by electricity, there was not a wire in this part. There was, at this point, a deadly discharge of an unknown force, just when, by coincidence, three men happened to be passing, or something more purposeful is suggested.

Down in a dark coal mine – and there is a seeming of the congruous between mysterious attacks and surroundings. Now I have a story of a similar occurrence at a point that was one of this earth's most crowded thoroughfares. See the *New York Herald* (Jan. 23, 1909). John Harding, who was the head of a department in John Wanamaker's store, was crossing Fifth Avenue, at Thirty-third Street, when he felt a stinging sensation upon his chest. There was no sign of a missile of any kind. Then he saw, near by, a man, who was rubbing his arm, looking around angrily. The other man told Harding that something unseen had struck him.

If this occurrence had been late at night, and, if only two persons were crossing Fifth Avenue, at Thirty-third Street, and if a force of intensity enough to kill had struck them, the explanation, upon the finding of the bodies, would probably be that two men had, by coincidence, died in one place, of heart failure. At any rate, see back to the case of the bodies on benches of a Harlem park. No reporter of the finding of these bodies questioned the explanation that two men, sitting near each other, had died, virtually simultaneously, of heart failure, by coincidence.

We emerge from seeming attacks upon more than one person at a time, into seeming definitely directed attacks upon single persons. *New York Herald Tribune* (Dec. 4, 1931) – Ann Harding, film actress, accompanied by her secretary, on her way, by train, to Venice, Florida. There came an intense pain in her shoulder. Miss Harding could not continue travelling, and left the train, at Jacksonville. A physician examined her and found that her shoulder was dislocated. The secretary was mystified, because she had seen the occurrence of nothing by which to explain, and Miss Harding could offer no explanation of her injury.

Upon Dec. 7, 1931 – see the *New York Times* (Dec. 8, 1931) – the German steamship *Brechsee* arrived at Horsens, Jutland. Captain Ahrenkield told of one of his sailors, who had been unaccountably wounded. The man had been injured during a storm, but he seemed to have been singled out by something other than stormy conditions. The captain had seen him, wounded by nothing that was visible, falling to the deck, unconscious. It was a serious wound, four inches long, that had appeared upon the sailor's head, and the captain had sewed it with an ordinary needle and thread.

In this case, unaccountable wounds did not appear upon several other sailors. Suppose, later, I tell of instances in which a number of persons were so injured. Mass psychology?

CHAPTER 4

Not a bottle of catsup can fall from a tenement-house fire-escape, in Harlem, without being noted – not only by the indignant people downstairs, but – even though infinitesimally – universally – maybe –

Affecting the price of pyjamas, in Jersey City: the temper of somebody's mother-in-law, in Greenland; the demand, in China, for rhinoceros horns for the cure of rheumatism – maybe –

Because all things are inter-related – continuous – of an underlying oneness –

So then the underlying logic of the boy – who was guilty of much, but was at least innocent of ever having heard of a syllogism – who pasted a peach label on a can of string beans.

All things are so inter-related that, though the difference between a fruit and what is commonly called a vegetable seems obvious, there is no defining either. A tomato, for instance, represents the merging-point. Which is it – fruit or vegetable?

So then the underlying logic of the scientist – who is guilty of much, but also is very innocent – who, having started somewhere with his explanation of "mass psychology," keeps right on, sticking on that explanation. Inasmuch as there is always a view somewhere, in defence of anything conceivable, he must be at least minutely reasonable. If "mass psychology" applies definitely to one occurrence, it must, even though almost imperceptibly, apply to all occurrences. Phenomena of a man alone on a desert island can be explained in terms of "mass psychology" – inasmuch as the mind of no man is a unit, but is a community of mental states that influence one another.

Inter-relations of all things – and I can feel something like the hand of Emma Piggot reaching out to the hand, as it were, of the asphyxiated woman on the mountainside. John Doughty and bodies on benches in a Harlem park – as oxygen has affinity for hydrogen. Rose Smith – Ambrose Small – the body of a shepherd named Funnell –

Upon the morning of April 10, 1893, after several men had been taken to a Brooklyn hospital, somebody's attention was attracted to something queer. Several accidents, in quick succession, in different parts of the city would not be considered strange, but a similarity was noted. See the *Brooklyn Eagle* (April 10, 1893).

Then there was a hustle of ambulances, and much ringing of gongs –

Alex. Burgman, Geo. Sychers, Lawrence Beck, George Barton, Patrick

Gibbons, James Meehan, George Bedell, Michael Brown, John Trowbridge, Timothy Hennessy, Philip Oldwell, and an unknown man –

In the course of a few hours, these men were injured, in the streets of Brooklyn, almost all of them by falling from high places, or by being struck by objects that fell from high places.

Again it is one of my questions that are so foolish, and that may not be so senseless – what could the fall of a man from a roof, in one part of Brooklyn, have to do with a rap on the sconce, by a flower pot, of another man, in another part of Brooklyn?

In the town of Colchester, England – as told in *Lloyd's Daily News* (London; April 30, 1911) – a soldier, garrisoned at Colchester, was, upon the evening of April 24th, struck senseless. He was so seriously injured that he was taken to the Garrison Hospital. Here he could give no account of what had befallen him. The next night, to this hospital, was taken another seriously injured soldier, who had been "struck senseless by an unseen assailant." Four nights later, a third soldier was taken to this hospital, suffering from the effects of a blow, about which he could tell nothing.

I have come upon a case of the "mass psychology" of lace curtains. About the last of March, 1892 – see the *Brooklyn Eagle,* (April 19, 1892) – people who had been away from home, in Chicago, returned to find that during the absence there had been an orgy of curtains. Lace curtains were lying about, in lumps and distortions. It was a melancholy prostration of virtues: things so flimsy and frail, yet so upright, so long as they are supported. Bureau drawers had been ransacked for jewellery, and jewellery had been found. But nothing had been stolen. Strewn about were fragments of rings and watches that had been savagely smashed.

There are, in this account, several touches of the ghost story. There are many records of similar wanton, or furious, destructions in houses where poltergeist disturbances were occurring. Also there was mystery, because the police could not find out how this house had been entered.

Then came news of another house, which, while the dwellers were away, had been "mysteriously entered." Lace curtains, in rags, were lying about, and so were remains of dresses that had been slashed. Jewellery and other ornaments had been smashed. Nothing had been stolen.

So far as the police could learn, the occupants of these houses had no common enemy. A rage against lace curtains is hard to explain, but the hatred of somebody, whose windows were bare, against all finery and ornaments, is easily understandable. Soon after rages had swept through these two houses,

15

other houses were entered, with no sign of how the vandal got in, and lace curtains were pulled down, and there was much destruction of finery and ornaments, and nothing was stolen.

New York Times (Jan. 26, 1873) – that, in England, during the Pytchley hunt, Gen. Mayow fell dead from his saddle, and that about the same time, in Gloucestershire, the daughter of the Bishop of Gloucestershire, while hunting, was seriously injured; and that, upon the same day, in the north of England, a Miss Cavendish, while hunting, was killed. Not long afterward, a clergyman was killed, while hunting, in Lincolnshire. About the same time, two hunters, near Sanders' Gorse, were thrown and were seriously injured.

In one of my incurable, scientific moments, I suggest that when diverse units, of, however, one character in common, are similarly affected, the incident force is related to the common character. But there is no suggestion that any visible hater of fox-hunters was travelling in England, pulling people from saddles, and tripping horses. But that there always has been intense feeling, in England, against fox-hunters is apparent to anyone who conceives of himself, as a farmer – and his fences broken, and his crops trampled by an invasion of red coats – and a wild desire to make a Bunker Hill of it.

In the *New York Evening World* (Dec. 26, 1930), it was said that Warden Lewis E. Lawes, of Sing Sing Prison, had been ill. The Warden recovered, and, upon Christmas morning, left his room. He was told that a friend of his, Maurice Conway, who had come to visit him, had been found dead in bed. Upon Christmas Eve, Keeper John Hyland had been operated upon, "for appendicitis," and was in a serious condition in Ossining Hospital. In the same hospital was Keeper John Wescott, who also had been stricken "with appendicitis." Keeper Henry Barrett was in this hospital, waiting to be operated upon "for hernia."

Probably the most hated man in the New York State Prison Service was Asael J. Granger, Head Keeper of Clinton Prison, at Dannemora. He had effectively quelled the prison riot of July 22, 1929. Upon this Christmas Day, of 1930, in the Champlain Valley Hospital, Plattsburg, N.Y., Granger was operated upon "for appendicitis." Two days later he died. About this time, Harry M. Kaiser, the Warden of Clinton Prison, was suffering from what was said to be "high blood pressure." He died, three months later (*New York Herald Tribune,* March 24, 1931).

The London newspapers of March, 1926, told of fires that had simultaneously broken out in several parts of Closes Hall, the residence of Captain B. Heaton, near Clitheroe, Lancashire (London *Daily Express,* March 30, 1926).

The fires were in the woodwork under the roof, and were believed to have been caused by sparks from the kitchen stove. These fires were in places that were inaccessible to any ordinary incendiary: to get to them, the firemen had to chop holes in the roof. Nothing was said of previous fires here. Maybe it is strange that sparks from a kitchen stove should simultaneously ignite remote parts of a house, distances apart.

A fire in somebody's house did not much interest me, but then I read of a succession of similars. In three months, there had been ten other mansion fires. "Scotland-yard recently made arrangements for all details of mansion fires to be sent to them, in order that the circumstances might be collated, and the probable cause of the outbreaks discovered" (London *Evening Standard,* March 10, 1926).

April 2, 1926 – Ashley Moor, a mansion near Leominster, destroyed by fire (*Daily Express,* April 3, 1926).

Somebody, or something, was burning mansions. How it was done was the mystery. There was a scare, and probably these houses were more than ordinarily guarded; but so well-protected are they, ordinarily, that some extraordinary means of entrance is suggested. In no report was it said that there was any evidence of how an incendiary got into the house. No theft was reported. For months, every now and then there was a mansion fire. Presumably the detectives of Scotland-yard were busily collating.

The London newspapers, of November 6th, told of the thirtieth mansion fire in about ten months (*Daily Express,* November 6, 1926).

There were flaming mansions, and there were flaming utterances, in England.

Sometimes I am a collector of data, and only a collector, and am likely to be gross and miserly, piling up notes, pleased with merely numerically adding to my stores. Other times I have joys, when unexpectedly coming upon an outrageous story that may not be altogether a lie, or upon a macabre little thing that may make some reviewer of my more or less good works mad. But always there is present a feeling of unexplained relations of events that I note; and it is the far-away, haunting, or often taunting, awareness, or suspicion, that keeps me piling on –

Or, in a feeling of relatability of seemingly most incongruous occurrences that nevertheless may be correlated into the service of one general theme, I am like a primitive farmer, who conceives that a zebra and a cow may be hitched together to draw his plough –

But isn't there something common about zebras and cows?

An ostrich and a hyena.

Then the concept of a pageantry – the ransack of the jungles for creatures of the wildest unlikeness to draw his plough – and former wild clatters of hoofs and patters of paws are the tramp of a song – here come the animals, two by two –

Or John Doughty, three abreast with the dead men of a Harlem park, pulling on my theme – followed by forty-five schoolgirls of Derby – and the fish dealer's housemaid, with her arms full of sponges and Turkish towels – followed by burning beds, most suggestively associated with her, but in no way that any conventional thinker can explain –

Or the mansion fires in England, in the year 1926 – and, in a minor hitch-up, I feel the relatability of two scenes:

In Hyde Park, London, an orator shouts: "What we want is no king and no law! How we'll get it will be, not with ballots, but with bullets!"

Far away in Gloucestershire, a house that dates back to Elizabethan times unaccountably bursts into flames.

CHAPTER 5

"Good morning!" said the dog. He disappeared in a thin, greenish vapour. I have this record, upon newspaper authority.

It can't be said – and therefore will be said – that I have a marvellous credulity for newspaper yarns.

But I am so obviously offering everything in this book, as fiction. That is, if there is fiction. But this book is fiction in the sense that *Pickwick Papers,* and *The Adventures of Sherlock Holmes,* and *Uncle Tom's Cabin,* Newton's *Principia,* Darwin's *Origin of Species, Genesis, Gulliver's Travels,* and mathematical theorems, and every history of the United States, and all other histories, are fictions. A library-myth that irritates me most is the classification of books under "fiction" and "non-fiction."

And yet there is something about the yarns that were told by Dickens that set them apart, as it were, from the yarns that were told by Euclid. There is much in Dickens' grotesqueries that has the correspondence with experience that is called "truth," whereas such Euclidean characters as "mathematical points" are the vacancies that might be expected from a mind that had had scarcely any experience. That dog-story is axiomatic. It must be taken on faith. And, even though with effects that sometimes are not much admired, I ask questions.

It was told in the *New York World* (July 29, 1908) – many petty robberies, in the neighbourhood of Lincoln Avenue, Pittsburgh – detectives detailed to catch the thief. Early in the morning of July 27th, a big, black dog sauntered past them. "Good morning!" said the dog. He disappeared in a thin, greenish vapour.

There will be readers who will want to know what I mean by turning down this story, while accepting so many others in this book.

It is because I never write about marvels. The wonderful, or the never-before-heard-of, I leave to whimsical, or radical, fellows. All books written by me are of quite ordinary occurrences.

If, say, sometime in the year 1847, a New Orleans newspaper told of a cat, who said: "Well, is it warm enough for you?" and instantly disappeared sulphurously, as should everybody who says that; and, if I had a clipping, dated sometime in the year 1930, telling of a mouse, who squeaked: "I was along this way, and thought I'd drop in," and vanished along a trail of purple sparklets; and something similar from the *St. Helena Guardian,* in 1905; and something like that from the *Madras Mail,* year 1879 – I'd consider the story of the polite dog no marvel, and I'd admit him to our fold.

But it is not that I take numerous repetitions, as a standard for admission –

The fellow who found a pearl in the oyster stew – the old fiddle that turned out to be a Stradivarius – the ring that was lost in a lake, and then what was found when a fish was caught –

But these often repeated yarns are conventional yarns.

And almost all liars are conventionalists.

One quality that the lower animals lack in common with human beings is creative imagination. Neither a man, nor a dog, nor an oyster ever has had any. Of course there is another view, by which is seen that there is in everything a touch of creativeness. I cannot say that truth is stranger than fiction, because I have never had acquaintance with either. Though I have classed myself with some noted fictionists, I have to accept that the absolute fictionist never has existed. There is fictional coloration to everybody's account of an "actual occurrence," and there is at least the lurk somewhere of what is called the "actual" in everybody's yarn. There is the hyphenated state of truth-fiction. Out of dozens of reported pearls in stews, most likely there have been instances; most likely once upon a time an old fiddle did turn out to be a Stradivarius; and it could be that once upon a time somebody did get a ring back fishwise.

But when I come upon the unconventional repeating, in times and places far apart, I feel – even though I have no absolute standards to judge by – that I am outside the field of ordinary liars.

Even in the matter of talking dogs, I think that the writer probably had something to base upon. Perhaps he heard of talking dogs. It is not that I think it impossible that detectives could meet a dog, who would say: "Good morning!" That's no marvel. It is "Good morning!" and disappearing in the thin, greenish vapour that I am making such a time about. In the *New York Herald Tribune* (Feb. 21, 1928), there was an account of a French bulldog, owned by Mrs. Mabel Robinson, of Bangor, Maine. He could distinctly say: "Hello!" Mrs. J. Stuart Tompkins, 101 West 85th Street, New York City, read of this animal, and called up the *Herald Tribune,* telling of her dog, a Great Dane, who was at least equally accomplished. A reporter went to interview the dog, and handed him a piece of candy (*New York Herald Tribune,* February 22, 1928). "Thank you!" said the dog.

In the city of Northampton, England – see *Lloyds' Weekly News* (London; March 2, 1912) – a detective chased a burglar, who had entered a hardware store. The burglar got away. The detective went back, and got into the store.

There were objects hanging on hooks, overhead. "By coincidence," just as the detective passed under one of them, it fell. It was a scythe-blade. It cut off his ear. Now I am upon familiar ground; there are suggestions in this story that correlate with suggestions in other stories.

"A bank in Blackpool was robbed, in broad daylight, on Saturday, in mysterious circumstances" – so says the London *Daily Telegraph* (Aug. 9, 1926). It was one of the largest establishments in town – the Blackpool branch of the Midland Bank. At noon, Saturday, while the doors were closing, an official of the Corporation Tramways Department went into the building, with a bag, which contained £800, in Treasury notes. In the presence of about twenty-five customers, he placed the bag upon a counter. Then the doorman unlocked the front door for him to go out and then return with another amount of money, in silver, from a motor van. The bag had vanished from the counter. It was a large, leather bag. Nobody could, without making himself conspicuous, try to conceal it. Nobody wearing a maternity cloak was reported.

In the afternoon, in a side street, near the bank, the bag was found and was taken to a police station. But the lock on it was peculiar and complicated, and the police could not open it. An official of the Tramways Department was sent for. When the Tramways man arrived with the key, no money was found in the bag. If a bag can vanish from a bank, without passing the doorman, I record no marvel in telling of money that vanished from a bag, though maybe the bag had not been opened.

Well, then, there's nothing marvellous about it, if from a locked drawer of Mrs. Bradley's bureau, money disappeared. *New York Times*, (Feb. 28, 1874) – Mrs. Lydia Bradley, of Peoria, Ill., "mysteriously robbed." There were other occurrences, and they, too, were anything but marvellous. Pictures came down from the walls, and furniture sauntered about the place. Stoves slung their lids at people. Such doings have often been reported from houses, in the throes of poltergeist disturbances. There are many records of pictures that couldn't be kept hanging on walls. Chairs and tables have been known to form in orderly fashion, three or four abreast, and parade. In Mrs. Bradley's home, the doings were in the presence of the housemaid, Margaret Corvell. So the girl was suspected, and one time, in the midst of pranks by things that are ordinarily so staid and settled, somebody held her hands. While her hands were held, a loud crash was heard. A piano, which up to that moment had been behaving itself properly, joined in. But the girl was accused. She confessed to everything, including the stealing of the money, except whatever had occurred when her hands were held. There are dozens of poltergeist cases, in which the girl –

oftenest a young housemaid – has confessed to all particulars, except things that occurred while she was held, tied, or being knocked about. Ignoring these omissions, accounts by investigators end with the satisfactory explanation that the girl had confessed.

In the *Home News* (Bronx; Sept. 25, 1927) is a story of "ghost-like depre-dations." In the town of Barberton, Ohio, lived an uncatchable thief. I call attention to an element often of openness, often of defiance, that will appear in many of our stories. It is as if there are criminals, and sometimes mischievous fellows, who can do unaccountable things and delight in mystifying their victims, confident that they cannot be caught. For ten years the uncatchable thief of Barberton had been operating, periodically. In some periods, as if to show off his talents, he returned to the same house half a dozen times.

In January, 1925, the police of London were in the state of mind of the rest of us, when we try to solve crossword puzzles that have been filled in with alleged Scotch dialect, obsolete terms, and names of improbable South Amer-ican rodents. Somebody was playing a game, unfairly making it difficult. The thing that he did were what a crossword author would call "vars." He was called a "cat burglar." Since his time, many minor fellows have been so named. The newspapers stressed what they called this criminal's uncanny ability to enter houses, but I think that the stress should have been upon his knowledge of just where to go, after entering houses. Whether he had the property of invisibility or not, residents of Mayfair reported losses of money and jewellery that could not be more mystifying, if an invisible being had come in through doors or win-dows without having to open them, and had strolled through rooms, sizing up the lay of things. He was called the "cat burglar," because there was no conven-tional way of accounting for his entrances, except by thinking that he had climbed up the sides of houses – always knowing just what room to climb to – climbing with a skill that no cat has ever had. Sometimes it was said that marks were seen on drain pipes and on window sills. Just so long as the police can say something, that is accepted as next best to doing something. Of course, in this respect, I'd not pick out any one profession.

The "cat burglar" piled up jewellery that would satisfy anybody's dream of expensive junk, and then he vanished, maybe not in a thin, greenish vapour, but anyway in an atmosphere of the unfair mystification of crosswords that have been made difficult with "vars" and "obs." Perhaps marks were found on drain pipes and on window sills. But only logicians think that anything has any exclusive meaning. If I had the power of invisibly entering houses, but pre-ferred to turn off suspicions, I'd make marks on drain pipes and window sills.

Everything that ever has meant anything has just as truly meant something else. Otherwise experts, called to testify at trials, would not be the fantastic exhibits that they so often are.

New York Evening Post (March 14, 1928) – people in a block of houses, in the Third District of Vienna, terrorised. They were "haunted nightly by a mysterious person," who entered houses, and stole small objects, never taking money, doing these things just to show what he could do. Then, from dusk to dawn, the police formed a cordon around this block, and at approaches to it stationed police dogs. The disappearances of small objects, of little value, continued. There were stories of this "uncanny burglar or maniac" having been seen, "running lizardwise along moonlit roofs." My own notion is that nothing was seen running along roofs. There was such excitement that the "highest authorities" of Vienna University offered their mentalities for the help of the baffled policemen and their dogs. I wish I could record an intellectual contest between college professors and dogs; there might be some glee from my malices. There are probably many college professors, who at times read of strange crimes, and sympathise with civilisation, because they had not taken to detective work. However, nothing more was said of the professors who offered to help the cops and the dogs. But there was a challenge here, and I am sorry to note that it was not accepted. It would have been a crowning show-off, if this perhaps occult sportsman had entered the homes of some of these "highest authorities" and had stolen from them whatever it is by which "highest authorities" maintain their authority, or had robbed them of their pants. But he did not rise to this opportunity. After we have more data, it will be my expression that probably he could not practice outside this one block of houses. However, he got into a house in which lived a policeman, and he went to the policeman's bedroom. He stole the policeman's revolver.

Upon the afternoon of June 18, 1907, occurred one of the most sensational, insolent, contemptible, or magnificent thefts in the annals of crime, as viewed by most Englishmen; or a crime not without a little interest to Americans. On a table, on the lawn back of the grandstand, at Ascot, the Ascot Cup was on exhibition, 13 inches high, and 6 inches in diameter; 20-carat gold; weight 68 ounces. The cup was guarded by a policeman and by a representative of the makers. The story is told in the London *Times* (June 19, 1907). Presumably all around was a crowd, kept at a distance by the policeman, though, according to the standards of the *Times,* in the year 1907, it was not dignified to go into details much. From what I know of the religion of the Turf, in England, I assume that there was a crowd of devotees, looking worshipfully at this icon.

It wasn't there.

About this time, there were a place and a time and a treasure that were worthy the attention of, or that were a challenge to, any magician. The place was Dublin Castle. Outside, day and night, a policeman and a soldier were on duty. Within a distance of fifty yards were the headquarters of the Dublin metropolitan police; of the Royal Irish Constabulary; the Dublin detective force; the military garrison. It was at the time of the Irish International Exhibition, at Dublin. Upon the 10th of July, King Edward and Queen Alexandra were to arrive to visit the Exhibition. In a safe in the strong room of the Castle had been kept the jewels that were worn by the Lord Lieutenant, upon State occasions. They were a barbaric pile of bracelets, rings, and other insignia, of a value of $250,000.

And of course. They had disappeared about the time of the disappearance of the Ascot Cup: sometime between June 11th and July 6th.

All investigations came to nothing. For about twenty-four years nothing new came out. Then, according to a dispatch from London to the *New York Times* (Sept. 6, 1931), there was a report of attempted negotiations with the Dublin authorities, or an offer by which, "on certain conditions," the jewels would be returned. If this rumour were authentic, the remarkable part is that the various jewelled objects had not been broken up, but for twenty-four years had been kept intact. This is the look of the stunt.

But what I am worrying about is the big dog who said "Good morning!" and disappeared in a thin, greenish vapour. I am not satisfied with my explanation of why I rejected him. Considering some of my acceptances, it seems illogical to turn down the dog who said "Good morning!" – except that only to the purist, or the scholar, can there be either the logical or the illogical. We have to get along with the logical-illogical, in our existence of the hyphen. Everything that is said to be logical is somewhere out of agreement with something, and everything that is said to be illogical is somewhere in agreement with something.

I need not worry about the big dog who said "Good morning!" If, considering some of my acceptances, I inconsistently turn him down, I am consistent with something else, and that is the need in every mind to turn down something – the need in every mind that believes, or accepts anything, to consider something else silly, preposterous, false, evil, immoral, terrible – taboo. It is not necessary that we should all agree in being revolted, shocked, or contemptuous. Some of us take Jehovah, and some of us take Allah, to despise, or to be amused with. To give us limits within which to seem to be, and to give it contrasts by which to seem to be, every mind must practice exclusions.

I draw my line at the dog who said "Good morning!" and disappeared in a thin, greenish vapour. He is a symbol of the false and arbitrary and unreasonable and inconsistent – though of course also the reasonable and consistent – limit, which everybody must somewhere set, in order to pretend to be.

You can't fool me with that dog-story.

Chapter 6

Conservatism is our opposition, but I am in considerable sympathy with conservatives. I am often lazy, myself.

It's evenings, when I'm somewhat played out, when I'm most likely to be most conservative. Everything that is highest and noblest in my composition is most pronounced when I'm not good for much. I may be quite savage, mornings; but, as my energy plays out, I become nobler and nobler, and lazier, and conservativer. Most likely my last utterance will be a platitude, if I've been dying long enough. If not, I shall probably laugh.

I like to read my evening newspaper comfortably. And it is uncomfortably that I come upon any new idea, or suggestion of the new, in an evening newspaper. It's a botheration, and I don't understand it, and it will cost me some thinking – oh, well, I'll clip it out, anyway.

But where are the scissors? But they aren't. Hasn't anybody a pin? Nobody has. There was a time when one could manoeuvre over to the edge of a carpet, without having to leave one's chair, and pull up a tack. But everybody has rugs, nowadays. Oh, well, let it go.

Something in a newspaper about a mysterious hair-clipper. This is a new department of data, though hair-stealing links with other mysterious thefts. Where's a pin? Oh, well, there's nothing in particular about this matter of hair-clipping. A petty thief stole hair to sell, of course. Vague suggestions hanging over from reading of various phrases of "black magic" – but, if there is a market for human hair, hair-clippers are accounted for – still –

And so I could go on, every now and then, for many years, feeling a haunt of a new idea, but feeling more comfortable, if doing nothing about it. But, daytimes, I go to libraries, and, if several times, close together, something that is new to me, in newspapers, attracts my attention, I get the power somewhere to make a note of it.

These vague, new ideas that flutter momentarily in every mind – sometimes they're as hard to catch as is the moment they flutter in. It's like trying to pin a butterfly without catching it. They're gone. They can't develop, because one doesn't, or can't, note them, and collect notes. We'd all be somewhat enlightened – if that would be any good to us – were it not for easy chairs. Where's a pin? Hereafter I'm going to have a pet porcupine around the house. One can't learn much and also be comfortable. One can't learn much and let anybody else be comfortable.

Two cases of hairdressers' windows broken, and women's switches stolen. Probably to sell to other hairdressers.

I noted this, just as an oddity:

London *Daily Chronicle* (July 9, 1913) – Paris – wealthy engineer, named Leramgourg, arrested. "At Leramgourg's residence, the police found locks of hair of 94 women."

I put this item with others upon freaks of collectors. In Oklahoma City, July, 1907, somebody collected ears. Bodies of three men – ears cut off. In April, 1913, a collector, who was known as *Jack the Slipper-snatcher*, operated in the subways of New York City. Girl going up the steps of a subway exit – one foot up from the step – the snatch of her slipper –

The fantastic, or the amusing – but it is as close to the appalling as is the beautiful to the hideous –

The murderer of the Conners child, in New York, in July, 1916, hacked hair from his victim.

I have only two records of male victims of hair-clippers. I conceive that once upon a time abundant whiskers were tempting. Where do manufacturers of false whiskers get their material? Both of these victims were children. There was a case of three gypsy women, who waylaid a boy, aged eight, and cut off his hair. That they were gypsies may be of occult suggestion, but this could be simply the theft of something that could be sold.

A case is told of, in the *People* (London; Jan. 23, 1921). The residents of Glenshamrock Farm, Auchinleck, Ayrshire, Scotland, awoke one morning to find that during the night a burglar had made off with various articles. There were screams from the bedroom of a young female member of the household. Upon awakening, she had learned that her hair had been cut off. I say that this case was told of – but a case of what? And, in the *New York Sun* (March 7, 1928) – a case of what? An old man had entered the home of Angelo Nappi, 83 ½ Garside Street, Newark, N.J., and had cut off the hair of his three little daughters.

Old age and youth – male and female – there is the haunt, in stories of hair-clippers, of something that is not of hair-selling. If *Jack the Slipper-snatcher* were in the second-hand business, he'd have manoeuvred girls into having both feet in the air.

I take a story from the *Medium and Daybreak* (20, 785). It was copied from the *Brockville Daily Times* (Ontario; Nov. 23, 1889). There were doings in the home of George Dagg, a farmer, living in the Township of Clarendon, Province of Quebec, Canada. With Dagg lived his wife, two young children, and a little girl, aged 11, Dinah McLean, who had been adopted from an orphan asylum. The report from which I quote was the result of investigations by Percy Woodcock. I know that that sounds fictitious, but just the same Percy Woodcock was a well-known painter. Also Mr. Woodcock was a spiritualist. It could be that he coloured as much on paper as on canvas.

The first of the "uncanny" occurrences – as they are so persistently called by persons who do not realise how common they are – was upon Sept. 15th. Window panes broke. There were unaccountable fires – as many as eight a day. Stones of unknown origin were thrown. A large stone struck one of the children, and "strange to say not hurting her in the least" –

And I give my opinion that, in comments upon my writings, my madness has been over-emphasised. Of course I couldn't pass any alienist's examination – but could any alienist? But when I come upon a detail like this of stones striking people harmlessly, in an Ontario newspaper, and have noted the same detail in a story in a Constantinople newspaper, and have come upon it in newspapers of Adelaide, South Australia, and Cornwall, England, and other places – and when I note that it is no standardised detail of ghost stories, so that probably not one of the writers had ever heard of anything of the kind before – I'd consider myself sane and reasonable in giving heed to this, if there were sanity and reasonableness.

"One afternoon little Dinah felt her hair, which hung in a long braid down her back, suddenly pulled, and on crying out, the family found her braid almost cut off, simply hanging by a few hairs. It had to be cut off entirely, and looked as if a person had grabbed the braid and sawed it off with a knife. On the same day the little boy began crying, and said somebody pulled his hair all over. Immediately it was seen by his mother that his hair had also had been cut off in chunks as it were all over his head."

Woodcock told of a voice that was heard. This is an element that does not appear in the great majority of cases of poltergeist disturbances. His story is of conversations that were carried on between him and an invisible being. There was a feud between the Daggs and neighbours named Wallace; and "the voice" accused Mrs. Wallace of having sent him, or her, or it, or whatever, to persecute the Daggs. Most of the time, the house was crowded. When this accusation was heard, a number of farmers went to the home of the Wallaces, and returned with Mrs. Wallace. The story is that "the voice" again accused Mrs. Wallace, but then made statements that were so inconsistent that it was not believed. It was an obscene voice, and Mr. Woodcock was shocked. He reasoned with it, pointing out that there were farmeresses present. And "the voice" was ashamed of itself. It repented. It sang a hymn and departed.

I take something from the *Religio-Philosophical Journal* (Oct. 4, Nov. 1 and 15, 1873), as copied from the *Durand Times* (Wisconsin) and other newspapers. Home of Mr. Lynch, 14 miles from Menomonie, Wisconsin – had moved from Indiana, a few years before, and was living with a second wife and the four children of the first wife's. She had died shortly before he had moved. Lynch went to town one day, and returned with a dress for his wife. Soon afterward, this dress was found in the barn, slashed to shreds. Objects all over the house vanished. Lynch bought another dress. This was found, in the barn, cut down to fit one of the children. Eggs rose from tables, tea cups leaped, and a pan of soft soap wandered from room to room. One of the children, a boy, aged six, was thought to be playing tricks, because phenomena centred around him. Nobody lambasted him until he confessed, but he was tied in a chair – tea cups as lively as ever.

There was the usual openness. No midnight mysteries of a haunted house. Sightseers were arriving in such numbers that there was no room in the house for them. Several hundred of them lounged outside, sitting on fences or leaning against anything that would hold them up, ready for a dash into the house, at any announcement of doings.

"One day one of the children, named Rena, was standing close to Mrs. Lynch. Her hair was sheared off, close to her scalp, and vanished."

There have been single instances, and there have been hairclipping scares that were attributed to "mass psychology." Also I have noted cases in which girls were accused of having cut off their own hair, hoping to take up some newspaper space. My only reason for doubt is the satisfactory endings of these accounts, with statements that the girls confessed.

There were accounts in the London newspapers, of Dec. 2 and 10, 1922, of a scare in places east and west of London. In a street, in Uxbridge, Middlesex, a woman found that her braid had been cut off. She had been aware of no such operation, but remembered that, in a crowd, her hat had been pushed over her eyes. According to the stories, women were terrorised by "a vanishing man." "Disappeared as if by magic." It is an *uncatchable* again, a defiant fellow, operating openly, as if confident that he could not be caught. Note that these are not ghost stories. They are stories of human beings, who seemed to have ghostly qualities, or powers. Dorris Whiting, aged 17, approaching her home, in the village of Orpington, saw a man, leaning on the gate. As she was passing him, he grabbed her, and cut off her hair. The girl screamed, and her father and brother ran to her. They searched, but the clipper was unfindable. A maid, employed by Mrs. Glanfield, of Crofton Hall, Orpington, was pounced upon by a man, who hacked off a handful of her hair. He vanished. There was excitement in Orpington, at the end of a bus route. A girl exclaimed that much of her hair had been cut off. Merely this does not seem mysterious; it seems that a deft fellow could have done this without being seen by the other passengers. But other girls were saying whatever girls say when they discover that their hair has been cut off. At Enfield, a girl named Brand, employed as a typist, at the Constitutional Club, was near the club house, one morning, about eight o'clock, when a man grabbed her and cut off her hair. "No trace of him was found, though the search was taken up a minute after the outrage."

I have noted occurrences in London, which look as if there was a desire, not generally for hair, or for anybody's hair, but for hair, and then more hair, of one victim. See the *Kensington Express* (London; Aug. 23, 1907). Twice a girl's hair had been clipped. In a London street, she felt a clip, the third time. The girl accused a man. He was arrested and was arraigned at the Mansion House. Neither the girl nor anybody else had seen him as a clipper, but he had walked "sharply away," and when accused had run. Nothing was said of either scissors or hair in any quantity found in his possession. The hair that had been cut off was not found. But "some hair was found on his jacket," and he was found guilty and was fined.

I have record of another case of "mass psychology." It is my expression that the description "mass psychology" does partly apply to it, just as would "horizontal ineptitude," or "metacarpal iridescence," or any other idea, or combination of ideas, apply, to some degree, to anything. In an existence of the hyphen, it is impossible to be altogether wrong – or right. This is why it is so hard to learn anything. It is hard to overcome that which can not be altogether wrong with that which can not be altogether right. I look forward to the time when I shall refuse to learn another thing, having accumulated errors enough.

In the *Spiritualist and Journal of Psychological Science* of July 21, 1876 (8, 339) was published a story of "mass excitement" in Nanking (Nanjing) and other cities of China. Uncatchables, who could not even be seen, were cutting off the pigtails of Chinamen, and there was panic. More of the story was told, but I preferred to take accounts from a local newspaper. I give details, as I found them, in various issues of the *North China Herald* (Shanghai) from May 20 to Sept. 16, 1876 (n.s., 16: 474, 506; 17: 122, 143, 191, 218, 270).

Panic in Nanking and other towns, and its spread to Shanghai – people believed that invisibles were cutting off their pigtails. It was said that, regard this story of the invisibles as one would, there was no doubt that a number of pigtails had been cut off, and that great alarm existed, in consequence. "Many Chinamen have lost their tails, and we can hardly admit that the imaginary sprites are real men with steel shears; for it could hardly happen that some one would not have been detected, before this, in the act of cutting. The most likely explanation is that agents, whoever they are, of the conspirators, whoever they may be, operate by means of some potent acid."

Panic spreading to Hangchow (Hangzhou) – "Numerous cases are reported, but few of them are authentic." "The cases are increasing daily."

In the streets of Wuchang (Wuhan) men, fearing attacks behind, were holding their pigtails in front of them. Quack doctors were advertising charms. Probably the reputable physicians, devoted to their own incantations, were indignant about this. The Military Commandant stationed soldiers in various parts of the city. "Suffice it to mention that, among much that is untrustworthy, there seem good grounds for believing that some children have actually lost part of their tails."

Sellers of charms suspected of cutting off pigtails, to stimulate business – mischievous children suspected – missionaries accused, and anti-Christian placards appearing in public places – rumours of drops of ink thrown in people's faces, "by some unknown agency," and people so treated dying – inhabitants of Woosih (Wuxi) and Soochow (Suzhou) mad with terror – the decapitation of suspected persons – arrests and torture. People had suspended work, and had organised into guards. At Soochow broke out "the crushing mania," or a belief that at night people were crushed in their beds. The beating of gongs was taken up so that the supply ran out, and anybody who wanted a gong had to wait for one to be made.

The standardised way of telling of such a scare is to elaborate upon the extremities at the climax of the excitement, and to ignore, or slightingly to touch upon, the incidents that preceded. There was a panic, or a mania, in China. Perhaps there was. I have no Chinaman's account. For all I know, some Chinaman may have sent an account to his newspaper, of us, beating gongs, during the parrot-disease scare, of the year 1930, having seen a janitor knocking off dust from the cover of an ash can. There was probably considerable excitement that was the product of delusions: nevertheless it does seem acceptable that there were cases of mysterious hair-clipping.

CHAPTER 7

Rabid vampires – and froth on their bloody mouths. See the *New York Times* (Sept. 5 and 29, 1931) – rabies in vampire bats, reported from the island of Trinidad. Or a jungle at night – darkness and dankness, tangle and murk – and little white streaks that are purities in the dark – pure, white froths on the bloody mouths of flying bats – or that there is nothing that is beautiful and white, aglow against tangle and dark, that is not symbolised by froth on a vampire's mouth.

I note that it is ten minutes past nine in the morning. At ten minutes past nine, tonight, if I think of this matter – and can reach a pencil, without having to get up from my chair – though sometimes I can scrawl a little with the burnt end of a match – I shall probably make a note to strike out those rabid bats, with froth on their bloody mouths. I shall be prim and austere, all played out, after my labours of the day, and with my horse powers stabled for the night. My better self is ascendant when my energy is low. The best literary standards are affronted by those sensational bats.

I now have a theory that our existence, as a whole, is an organism that is very old – a globular thing within a starry shell, afloat in a super-existence in which there may be countless other organisms – and that we, as cells in its composition, partake of, and are ruled by, its permeating senility. The theologians have recognised that the ideal is the imitation of God. If we be a part of such an organic thing, this thing is God to us, as I am God to the cells that compose me. When I see myself, and cats, and dogs losing irregularities of conduct, and approaching the irreproachable, with advancing age, I see that what is ennobling us is senility. I conclude that the virtues, the austerities, the proprieties are ideal in our existence, because they are imitations of the state of a whole existence, which is very old, good, and beyond reproach. The ideal state is meekness, or humility, or the semi-invalid state of the old. Year after year I am becoming nobler and nobler. If I can live to be decrepit enough, I shall be a saint.

It may be that there are vampires other than the vampire bats. I have wondered at the specialisation of appetite in the traditional stories of vampires. If blood be desired, why not the blood of cattle and sheep? According to many stories there have been unexplained attacks upon human beings; also there have been countless outrages upon other animals.

Possibly the remote ancestors of human beings were apes, though no evolutionist had made clear to me reasons for doubting the equally plausible theory that apes have either ascended, or descended, from humans. Still, I think some humans may have evolved from apes, because the simians openly imitate humans, as if conscious of a higher state, whereas the humans who act like apes are likely to deny it when criticised. Slashers and rippers of cattle may be throw-backs to the ape-era. But, though it is said that, in the Kenya Colony, Africa, baboons sometimes mutilate cattle, I'd not say that the case against them has been made out. London *Daily Mail* (May 18, 1925) – that, for some years, an alarming epidemic of sheep-slashing and cattle-ripping had been breaking out, in the month of April, on Kenya stock ranches. Natives were blamed, but then it was learned that their cattle, too, had been attacked. Then it was said to be proved that chacma baboons were the marauders. Possibly the baboons, too, were unjustly blamed. Then what? The wounds were long, deep cuts, as if vicious slashes with a knife; but it was explained that baboons kill by ripping with their thumb nails.

The most widely known case of cattle-mutilation is that in which was involved a young lawyer, George Edalji, son of a Parsee, who was a clergyman in the village of Wyrley, Staffordshire. The first of a series of outrages occurred upon the night of Feb. 2, 1903. A valuable horse was ripped. Then, at intervals, up to August 17th, there were mutilations of horses, cows, and sheep. Suspicion was directed to Edalji, because of anonymous letters, accusing him.

After the mutilation of a horse, Aug. 17th, Edalji was arrested. The police searched his house, and, according to them, found an old coat, upon which were bloodstains. In the presence of Edalji's parents and his sister, the police said that there were horse hairs upon this coat. The coat was taken to the police station, where Dr. Butter, the police surgeon, examined it, reporting that upon it he had found twenty-nine horse hairs. The police said that shoes worn by Edalji exactly fitted tracks in the field, where the horse had been mutilated. They learned that the young man had been away from home, that night, "taking a walk," as told by him. The case against Edalji convinced a jury, which found him guilty, and he was sentenced to seven years, penal servitude.

I now have a theory that our existence is a phantom – that it died, long ago, probably of old age – that the thing is a ghost. So the unreality of its composition – its phantom justice and make-believe juries and incredible judges. There seems to be a ghostly justice surviving in the old spook, having the ghost's liking for public appearances, at times. Let there be publicity enough, and Justice prevails. In a Dreyfus case, when the attention of the world is attracted, Justice, after much delay, and after a fashion, appears. Probably in the prison with Edalji were other prisoners who had been sent there, about as he had been sent. They stayed there. But Sir Arthur Conan Doyle, with much publicity, took up Edalji's case (London *Daily Telegraph,* January 11 and 12, 1907). In his account, in Max Pemberton's *Great Stories of Real Life* (30), Doyle says that when the police inspector found the old coat, upon which, according to him, there were horse hairs, Mrs. Edalji and Miss Edalji examined it and denied that there was a horse hair upon it: that Edalji's father said: "You can take the coat. I am satisfied there is no horse hair upon it." Doyle's statements imply that somewhere near the police station was a stable. As to the statement that Edalji's shoes exactly fitted tracks in the field, where the horse was ripped, Doyle says that the outrage occurred just outside a large colliery, and that hundreds of excited miners had swarmed over the place, making it impossible to pick out any one track. Because of Doyle's disclosures – so it is said – or because of the publicity, the government appointed a committee to investigate, and the report of this committee was that Edalji had been wrongfully convicted.

Sometimes slashers of cattle have been caught, and, when called upon to explain, have said that they had obeyed an "irresistible impulse." The better-educated of these unresisting ones transform the rude word "slasher" into "vivisectionist," and, instead of sneaking into fields at night, work at regular hours, in their laboratories. There are persons who wonder at the state of mind of the people in general, back in times when the torture of humans was sanctioned. The guts of a man were dragged out for the glory of God. "Abdominal exploration" of a dog is for the glory of Science. The state of mind that was, and the state of mind that is, are about the same, and the unpleasant features of anything are glossed over, so long as mainly anything is glorious.

According to a reconsideration, by the English government, in the Edalji case, the slasher of cattle, at Wyrley, remained uncaught. In the summer of 1907, in the same region, again there was slashing.

Aug. 22, 1907 – a horse mutilated, near Wyrley. It was said that blood had been found on the horns of a cow, and that the horse had been gored. Five nights later, two horses, in another field, were slashed so that they died. Sept. 8 – horse slashed, at Breenwood, Staffordshire. A young butcher, named Morgan, was accused, but he was able to show that he had been in his home, at the time. For about a month injuries to horses continued to be reported. They had been injured "by barbed wires," or "by nails projecting from fences."

CHAPTER 8

Some time in the year 1867, a fishing smack sailed from Boston. One of the sailors was a Portuguese, who called himself "James Brown." Two of the crew were missing and were searched for. The captain went into the hold. He held up his lantern and saw the body of one of these men, in the clutches of "Brown," who was sucking blood from it. Near by was the body of the other sailor. It was bloodless. "Brown" was tried, convicted, and sentenced to be hanged, but President Johnson commuted the sentence to life imprisonment. In October, 1892, the vampire was transferred from the Ohio Penitentiary to the National Asylum, Washington, D.C., and his story was re-told in the newspapers. See *Brooklyn Eagle* (Nov. 4, 1892).

Ottawa Free Press (Sept. 17, 1910) – that, near the town of Galazanna, Portugal, a child had been found dead, in a field. The corpse was bloodless. The child had been last seen with a man named Salvarrey. He was arrested, and confessed that he was a vampire.

See the *New York Sun* (April 14, 1931) for an account of the murders of nine persons, all but one of them females, which in the year 1929 terrorised the people of Düsseldorf, Germany. The murderer, Peter Kurten, was caught. At his trial, he made no defence and described himself as a vampire.

I have a collection of stories of children, upon whom, at night, small wounds appeared. Rather to my own wonderment, considering that I am a theorist, I have not jumped to the conclusion that these stories are data of vampires, but have thought the explanation of rat bites satisfactory enough. But, in the *Yorkshire Evening Argus* (March 13, 1924), I came upon a rat story that seems queer. Inquest upon the death of Martha Senior, aged 68, of New Street, Batley. "On the toes and fingers were a lot of wounds that rather suggested rat bites." It was said that these little wounds could have had nothing to do with the woman's death, which, according to the coroner, was from valvular heart disease. The only explanation acceptable to the coroner was that, before the police took charge of the body, the woman must have been dead a considerable time, during which rats mutilated the corpse. But Mrs. Elizabeth Lake, a neighbour, testified that she had found Mrs. Senior lying on the floor, and that Mrs. Senior had told her that she was dying. The statement meant that the woman had been attacked by something, before dying. The coroner disposed of it by saying that the woman must have been dead a considerable time, before the body was found, and that Mrs. Lake was mistaken in thinking that Mrs. Senior had spoken to her.

The fun of everything, in our existence of comedy-tragedy – and I was suspicious of the story of the terrorised Chinamen, as told by English reporters, because it was a story of panic that omitted the jokes – mania without the smile. Every fiendish occurrence that gnashes its circumstances, and sinks its particulars into a victim, wags a joke. In June, 1899, there was, in many parts of the U.S.A., much amusement. Something, in New York City, Washington, and Chicago, was sending people to hospitals. I don't recommend the beating of a gong to drive away a hellish thing, but I think that the treatment is as enlightened as is giving to it a funny name. Hospitals of Ann Arbor, Mich.; Toledo, Ohio; Rochester, N.Y.; Reading, Pa. –

The "kissing bug", it was called.

The story of the origin of the "kissing bug" scare-joke is that, upon the 19th of June, 1899, a Washington newspaper man, hearing of an unusual number of persons, who, at the Emergency Hospital, had applied for treatment for "bug bites," investigated, learning of "a very noticeable number of patients," who were suffering with swellings, mostly upon their lips, "apparently the result of an insect bite." According to Dr. L.O. Howard, writing in *Popular Science Monthly* (56, 31), there were six insects, in the United States, that could inflict dangerous bites, or punctures, but all of them were of uncommon occurrence. So Dr. Howard rejected the insect-explanation. In his opinion there had arisen a senseless scare, like those of former times, in southern Europe, when hosts of hysterical persons imagined that tarantulas had bitten them.

This is "mass psychology" again – or the Taboo-explanation. To the regret of my contrariness, it is impossible for me utterly to disagree with anybody. I think with Dr. Howard that the "kissing bug" scare was like the tarantula scares. But it could be that some of those people of southern Europe did not merely imagine that something was biting them. If somebody should like to write a book, but is like millions of persons who would like to write books, but fortunately don't know just what to write books about, I suggest a study of scares, with the idea of showing that they were not altogether hysteria and mass psychology, and that there may have been something to be scared about.

New York Herald (July 9, 1899) – names and addresses of 11 persons, who upon one day (8th of July) had either scared their bodies into producing swellings, or had been bitten by something that the scientists refused to believe existed. And people who were bitten captured insects. *Entomological News* (10, 205) – some of these insects, which were sent to the Academy of Natural Sciences of Philadelphia, were house flies, bees, beetles, and even a butterfly. There are wings of vampires that lull with scientific articles. See Taboo, as represented by Dr. E. Murray-Aaron, writing in the *Scientific American* (n.s., 81, 54) – nothing but sensation-mongering from Richmond, Va., to Augusta, Me.

There was a sensational horse, in Cincinnati. His jaw swelled. Would a child, aged four, be too young for "mass psychology"? I suppose not. I am not denying that there was much mass psychology in this. Cedar Falls, Iowa – a four-year-old child bitten. Trenton, N.J. – Helen Lersch, two years old, bitten – died. Bay Shore, L.I. – a child, aged two, bitten.

Later, I shall give instances of sizeable wounds that have appeared upon people; but, in this chapter, I am considering tiny punctures that may not have been either rat bites or insect stings. An account in the *Chicago Tribune* (July 11, 1899) is suggestive of traditional vampire stories. A woman, in Cleveland, had been bitten. "Two red spots showed where she had been stung around which a dark circle formed."

I don't know whether I am of a cruel and bloodthirsty disposition, or not. Most likely I am, but not more so than any other historian. Or, conforming to the conditions of our existence, I am amiable-bloodthirsty. In my desire for vampires, which is not in the least a queer desire, inasmuch as I have a theory that there are vampires, I was not satisfied with the "kissing bug": what I wanted was an account of hospital cases, not in the summer time. The insect-explanation, even though it was not upheld by Taboo, is too much at home, in the summer time. I needed an account, not in the summer time, to fill out my collection of data. Any collector will understand how pleased I was to come upon – London *Daily Mail* (April 20, 1920) – an account of human suffering. "A number of people in country places have been bitten by some mysterious creature with a very poisonous fang. It is rare for any sort of poisonous bite or sting to occur before summer, and as a rule the culprit is known. This spring doctors have attended case after case, where the swellings have been sudden and severe, though there is little sign of the bite itself." I have record of several winter time cases. See *La Nature* (Paris; 1897, I, Supp., Jan. 16, 1897, 25) – that, while filling a stove with coal, in a house in the Rue de la Tour, Paris, a concierge had felt a stinging sensation upon his arm, which swelled. He was taken to a hospital, where he died. People in the house said that they had seen gigantic wasps entering the house by way of stove pipes.

But the most mysterious of cases of insect bites, or alleged insect bites, is that of the small wound that led to the death of Lord Carnarvon, if be accepted that his death, and the deaths of fourteen other persons, were in any especial way related to the opening, or the violation, of the tomb of Tut-Ankh-Amen. Lord Carnarvon was stung by what was supposed to be an insect. What was said to be blood poisoning set in. What was said to be septic pneumonia followed.

The stories of the "kissing bug" differ from vampire stories, in that victims were painfully wounded. But there was an occurrence in Upper Broadway, New York City, May 7th, 1909, that may be more in agreement. It seems possible that a woman could, in a street crowd, viciously jab several persons with a hat pin, without being detected: but it does seem unlikely that she could enjoy such a stroll, jabbing at least five men and a woman, before being interfered with. A Broadway policeman learned that upon somebody a small wound, as if made by a hat pin, had appeared. Four other men and a woman joined the crowd and showed that they had been similarly wounded. The policeman arrested, as the cause of the excitement, a woman, who told that her name was Mary Maloney and gave a false address (*New York Sun,* May 8, 1909).

Perhaps she had no address. She may have been guilty, but perhaps she was shabby. If somebody must be arrested, it is wise to pick out one who does not look very self-defensive. "Plead guilty, and you'll get off with a light sentence." It is dangerous to be anywhere near any scene of crime, considering the way detectives pick up "suspects," even an hour or so later, obviously arguing that when somebody commits a crime, he hangs around to be suspected.

I have never been jabbed with a hat pin, but I have sat on pointed things, and my responses were so energetic that I suspect that at least six persons were not jabbed with a hat pin, before the jabber was caught. See data to come, that indicate that people may be – by some means at present not understood – wounded, and not know it until later. Also that a woman was accused makes me doubt that the marauder was caught. Women don't do such things. I have a long list of *Jacks,* ranging from rippers and stranglers to the egg throwers and ink squirters: but Mary Maloney is the only alleged *Jill* in my collection. Women don't do such things. They have their own deviltries.

Upon Dec. 4th, 1913, Mrs. Wesley Graff, who sat in a box, in the Lyric Theatre, New York City, felt something scratching her hand. She felt a pain like the sting of a wasp, and, staggering from her chair, fainted, first accusing a young man near her. The manager of the theatre held the young man, and called the police. Policemen searched, and found, on the floor, a common darning needle. It was their theory that the young man was a white slaver, who by means of a hypodermic injection, had sought to render a victim insensible, probably having waiting outside, a cab, to which he, explaining that he was her companion, would carry her. There were marks upon Mrs. Graff's arm, but it seems that they were not made by a darning needle.

With the idea that the needle might be tipped with a drug, the police sent it to a chemist. To my astonishment, I record that he reported that he had found neither drug, nor poison, on it. A strange circumstance is that, at this place, where a woman was wounded somewhat as if by a darning needle, was found this darning needle, which was suggestive of a commonplace explanation.

Then arose the story that a gang of white slavers was operating in the city. But in the newspapers were published interviews with physicians, who stated that they knew of no drug by which women could be affected so as to make them easily abductable, because the pain of an injection would give minutes of warning, before a victim could be rendered helpless. But it may be that something, or somebody, was abroad, mysteriously wounding women. In the *Brooklyn Eagle* (Dec. 6, 1913), it was said that in a period of two weeks, the Committee of Fourteen, of New York City, had heard a dozen complaints of mysterious, minor attacks upon women, and had investigated, but had been unable to learn anything definite in any case.

See back to the story of the Cleveland woman, and marks of "two red spots." Upon Mrs. Graff's arm were two little punctures. Dec. 29 – girl named Marian Brindle said that something stung her. Upon her arm were two little punctures.

It may be that, in the period of the scare in New York City, the first occurrence of which was in November, 1913, a vampire was abroad. It could be that we pick up the trail more than a year before this time. In October, 1912, Miss Jean Milne, aged 67, was living alone in her home, in West Ferry, Dundee, Scotland. London *Times* (Nov. 5, 1912) – the finding of her body. The woman was beaten, presumably with a poker, which was found, according to the account in the *Times;* but it was said that, though she had been struck on the head, her skull was not fractured, so her death was not altogether accounted for. There was more of this story, in the London *Weekly Dispatch* (Nov. 24, 1912). Upon this body were found perforations, as if having been made by a fork.

Late at night, Feb. 2, 1913, the body of a woman was found on the tracks of the London Underground Railway, near the Kensington High-street station. The body had been run over, and the head had been cut off. The body was identified as that of Miss Maud Frances Davies, who, alone, had been travelling around the world, and, earlier in the day, had, upon a ship train, arrived in London. She had friends and relatives in South Kensington, and presumably she was on her way to visit them. But the explanation at the inquest was that she had probably committed suicide by placing her neck upon a rail (London *Times,* Feb. 6, 1913).

"Dr. Townsend said the body was decapitated. Over the heart he found a number of small punctured wounds, over a dozen of which had penetrated the muscles and one had entered one of the ventricle cavities of the heart. These punctures had been caused during life with a sharp instrument, such as a hat-pin. They were not enough to cause death, but had been made a few hours previously."

Upon December 29th, of this year, 1913, a woman, known as "Scotch Dolly," was found dead in her room, 18 Ethan Street, S.E. London. A man, who had lived with her, was arrested, but was released, because he was able to show that, before the time of her death, he had left the woman. Her face was bruised, but she had seldom been sober, and the man, Williams, before leaving her, had struck her. The verdict was that she had died of heart failure, "from shock" (*South London Press,* January 2 and 16, 1914; London *Daily Mail,* January 2 and 20, 1914).

Upon one of the woman's legs was found a series of 38 little, double wounds. They were not explained. "The Coroner: 'Have you ever had a similar case, yourself?' Dr. Spilsbury: 'No, not exactly like this.'"

Chapter 9

Upon April 16, 1922, a man was taken to Charing Cross Hospital, London, suffering from a wound in his neck. It was said that he would tell nothing about himself, except that, while walking along a turning, off Coventry Street, he had been stabbed. Hours later, another man, who had been wounded in the neck, entered the hospital. He told, with a foreign accent, that in a turning, off Coventry Street, he had been so wounded. He signed his name in the hospital register, as Pilbert, but would, it was said, give no other information about the assault upon him. Late in the day, another wounded man was taken to this hospital, where according to the records, he refused to tell anything about what had befallen him, except that he had been stabbed in the neck, while walking along a turning, off Coventry Street.

In the pockets of these men were found racing slips. The police explained that probably all of them were victims of a turf-feud.

It is, considering many other data, quite thinkable that, instead of refusing to tell how they had been wounded, these men were unable to tell, but that this inability was so mysterious that the hospital authorities recorded it as a refusal. See the London *Daily Express* (April 17, 1922) and the *People* (April 23, 1922).

In a London hospital, there is small chance for an unconventional record, and probably in no London newspaper would have been published any reporter's notion of the lurk of an invisible and murderous thing, in a turning, off Coventry Street. But, in the London *Daily Mail* (Sept. 26, 1923), there was an account of something like this, but far away. It was a facetious account. Murderous things always have, somewhere, been regarded humorously. Or fondly. No address was published, or probably this one would have received letters from women, wanting to marry it. The story was that, in September, 1923, there was a *Mumiai* scare in India. *Mumiais* are invisibles that grab people. They have no sense of the mystic: don't dwell in enchanted woods, nor feel out for victims from old towers, or ruins, they grab people. Coolies, in the city of Lahore, believed that a *Mumiai* was abroad. There was a panic in Lahore, and it fed upon screams of rickshaw men, who thought that they were grabbed.

Probably the *Daily Mail* published this story, because of wavelets of gratification that arose from it, at London breakfast tables. It is usually thought that the value of coolies is only in their willingness to work for a few cents a day; but I have a notion that they have another function, or that, if it were not for coolies, and their silly superstitions that give the rest of us some sense of superiority to keep going on, millions of the rest of us would lie down and die of chagrin. Sometime I shall develop a theory of evolution in aristocratic terms, showing that things probably made of themselves oysters and lions and hyenas, just for the thrill of gratification in being able to say that at least they weren't elephants, or worms, or human beings. I know how it is, myself, and have compensations, in thinking of silly, credulous people who believe that a dog ever said "Good Morning!" and disappeared in a thin, greenish vapour.

Away back in the year 1890, the Japanese were coolies. Then they showed such talents for slaughter that now they are respected everywhere. But, in the year 1890, the Japanese were supposed to be little more than a nation of artists. A story of a panic in Japan was something to smile smugly about. I take a story from the *Religio-Philosophical Journal* (May 17, 1890), as copied from the newspapers. People in Japan thought that, sometimes in the streets, and sometimes in their houses, an invisible thing was attacking them. They thought that upon persons were appearing wounds, each a slash about an inch long. They thought that, at the time of an attack, little pain was felt.

Possibly a Jap, educated according to what is supposed to be an education, having his ideas as to the identity and geographical distribution of coolies, has looked over the files of American newspapers, and has come upon accounts of a series of occurrences in New York City, in the winter of 1891-92, and has been amused to note the mystery that New York reporters infused into their accounts of woundings of men, in the streets of New York. The reporters told of a "vanishing man." The assassin "disappeared marvellously." As noted in the *New York Sun* (Jan. 14, 1892), five men had been stabbed by an unknown assailant. There were other attacks. The police were blamed, and in the downtown precincts of the city, the most important order, each day, was to catch the stabber.

Jan. 17 – Slasher captured. The police were out to get him, and one of them got an unterrifying-looking little fellow, named Dowd. It was said that he had been caught, stabbing a man (*New York Sun,* Jan. 17, 1892).

In the mixture of all situations, it is impossible to be unable to pick out grounds for reasonably believing, or disbelieving, anything. Say that it is our preference to believe – or to accept – that it was not the "marvellously disappearing" slasher who was caught, but somebody else who would do just as well. Then we note that, twenty minutes earlier, another policeman had caught a man, who had, this policeman said, seized somebody, and was about to stab him. Or June, 1899 – and two men were out to catch the "kissing bug" – and one of them caught a beetle, and the other nabbed a butterfly. The policeman of the first arrest was ignored; the captor of Dowd was made a roundsman.

Dowd pleaded not guilty. He said that he had had nothing to do with the other assaults, and had drawn his knife only in this one case, which had been a quarrel. His lawyer pleaded not guilty, but insane. He was found insane and was sent to the asylum for insane criminals, at Auburn, N.Y.

The outrages in New York stopped. *Brooklyn Eagle* (March 12, 1892) – dispatch from Vienna, Austria – "This city continues to be shocked by mysterious murders. The latest victim is Leopold Buchinger, who was stabbed to the heart by an undetected assassin, in one of the most public places in Vienna. This makes the list of such tragedies five in number, and there is a growing feeling of terror among the public."

Say that it's an old castle, hidden away in the Balkan forest – and somebody was wounded, at night – but, as if lulled by a vampire's wings, felt no pain. This would be only an ordinarily incredible story.

In November, 1901, a woman told a policeman, of Kiel, Germany, that, while walking in a street in Kiel, she learned that she had been unaccountably wounded. She had felt no pain. She could not explain.

The police probably explained. If a doctor was consulted, he probably explained learnedly.

Another woman – about thirty women – "curious and inexplicable attacks." Then men were similarly injured. About eighty persons, openly, in the streets, were stabbed by an uncatchable – an invisible – or it may be the most fitting description to say that, upon the bodies of people of Kiel, wounds appeared. See the London *Daily Mail* (Dec. 7, 1901) . . "The extraordinary thing about the mystery is that some marvellously sharp instrument must have been used, because the victims do not seem to know that they are wounded, until several minutes after the attack."

And yet I think that something of an explanation of these *Jacks* is findable in every male's recollections of his own boyhood – the ringing of door bells, just to torment people – stretching a string over sidewalks, to knock off hats – other, pestiferous tricks. It is not only "just for fun"; there is an engagement of the imagination in these pranks. It will be my expression that, when the more powerful and more definite imagination of an adult human similarly engages and concentrates, phenomena that will be considered beyond belief, or acceptance, by readers who do not realise of what common occurrence they are, develop.

We have had stories of series of accidents, and perhaps my suspicion that they were not mere coincidences has been regarded at least tolerantly. I have data upon three automobile accidents that occurred at times not far apart; and, as to this series, I note a seeming association with minor attacks upon other automobiles, and upon people, that suggests the doings of one criminal. If so, he will have to be called *occult,* whether we take readily to, or are much repelled by, that term.

Upon the night of April 9th, 1927, Alexander Nemko and Pearl Devon were motoring through Hyde Park, London, when their car dashed down an incline, and plunged into the Serpentine. The car sank in fifteen feet of water. Though terrified and drowning, Nemko had his wits with him, so that he opened the door of the car and dragged his companion to the surface, and, with her, swam ashore.

There was nothing in the lay of the land by which to explain. The newspapers noted that there had never been an accident here before. "The steering gear apparently failed," was Nemko's attempt to explain. Perhaps it is queer that right at this point, so near a body of water, the steering gear failed; but, considered by itself, as mysteries usually are considered, there is little that can be said against Nemko's way of explaining (London *Daily Mail,* April 11, 1927; London *Daily Express,* April 11, 1927).

Two nights later, a taxicab plunged into the Thames, at Walton. The passenger swam ashore, but the driver was, it seems, drowned. His body was dredged for but was not found. The passenger, who must have been jostled past having any clear remembrance of what occurred, explaining that, at the brink of the river, the rear wheels of the car had dropped into a deep rut and that the car jolted into the river (London *Evening Standard,* April 12, 1927).

Upon May 3rd – see the London *Evening Standard* (May 6) – William Farrance and Beatrice Villes, of Linom Road, Clapham, London, were driving near Tunbridge Wells, when the car suddenly plunged toward a hedge, at the left of the road. Farrance succeeded in forcing the car to the right. Again something drove it toward the hedge. Farrance was powerless to stop it, and it broke through the hedge, overturning, killing the girl.

A schoolgirl, Beryl de Meza, was shot by somebody unknown and unseen, while playing in the street, near her home, at Hampstead, London (London *Daily Mail,* April 13, 1927; London *Observer,* May 8, 1927).

At Sheffield, there was an occurrence that was atrocious, but that may not be uncanny, but that attracts my attention because of the fiendishness of something else with which it associates. At the Soho Grinding Wheel Works, it was found, morning of April 19th, that grinding wheels had been chipped, and that belting had been stripped from pulleys. Nails had been driven, points upward, in chairs upon which the grinders sat. Tools had been thrown into motors, and currents had been turned on, causing much damage. All this looks like sabotage, malicious but scarcely "fiendish"; but in a building next door there had been doings that are so describable. Chickens had been tortured; combs cut off, legs broken, the head of one burned; others mutilated, and their injuries smeared with white paint (London *Daily Mail,* April 21, 1927).

London *Evening Standard* (May 5) – "Mystery of four shooting affairs." A boy, playing in Mitchum Park, London, was shot in the head, by an air gun, it was thought, though no air gun pellet was found. At Tooting Bec-common, an "air gun pellet" – though it was not said that an air gun pellet was found – passed through the wind shield of a motor car. In Stamford two men were shot by an unknown assailant. London *Sunday Express* (May 8) – Mr. George Berlam, of Leigh-on-Sea, motoring on the road from London to Southend – he heard a report, and his wind shield was splintered. In accounts of the punctured wind shield, at Tooting Bec-common, the driver of the car was quoted as saying that he had heard a report, and at the same time a laugh, "though nobody was about, at the time."

Wounds have appeared upon people. Usually the explanation is that they were stabbed. Objects have been mutilated. Window panes and automobile windshields have been pierced, as if by bullets, but by bullets that could not be found. Such were the doings of the "phantom sniper of Camden" (N.J.). He appeared first, in November, 1927; but the first clipping that I have, relating to him, is from the *New York Evening Post* (Jan. 26, 1928) – a store window pierced by a bullet – the eighth repeated occurrence. Later, the stories were definitely of a "phantom sniper" and his "phantom bullets."

New York Herald Tribune (Feb. 9, 1928) – Collingswood, N.J., Feb. 8 – "The 'phantom sniper,' if it was the work of South Jersey's mysterious marksman, scored his most sensational attack tonight when a window in the home of William T. Turnbull was shattered by what appeared to be a charge of shot.

"Police at first believed it an attempted assassination, but, as in all the other cases, no missile was found.

"Turnbull, a Philadelphia stockbroker, and a former president of the Collingswood Borough Council, who was seated near the window, reading, was splattered with glass. He said that an automobile had stopped in front of the house a few minutes before. The absence of any grains of shot added to the mystery."

I have sent letters of enquiry to all persons mentioned in the various reports. I received not one answer. It may be preferable to some readers to think that there are no such persons. Still, I note that not one of these letters was dead-lettered back to me.

The attacks continued until Feb. 28, 1928. Window panes and wind shields of automobiles were pierced by something that made no report of a gun, and that was unfindable. Something, or somebody, who was unseen, caused excitement in half a dozen towns from Philadelphia to Newark. Even if I could persuade myself that I am over-fanciful in my own notions, the seemingly veritable stories of a missile-less gun would be interesting. Authorities in New Jersey towns, noting the range of the malefactor, were especially watchful of motorists; but it is my notion that he had no need of anything on wheels in which to do his travelling. I noticed a similar range, in the doings in England, in April and May, 1927.

Snipings by the "Camden phantom" were the show-off, and nobody was injured by him; but a more harmful fellow operated in Boston, beginning about Nov. 1, 1930. I think that these sportsmen, who possibly are sentimental opponents to the shooting of game birds and deer, and practice their cruelties in ways that seem to them less condemnable, divide into the occult, and into more imaginative fellows who have found out how to practice occultly. In Boston, a noiseless weapon was used, but, this time, in two weeks, two men and a woman were seriously injured, and bullets of small calibre were removed from their wounds. These attacks so alarmed people that policemen, armed with riot guns, lined the roads south of Boston, with orders to catch the "silent sniper." The attacks continued until about the middle of February, 1931. Nobody was caught.

In this period (Nov. 12, 1931) a dispatch to the newspapers, from Bogota, Colombia, told of a "puzzling crime wave." In the hospitals were forty-five persons, suffering from stab wounds. "The police were unable to explain what appeared to be a general attack, but they arrested more than 200 persons."

Another occurrence of "phantom bullets," in the State of New Jersey, was told of, in the *New York Herald* (Feb. 2, 1916). Mr. and Mrs. Charles F. Repp, of Glassboro, N.J., had been fired upon by "phantom bullets." This was a special attack upon one house. There were sounds of breaking glass, and bullet holes were found in window panes, but nothing beyond the window panes was marked. It is such a circumstance as was told of in accounts of the "Camden sniper." It is as if somebody fired, not only with a missileless gun, or with invisible bullets, but as if with intent only to perforate windows, and with effects controlled by, and limited by, his intent. Consequently, instead of thinking of a shooting at window panes, I tend simply to think that holes appeared in window glass. Nobody in the house was injured; but Mr. and Mrs. Repp were terrified, and they fled. Members of the Township Committee investigated, and they reported that, though no bullets were findable, the windows "were broken much as a window usually is, when a bullet crashes through it."

That's the story. Of witnesses, I.C. Soddy and Howard R. Moore were mentioned. I sent letters of enquiry to all persons whose names were given, and received not one reply. There are several ways of explaining. One is that it is probable that persons who have experiences such as those told in this book, receive so many "crank letters" that they answer none. Dear me – once upon a time, I enjoyed a sense of amusement and superiority toward "cranks." And now here am I, a "crank," myself. Like most writers, I have the moralist somewhere in my composition, and here I warn – take care, oh, reader, with whom you are amused, unless you enjoy laughing at yourself.

It seemed to me doubtful that a woman could go along Upper Broadway, and jab, with a hat pin, five men and a woman, before being caught. There has been a gathering of suggestions of not ordinary woundings. In *Lloyd's Weekly News* (London; Feb. 21, 1909), there was an account of a panic in Berlin. Many women, in the streets of the city, had been stabbed. It was said that the assailant had been seen, and he was described as "a young man, always vanishing." If he was seen, he is another of the "uncatchables." In this newspaper of February 23, it was said that 73 women had been stabbed, all except four of them not seriously.

We have had data that suggest the existence of vampires, other than humans of the type of the Portuguese sailor; but the brazen and serialised – sometimes murderous, but sometimes petty – assaults upon men and women are of a different order, and seem to me to be the work of imaginative criminals, stabbing people to make mystery, and to make a stir. I feel that I can understand their motives, because once upon a time I was an imaginative criminal, myself. Once upon a time I was a boy. One time, when I was a boy, I caught a lot of flies. There was nothing of the criminal, nor of the malicious, in what I did, this time, but it seems to give me an understanding of the "phantom" stabbers and snipers. I painted the backs of the flies red and turned them loose. There was an imaginative pleasure in thinking of flies, so bearing my mark, attracting attention, causing people to wonder, spreading far, appearing in distant places, so marked by me.

In some of our stories there is much suggestion that there was no "vanishing man" – that wounds appeared upon people, as appeared – or as it was said to have appeared – a wound on the head of a sailor. See back to the story told by the captain of the *Brechsee*. Or that wounds appeared upon people, and that the victims, examined by the police, were more or less bullied into giving some kind of description of an assailant. However, some of the stories of the "vanishing man" look as if he, too, may be. There may be several ways of doing these things. Early in the year 1907, a "vanishing man" was reported from the town of Winchester, England. I take from the *Weekly Dispatch* (London; Feb. 10, 1907). Women of Winchester were complaining of an"uncatchable," who was committing petty assaults upon them, such as rapping their hands. "A mysterious feature of the affair is that the man disappears, as if by magic."

The "phantom stabber" of Bridgeport, Conn., appeared first Feb. 20th, 1925, and the last of his attacks, of which I have record, was upon June 1st, 1928. That was a long time in which to operate, uncaught. In the daytime, mostly, though sometimes at night, girls were stabbed: in the streets, in such public places as a department store and the entrance of a library. Descriptions of the assailant were indefinite. In almost all instances the wounds were not serious. One of the stories, as told in the *New York Herald Tribune* (Aug. 28, 1927), is typical of the circumstances of publicity, or of the confidence of an assailant that he could not be caught. If my stories will be regarded as ghost stories, a novelty about them is the eerieness of crowded thoroughfares – a lurk near Coventry Street, London, and the sneak of an invisible in Broadway, New York. I expect sometime to hear of a haunted subway, during rush hours. Edgar Allan Poe would say of me that I'm no artist and don't know how to infuse atmo-sphere. One would think that I had never heard of the uncanniness of dark nights in lonely places. Some of the stories are of desperate plays for notoriety. I have a story now, not of doings in a graveyard, but in a department store. Bridgeport, Conn. – staged on a staircase, with an audience of hundreds of persons, there was a very theatrical performance. A review of this melodrama was published in the *Herald Tribune* –

"The stabber who has terrorized Bridgeport for the last thirty months appeared this afternoon and claimed his twenty-third victim in a crowded down-town department store. The victim was Isabelle Pelskur, fourteen, 539 Main Street, messenger girl employed in the D.M. Read store. The girl was stabbed in the store where she was employed.

"The stabbing occurred at 4:50, just two minutes before closing time of the store. Already some of the store doors had been locked, and the large crowd of shoppers were being ushered from the store. The employees were leaving their counters, and the victim had started up the stairs from the arcade side of the first floor to the women's dressing room.

"The girl had scarcely ascended more than half a dozen steps when she was attacked by an assailant who lunged his sharp blade into her side, causing a severe wound."

He got away. Nobody reported having seen him escaping. The girl could give only a "meagre" description of him.

CHAPTER 10

Relatively to the principles of modern science, werewolves can not be. But I know of no such principle that is other than tautology or approximation. It is myth-stuff. Then, if relatively to a group of phantoms, werewolves can not be, there are at least negative grounds for thinking that they are quite likely.

Relatively to the principles, or lack of principles, of ultra-modern science, there isn't anything that can't be, even though also it is not clear how anything can be.

So my acceptance, or pseudo-conclusion, is that werewolves are quite likely-unlikely.

Once upon a time, when minds were dosed with the pill-theory of matter, werewolves were said to be physically impossible. Very little globes were said to be the ultimates of matter and were supposed to be understandable, and people thought they knew what matter is. But the pills have rolled away. Now we are told that the ultimates are waves. It is impossible to think of a wave. One has to think of something that is waving. If anybody can think of crime, virtue, or colour, independent of somebody who is criminal, virtuous, or coloured, that thinker – or whatever – may say that he knows what he is talking about, in denying the existence of anything, upon physical grounds. To say that the "ultimate waves" are electrical comes no closer to saying something. If there is no definition of electricity better than that of saying that it is a mode of motion, we're not enlighteningly told that the "ultimate waves" are moving motions.

My suspicion is that we've got everything reversed; or that all things that have the sanction of scientists, or that are in agreement with their myths, are ghosts; and that things called "ghosts," are, because they are not in agreement with the spooks of science, the more nearly real things. I now suspect that the spiritualists are reversedly right – that there is a ghost-world – but that it is our existence – that when spirits die they become human beings.

I now have a theory that once upon a time, we were real and alive, but departed into this state that we call "existence" – that we have carried over with us from the real existence, from which we died, the ideas of truth, and of axioms and principles and generalisations – ideas that really meant something when we were really alive, but that, of course, now, in our phantom-existence – which is demonstratable by any X-ray photograph of any of us – can have only phantom-meaning – so then our never-ending, but always frustrated search for our lost reality. We come upon chimera and mystification, but persistently have beliefs, as retentions from an experience in which there were things to believe in. I'd not say that all of us are directly ghosts: most of us may be the descendants of the departed from a real existence, who, in our spook-world, pseudo-propagated.

Once upon a time – but in our own times – there were two alleged marvels that were sources of uncommon contempt, or amusement, to scientists: they were the transformation of elements into other elements, and the transformation of human animals into other animals.

The history of science is a record of the transformations of contempts and amusements.

I think that the idea of werewolves is most silly, degraded, and superstitious; therefore I incline toward it respectfully. It is so laughable that I am serious about this.

Marauding animals have often unaccountably appeared in, or near, human communities, in Europe and the United States. The explanation of an escape from a menagerie has, many times, been unsatisfactory, or has had nothing to base upon. I have collected notes upon these occurrences, as *teleportations,* but also there may be *lycanthropy.*

Nobody has ever been finally reasonable, and it is impossible for me to be absolutely unreasonable. I can tell no yarn that is wholly a yarn, if it be my whim, or inspiration, to come out for the existence of werewolves.

What is there that absolutely sets apart the story of a man who turned into an ape, or a hyena, from the story of a caterpillar that became a butterfly? Or rascals who almost starve to death, and then learn to take on the looks of philanthropists? There are shabby young doctors and clergymen, who turn so sleek, after learning the lingo of altruists, that they have the appearance of very different animals. Or the series of portraits of Napoleon Bonaparte – and so much of his mind upon classical models – and the transformation of a young haggard man into much resemblance to the Roman Emperor Augustus.

It is a matter of common belief that men have come from animals called "lower," not necessarily from apes, though the ape-theory seems to fit best, and is the most popular. Then why not that occasionally a human sloughs backward? Data of reversions, not of individuals, but of species, are common in biology.

I have come upon many allusions to the "leopard men" and the "hyena men" of African tribes, but the most definite story that I know of is an article by Richard Bagot, in the *Cornhill Magazine* of Oct. 1918 (n.s., 3, 45, 353), upon the alleged powers of natives of Northern Nigeria to take on the forms of lower

animals. An experience attributed to Capt. Shott, D.S.O., is told of. A particular of the traditional werewolf story is that when a werewolf is injured, the
injury appears upon a corresponding part of the human being of its origin.
Bagot told of Capt. Shott's experience, alleged experience, whatever, with "one
enormous brute" that had been shot, and had made off, leaving tracks that were
followed. The hunters came to a spot where they found the jaw of the animal,
lying in a pool of blood. The tracks went on toward a native town. The next day a
native died. His jaw had been shot away.

There have been many appearances of animals that were unexplained –
anyway until I appeared upon the horizon of this field of data. It seems to me
that my expressions upon *Teleportations* are somewhat satisfactory in most of
the cases – that is, that there is a force, distributive of forms of life and other
phenomena that could switch an animal, say from a jungle in Madagascar to
a back yard somewhere in Nebraska. But theories of mine are not so god-like as
to deny any right of being for all other theories. I'd not be dogmatic and say
positively that once upon a time a lemur was magically transported from
Africa to Nebraska: possibly somebody in Lincoln, Nebraska, had been
transformed into a lemur, or was a werelemur.

Whatever the explanation may be, the story was told, in the *New York
Sun* (Nov. 12, 1931). Dr. E.R. Mathers, of Lincoln, Nebraska, had seen a
strange, small animal in his yard, acting queerly. The next day he found the
creature dead. The body was taken to Dr. I.H. Blake, of the University of Nebraska, who identified it as that of an African lemur of the *Galaga* group. A
lemur is a monkey-like animal, with a long snout: size about that of a monkey.

I wrote to Dr. Mathers about this, and, considerably to my surprise,
because mostly my "crank" letters are very properly ignored, received an
answer, dated Nov. 21, 1931. Dr. Mathers verified the story. The lemur, stuffed
and mounted, is now upon exhibition in the museum of the University of
Nebraska, at Lincoln. Where it had come from had not been learned. There
was no story of an escape, anywhere, that could match this appearance in a
back yard. Accounts had been spread-headed, with illustrations, in the *Lincoln
State Journal* (Oct. 23) and in the *Sunday State Journal* (Oct. 25); but, not even
in some other back yard had this animal been seen, according to absence of
statements. I neglected to ask whether, at the time of the appearance of
the lemur, the disappearance of any resident of Lincoln was reported.

Suppose, at a meeting of the National Academy of Sciences, I should
read a paper upon the transformation of a man into a hyena. There would be
only one way of doing that. I recommend it to unrecognised geniuses, who

can't otherwise get a hearing. It would have to be a hold-up.

But, without having to pull a gun, at the meeting of the N.A.S. at New Haven, Conn., Nov. 18, 1931, Dr. Richard C. Tolman suggested that energy may be transforming into matter.

If one can't think of a man transforming into a hyena, let one try to think of the motions of a thing turning into a thing.

My expression is that, in our existence of the hyphen, or of intermediateness between so-called opposites, there is no energy, and there is no matter; but that there is matter-energy, manifesting in different degrees of emphasis one way or the other:

That it is not thinkable that energy could turn into matter: but that it is thinkable that energy-matter could, by a difference of emphasis, turn into matter-energy –

Or that there is no man who is without the hyena-element in his composition, and that there is no hyena that is not at least rudimentarily human – or that at least it may be reasoned that, by no absolute transformation, but by a shift in emphasis, a man-hyena might turn into a hyena-man.

The year 1931 – and there were everywhere, but most notably in the U.S.A., such shifts, or reversions, from the state that is called "civilisation," that there was talk of repealing laws against carrying weapons, and of the arming of citizens to protect themselves, as if such cities as New York and Chicago were frontier towns. Out of policemen – in all except physical appearance – had come wolves that had preyed upon nocturnal women. There were chases of savages through the streets of New York City. Jackals on juries picked up bits from kills by bigger beasts, and snarled their jackal-verdicts.

New York Times (June 30, 1931) – "Police at Mineola hunt ape-like animal – hairy creature about four feet tall."

Out of judges had come swine.

County Judge W. Bernard Vause found guilty of using the mails to defraud, and sentenced to six years in Atlanta Penitentiary. Federal Judge Grover M. Moscowitz was censured by the House of Representatives. The Magistrates, who, facing charges of corruption, resigned, were Mancuso, Ewald, McQuade, Goodman, Simpson. Vitale was removed. Crater disappeared. Rosenbluth went away, for his health's sake.

And, near Mineola, Long Island, a gorilla was reported.

The first excitement was at Lewis & Valentine's nursery – story told by half a dozen persons – an ape that had come out of the woods, had looked them over, and had retreated. It seems that the police hadn't heard of "mass psychology"; so they had to explain less learnedly. Several days later, they were so impressed with repeating stories that a dozen members of the Nassau County Police Department were armed with shot guns and were assigned to ape-duty.

No circus had appeared anywhere near Mineola, about this time; and from neither any zoo, nor from anybody's smaller menagerie, had the escape of any animal been reported. Ordinarily let nothing escape, or let nothing large, wild, and hairy appear, but let it be called an ape, anyway – and, upon the rise of an ape-scare, one expects to hear of cows reported as gorillas: trees, shadows, vacancies taking on ape-forms. But – *New York Herald Tribune* (June 27, 1931) – Mrs. E.H. Tandy, of Star Cliff Drive, Malverne, reported something as if she had not heard of the ape-scare. She called up the police station, saying that there was a lion in her back yard. The policeman, who incredulously received this message, waited for another policeman to return to the station, and share the joke. Both waited for the arrival of a third disbeliever. The three incredulous policemen set out, several hours after the telephone call, and by that time there wasn't anything to disturb anybody's conventional beliefs, in Mrs. Tandy's back yard.

There was no marauding. All the stories were of a large and hairy animal that was appearing and disappearing –

And appearing and disappearing in the vast jungles not far from Mineola, Long Island, were skunks that were coming from lawyers. Some of them were caught and rendered inoffensive by disbarment. There was a capture of several dozen medical hyenas, who had been picking up livings in the trains of bootleggers. It could be that an occurrence, in New Jersey, was not at all special, but represented a slump back toward a state of about simian development. There was an examination of applicants for positions in the schools of Irvington. In mathematics, no question beyond arithmetic was asked; in spelling, no unusual word was listed. One hundred and sixteen applicants took the examination, and all failed to pass. The average mark was 31.5. The creep of jungle-life stripped clothes from people. Nudists appeared in many places. And it was not until later in the year, that the staunchest opponent of disclosures spoke out in the name of decency, or swaddling – or when Pope Pius XI refused to receive Mahatma Gandhi, unless he'd put on pants.

Upon the 29th of June, the ape-story was taken so seriously, at Mineola, the Police Captain Earle Comstock ordered out a dozen special motor patrols, armed with revolvers and sawed-off shot guns, with gas and ball ammunition, led by Sergeant Berkley Hyde. A posse of citizens was organized, and it was joined by twenty nurserymen, who were armed with sickles, clubs, and pitchforks. Numerous footprints were found. "The prints seemed to be solely those of the hind feet, and were about the size and shape of a man's hand, though the thumb was set farther back than would be the case with a man's hand." However, no ape was seen. As to prior observations, Policeman Fred Koehler, who had been assigned to investigate, reported statements by ten persons.

The animal disappeared, about the last of June. Upon July 18th, it was reported again, and by persons who were out of communication with each other. It was near Huntington, L.I. A nurseryman, named Stockman, called up the police, saying that members of his family had seen an animal, resembling a gorilla, running through shrubbery. Then a farmer, named Bruno, three miles away, telephoned that he had seen a strange animal. Policemen went to both places, and found tracks, but lost them in the woods. The animal was not reported again.

And I suppose I shall get a letter from somebody in Long Island asking me not to publish his name, unless I consider that positively necessary, but assuring me that, of all the theorists, who had tried to explain the Ape of Mineola, only I have insight and penetration –

Or an impulse that had come upon him, in June, 1931, to climb trees, and to chatter, and to pick over the heads of his neighbours – and then blankness. He had awakened from a trance, and had found on his carpet tracks of "thumbed footprints." A peculiar, greenish mud. He had gone to Lewis and Valentine's nursery, and there he had seen a patch of this mud, which was not known to exist anywhere else.

And, if I don't take seriously this letter that I shall probably receive from somebody in Long Island, it will be because probably also I shall hear from somebody else, telling me that above all he shrinks from notoriety, but that personal considerations must be swept aside for the sake of science – that, as told in the newspapers, somebody had slung a brick, hitting the retreating ape, and that he had been unable to sit down, next morning.

But the germination of a new idea, I'm feeling. I have wondered about occultly stealing a money-bag from a bank. But that is so paltry, compared with abilities, not considered occult, by which respectable operators steal banks. Or psychically dislocating somebody's shoulder, in a petty revenge – whereas, politically, and upon the noblest of idealistic principles, whole nations may be dislocated. But, when it comes to the Miracle of Mineola, I feel the stirrings of Usefulness –

Or the makings of a new religion – founded as solidly as any religion ever has been founded –

All ye who are world-weary – unsatisfied with mere nudism, which isn't reverting far enough – unsatisfied with decadence in creeds and politics of today, which conceivably might be more primitive – conceiving that, after all, the confusion in the sciences isn't blankness, and that the cave-arts are at least scrawling something – all ye who are craving a more drastic degeneration – and a possible answer to your prayer –

"Make me, oh, make me, an ape again!"

What I need, to keep me somewhat happy, and to some degree interested in my work, is opposition. If lofty and academic, so much the better: if sanctified, I'm in great luck. I suspect that it may be regrettable, but, though I am much of a builder, I can't be somewhat happy, as a writer, unless also I'm mauling something. Most likely this is the werewolf in my composition. But the science of physics, which, at one time, was thought forever to have disposed of werewolves, vampires, witches, and other pets of mine, is today such an attempted systemisation of the principles of magic, that I am at a loss for eminent professors to be disagreeable to. Upon the principles of quantum mechanics, one can make reasonable almost any miracle, such as entering a closed room without penetrating a wall, or jumping from one place to another without traversing the space between. The only reason the exponents of ultra-modern mechanics are taken more solemnly than I am is that the reader does not have to pretend that he knows what I am writing about. There are alarmed scientists, who try to confine their ideas of magic to the actions of electronic particles, or waves; but, in the *Physical Review* (s. 2, 37, 780) was published a letter from Prof. Einstein, Prof. R.C. Tolman, and Dr. Boris Podolsky that indicated that this refinement can not be maintained. Prof. Einstein applies the Principle of Uncertainty not only to atomic affairs, but to such occurrences as the opening and shutting of a shutter on a camera.

There can be no science, or pretended science, except upon the basis of ideal certainty. Anything else is to some degree guesswork. As a guesser, I'll not admit my inferiority to any scientist, imbecile, or rabbit. The position today of what is said to be the science of physics is so desperate, and so confused, that its exponents are trying to incorporate into one system both former principles and the denial of them. Even in the anaemia and frazzle of religion, today, there is no worse state of desperation, or decomposition. The attempt to take the principle of uncertainty – or the principle of unprincipledness – into science is about the same as would be an attempt by theologians to preach the word of God, and also include atheism in their doctrines.

As an Intermediatist, I find the principle of uncertainty unsatisfactorily expressed. My own expressions are upon the principled-unprincipled rule-misrule of our pseudo-existence by certainty-uncertainty –

Or, whereas it seems unquestionable that no man has ever been transformed into a hyena, we can be no more than sure-unsure about this.

About the first of January, 1849, somebody, employed in a Paris cemetery, came upon parts of a human body, strewn on the walks. Up in the leafless trees dangled parts of a body. He came to a new-made grave, from which, during the night, had been dug the corpse of a woman. This corpse had been torn to pieces, which, in a frenzy, had been scattered. For details, see *Galigani's Daily Messenger* (Paris; March 10, 23, 24, 1849).

Several nights later, in another Paris cemetery, there was a similar occurrence.

The cemeteries of Paris were guarded by men and dogs, but the ghoul eluded them and dug up bodies of women. Upon the night of March 8th, guards outside the cemetery of St. Parnasse saw somebody, or something, climbing a wall of the cemetery. Face of a wolf, or a clothed hyena – they could give no description. They fired at it, but it escaped.

Near a new-made grave, at St. Parnasse, they set a spring- gun. It was loaded with nails and bits of iron, for the sake of scattering. One morning, later in March, it was found that, during the night, this gun had discharged. Part of a soldier's uniform that had been shot away was found.

A gravedigger heard of a soldier, who had been taken to a Paris hospital, where he had told that he had been shot by an unknown assailant. It was said that he had been wounded by a discharge of nails and bits of iron.

The soldier's name was Francis Bertrand. The suspicion against him was considered preposterous. He was a young man of twenty-five, who had advanced himself to the position of Sergeant-Major of Infantry. "He bore a good name, and was accounted a man of gentle disposition, and an excellent soldier."

But his uniform was examined, and the fragment of cloth that had been found in the cemetery fitted into a gap in the sleeve of it.

The crime of the ghoul was unknown, or was unrecognised, in French law. Bertrand was found guilty, and was sentenced to imprisonment for one year, the maximum penalty for the only charge that could be brought against him. Virtually he could explain nothing, except that he surrendered to an "irresistible impulse." But there is one detail of his account of himself that I especially notice. It is that, after each desecration, there came to him another "irresistible impulse." That was to make for shelter – a hut, a trench in a field, anywhere – and there lie in a trance, then rising from the ghoul into the soldier.

I have picked up another item. It is from the *San Francisco Daily Evening Bulletin* (June 27, 1874) – "Bertrand, the Ghoul is still alive; he is cured of his hideous disease, and is cited as a model of gentleness and propriety."

CHAPTER 11

Damn the particle, but there is salvation for the aggregate.

A gust of wind is wild and free, but there are handcuffs on the storm.

During the World War, no course of a single bullet could have been predicted absolutely, but any competent mathematician could have written the equations of the conflict as a whole.

This is the attempt by the theologians of science to admit the Uncertainty Principle, and to cancel it. Similarly reason the scientists of theology:

The single records of the Bible may not be altogether accurate, but the good, old book, as a whole, is Immortal Truth.

Says Dr. C.G. Darwin, in *New Conceptions of Matter* (101):

"We cannot say exactly what will happen to a single electron, but we can confidently estimate the probabilities. If an experiment is carried out with a thousand electrons, what was a probability for one becomes nearly a certainty. Physical theory confidently predicts that the millions of millions of electrons in our bodies will behave even more regularly, and that to find a case of noticeable departure from the average we should have to wait for a time quite fantastically longer than the estimated age of the universe."

This reasoning is based upon the scientific delusion that there are final bodies, or wholes.

Arthur B. Mitchell, of 472 McAllister Avenue, Utica, N.Y., goes out for the evening. It can't be said exactly what will happen to a single cell of Mr. Mitchell's composition, but every wink of an eye, or scratch of an ear, of this body, as a whole, can be foretold.

But now we have a change of view, as to this body that had been regarded as a whole. Now Mr. Mitchell is regarded as one of many units in this community known as Utica. Now the admission is that Mr. Mitchell's conduct may be slightly irregular, but the contention is that the politics of Utica, as a whole, is never a surprise.

But surprising things, in Utica, are reported. Well, Utica is only one of the many communities that make up the State of New York. But the State of New York –

My own expression is that ours in an intermediate existence, poised, or fluctuating back and forth between two unrealisable extremes that may be called *positiveness* and *negativeness;* a hyphenated state of goodness-badness, coldness-heatness, equilibrium-inequilibrium, certainty-uncertainty. I conceive of our existence as an organism in which positivising and negativising manifestations, or conflicts, are metabolic. Certainty, or regularity, exists to a high degree, in the movements of the planets, but not absolutely, because of small, unformulable digressions; and negativeness exists to a high degree, in the freaks of a cyclone, though not absolutely, because a still more frenzied state of eccentricity can always be thought of.

My expression is that there are things, beings, and events that conform strikingly to regularised generalisations, but that also there are outrageous, silly, fiendish, bizarre, idiotic, monstrous things, beings, and events that illustrate just as strikingly universal imbecility, crime, or unformulability, or fantasy.

In the London newspapers, last of March, 1908, was told a story, which, when starting off, was called "what the coroner for South Northumberland described as the most extraordinary case that he had ever investigated" (London *Weekly News,* March 29, 1908). The story was of a woman, at Whitley Bay, near Blyth, England, who, according to her statement, had found her sister, burned to death on an unscorched bed. This was the equivalence of the old stories of "spontaneous combustion of human bodies." It was said that the coroner was at first puzzled by this story; but that he learned that the woman who told it had been intoxicated, and soon compelled her to admit that she had found her sister, suffering from burns, in another part of the house, and had carried her to her bed room.

But, in my experience with Taboo, I have so many notes upon coroners, who have seen to it that testimony was what it should be; and so many records of fires that, according to all that is supposed to be known of chemical affinity, should not have been, that, between what should and what shouldn't, I am so confused that all that I can say about a story of a woman who burned to death on an unscorched bed is that it is possible-impossible.

Looking over data, I note a case that has no bearing on the story of the burning woman on the unscorched bed, but that is a story of strange fires, or of fires that would be strange, if stories of similar fires were not so common. It is a case that interests me, because it aligns with the stories of Emma Piggot and John Doughty. There was an occurrence, and it was followed by something else that seems related; but, in terms of common knowledge, it can not be maintained that between the first occurrence and the following occurrences there was relationship. Most of the story was told in the London *Times* (August 21, 1856); but, whenever it is possible for me to do so, I go to local newspapers for what I call data. I take from various issues of the *Bedford Times and Huntingdon Express* (Aug. 23 and 30, 1856) and the *Bedford Mercury* (Aug. 16, 23, 30; Sept. 20, 1856).

Upon the 12th of August, 1856, a resident of Bedford, named Alfred Morton, was absent from home. He was upon a business trip to Ireland. At home were Mrs. Morton and the housemaid, Anne Fennemore. To fumigate the house, the girl burned sulphur, in an earthenware jar, on the floor. The burning sulphur ran out on the floor, and set the house afire. This fire was put out.

About an hour later, a mattress was found burning, in another room. But the fire from the sulphur had not extended beyond one room, and this mattress was in another part of the house. Smoke was seen, coming from a chest. Later, smoke was seen coming from a closet, and in it linen was found burning. Other isolated fires broke out. Morton was sent for, and returned, upon the evening of the 16th. He took off damp clothes and threw them on the floor. Next morning these clothes were found afire. Then came a succession of about forty fires, in curtains, in closets, and in bureau drawers. Neighbours and policemen came in, and were soon fearful for their safety. Not only objects around them flamed; so flamed their handkerchiefs.

There were so many witnesses, and so much talk in the town, that there was an investigation. Considering that nobody was harmed, it seems queer to read that the investigation was a coroner's inquest, but the coroner was the official who took up the investigation. Witnesses told of such occurrences as picking up a pillow and setting it down – pillow flaming. There was an attempt to explain, in commonplace terms; but nothing that could suggest arson was found, and Morton had insured neither the house nor the furniture. The outstanding puzzlement was that an ordinary fire seemed to be in some way related to the fires that followed it, but in no way that could be defined. The verdict of the jury was that the fire from the burning sulphur was accidental, but that there was no evidence to show what had caused the succeeding fires.

This story attracted attention in London. After the first account, in the *Times* (Aug. 23; Sept. 16 and 20, 1856), there was considerable correspondence. At the inquest, two physicians had given their opinion that the sulphur fire must have been the cause of the other fires – or that inflammable, sulphurous fumes had probably spread throughout Morton's house. But the jury had refused to accept this explanation, because of testimony that chairs and sofas that had been carried out into the yard had flamed. The fires were in a period of five days, and it is probable that in that length of time any permeation by fumes would have been detected. In the discussion in the *Times* it was pointed out that sulphurous fumes are oxides and are not inflammable.

However, I come to another fire, and maybe I'll explain this one.

It was upon the night of January 21, 1909. Upon this night, a small-town woman exasperated a New York hotel clerk. Perhaps I explain her unusual behaviour by thinking that, having come from a small town, she started picturing the dangers of the big city, and let her imaginings become an obsession. The woman was Mrs. Mary Wells Jennings, of Brewster, N.Y. Place – the Greek Hotel, 30 E. 42nd Street. See the *Brooklyn Eagle* (Jan. 22, 1909). Mrs. Jennings asked the night clerk to change her room, saying that she feared fire. The clerk assigned her to another room. Not long afterward – wouldn't he let her have another room? So another room. Again she annoyed the clerk. Room changed again. A few hours later, in an unoccupied room, where, during alterations, paints were stored, a fire broke out.

St. Louis Globe-Democrat (Dec. 16, 1889) – "In some mysterious way, a fire started in the mahogany desk in the centre of the office of the Secretary of War, at Washington, D.C. Several official papers were destroyed, but it was said that they were of no especial value, and could be replaced. Secretary Proctor can not understand how the fire originated, as he does not smoke, and keeps no matches about his desk."

It may be that there have been other cases, in which, "in some mysterious way" have been destroyed papers that were of no especial value, and could be replaced. Upon Sept. 16, 1920, London newspapers told of three fires that had broken out simultaneously in different departments of the government office, in Tothill Street, Westminster, London. It was not said that papers of no especial value had been destroyed, but it was said that these simultaneous fires had not been explained. London *Sunday Express* (May 2, 1920) – "Upon the night of April 28, fire of mysterious origin broke out at the War Office, Constantinople, where the archives are stored. The iron doors were locked, and it was impossible to gain entrance to the building until afternoon. Many important documents were destroyed."

The body of a girl – and the body of a crow – and a newspaper correspondent's vague feeling of an unknown relationship –

A woman who was away from home –

Upon the night of April 6, 1919 – see the *Dartford Chronicle and District Times* (April 11, 1919) – Mr. J. Temple Johnson was alone in his home, Hawley Manor, near Dartford. His wife went abroad. Particulars of the absence of his wife, or of anything leading to the absence of his wife, are missing. Something had broken up this home. The servants had been dismissed. Johnson was alone.

At 2:40 o'clock, morning of April 7th, the firemen were called to Hawley Manor. Outside Johnson's room, the house was blazing; but in his room there was no fire. Johnson was dead. His body was scorched; but upon his clothes there was no trace of fire.

CHAPTER 12

From the story of J. Temple Johnson, I pick up that this man, with his clothes on, was so scorched as to bring on death by heart failure, by a fire that did not affect his clothes. This body was fully clothed, when found, about three o'clock in the morning. Johnson had not been sitting up, drinking. There was no suggestion that he had been reading. It was commented upon, at the inquest, as queer, that he should have been up and fully clothed, about three o'clock in the morning. The verdict, at the inquest, was of death from heart failure, due to inhaling smoke. The scorches were large red patches on the thighs and lower parts of the legs. It was much as if, bound to a stake, the man had stood in a fire that had not mounted high.

In the burning house, nothing was afire in Johnson's room. Nothing was found – such as charred fragments of nightclothes – to suggest that, about three o'clock, Johnson awakened by a fire elsewhere in the house, had gone from his room, and had been burned, and had returned to his room, where he had dressed, but had then been overcome.

It may be that he had died hours before the house was afire.

It has seemed to me most fitting to regard all accounts in this book, as "stories." There has been a permeation of the fantastic, or whatever we think we mean by "untrueness." Our stories have not been realistic. And there is something about the story of J. Temple Johnson that, to me, gives it the look of a revised story. It is as if, in an imagined scene, an author had killed off a character by burning, and then, thinking it over, as some writers do, had noted inconsistencies, such as a burned body, and no mention of a fire anywhere in the house – so then, as an afterthought, the fire in the house – but, still, such an amateurish negligence in the authorship of this story, that the fire was not explained.

To the firemen, this fire in the house was as unaccountable as, to the coroner, was the burned body in the unscorched clothes. When the firemen broke into Hawley Manor, they found the fire raging outside Johnson's room. It was near no fireplace; near no electric wires that might have crossed. There was no odour of paraffin, nor was there anything else suggestive of arson, or of *ordinary* arson. There had been no robbery. In Johnson's pockets were money and his watch. The fire, of unknown origin, seemed directed upon Johnson's room, as if to destroy, clothes and all, this burned body in the unscorched clothes. Outside, the door of this room was blazing, when the firemen arrived.

We have had other stories of unaccountable injuries. According to them, men and women have been stabbed, but have not known until later that they were wounded. There was no evidence to indicate that Johnson knew of his scorched condition, tried to escape, or called for help.

There are stories of persons who have been found dead, with bullet wounds, under clothing that showed no sign of passage of bullets. The police-explanation has been of persons who were killed, while undressed, and were then dressed by the murderers. *New York Times* (July 1, 1872) – mysterious murder, at Bridgeport, Conn., of Capt. Colvocoresses – shot through the heart – clothes not perforated. *Brooklyn Eagle* (July 8, 10, and 13, 1891) – Carl Gros found dead, near Maspeth, L.I. – no marks in the clothes to correspond with wounds in the body. Man found dead in Paris, Feb. 14, 1912 – bullet wound – no sign of bullet passing through his clothes.

I have come upon so many stories of showers of stones that have entered closed rooms, leaving no sign of entrance in either ceilings or walls, that I have not much sense of strangeness in the idea that bullets, or a knife, could pierce a body, under uncut clothes. There are stories of bullets that have entered closed rooms, without disturbing the materials of walls or ceilings.

Dispatch, dated March 3, 1929, to the *San Francisco Chronicle* (March 4, 1929) – clipping sent to me by Miriam Allen de Ford, of San Francisco – "Newton, N.J. – The county prosecutor's office here is baffled by the greatest mystery in its history. For days a rain of buckshot, at intervals, has been falling in the office of the Newton garage, a small room with one door and one window. There are no marks on the walls or ceiling, and there are no holes in the room, through which the shot could enter."

About two years later, being not very speedy in getting around to this, I wrote to the County Prosecutor, at Newton, and received a reply, signed by Mr. George R.Vaughan – "This occurrence turned out to be a hoax, perpetrated by some local jokesters."

There is a story, in the *Charleston News and Courier* (Nov. 12 and 20, 1886), not of bullets falling in a closed room, but, nevertheless, of unaccountable bullets – two men in a field, near Walterboro, Colleton Co., S.C. – small shot falling around them. They thought that it was a discharge from a sportsman's gun, but the rain of lead continued. They gathered specimens, which they took to the office of the *Colleton Press.*

Religio-Philosophical Journal (March 6, 1880) – copying from the *Cincinnati Inquirer* – that, at Lebanon, Ohio, people of the town were in a state of excitement: that showers of birdshot were falling from the ceiling of John W. Lingo's hardware store. A committee was appointed, and according to its report, the phenomenon was veritable: slow-falling volleys of shot, not of the size of any sold in the store, were appearing from no detectable point of origin. There was another circumstance, and it may have had much to do with the phenomenon: about five years before, somebody, at night, had entered this store, and had been shot by Lingo, escaping without being identified.

In the *Religio-Philosophical Journal* (April 24, 1880), a correspondent, J.H. Marshall, wrote, after having read of the Lingo case, of experiences of his, in the summer of 1867. Bullets fell in every room in his house, forcefully, but not with gunshot velocity – large birdshot – broad daylight – short intervals, and then falls that lasted an hour or more. Many bullets appeared, but when Marshall undertook to gather them, he could never find more than half a dozen. About the same time raps were heard.

How bullets could enter closed rooms is no more mysterious than is the howness of Houdini's escape from prison cells, though, according to all that was supposed to be known of physical confinements, that was impossible. In Russia, Houdini made, from a prison van, an escape that involved no expert knowledge, nor dexterity, in matters of locks. He was put into this van, and the door was soldered. He appeared outside, and the police called it an unfair contest, because, so to pass through solid walls, he must have been a spirit. Anyway, this story is told by Will Goldston, President of the Magicians' Club, in London (*Sunday Express,* November 7, 1926).

I have a story of a horse that appeared in what would, to any ordinary horse, be a closed room. It makes one nervous, maybe. One glances around, and would at least not be incredulous, seeing almost any damned thing, sitting in a chair, staring at one. I'd like to have readers, who consider themselves superior to such notions, note whether they can resist just a glance. The story of the horse was told in the London *Daily Mail* (May 28, 1906). If anyone wants to argue that it is all fantasy and lies, I think, myself, that it is more comfortable so to argue. One morning, in May, 1906, at Furnace Mill, Lambhurst, Kent, England, the miller, J.C. Playfair, went to his stable, and found horses turned around in their stalls, and one of them missing. It is common for one who has lost something, to search in all reasonable places, and then, in desperation, to look into places where not at all reasonably could the missing thing be. Adjoining the stable, was a hay room: the doorway was barely wide enough for a man to enter. Mr. Playfair, unable to find a trace of the missing horse, went to the hay room doorway, probably feeling as irrational as would somebody, who had lost an elephant, peering into a kitchen closet. The horse was in the hay room. A partition had to be knocked down to get him out.

There were other occurrences that could not be. Heavy barrels of lime, with nobody perceptibly near them, were hurled down the stairs. This was in the daytime. Though occasionally I do go slinking about, at night, with our data, mostly ours are sunlight mysteries. The mill was an isolated building, and nobody – at least nobody seeable – could approach it unseen. There were two watch-dogs. A large water butt, so heavy that to move it was beyond human strength, was overthrown. Locked and bolted doors opened. I mention that the miller had a young son.

About the middle of March, 1901 – that a woman was stabbed to death, in a fiction – or in a scene like an imagined scene that did not belong to what we call "reality." The look of the story of Lavinia Farrar is that it, too, was "revised," and by an amateurish, or negligent, in some unknown way hampered, "author," who, in an attempt to cover up his crime, bungled – or that this woman had been killed inexplicably, in commonplace terms, and that, later, means were taken, but awkwardly, or almost blindly, and only by way of increasing mystery, to make the murder seem understandable in terms of common human experience.

Cambridge Daily News (England; March 16, 1901) – that Lavinia Farrar, aged 72, a blind woman, of "independent means," had been found dead on her kitchen floor, face bruised, nose broken. Near her body was a blood-stained knife, and there were drops of blood on the floor. The body was dressed, and, until the post-mortem examination, no wound to account for the death was seen. At the inquest, two doctors testified that the woman had been stabbed to the heart, but that there was no puncture in her garments of which there were four. The woman, undressed, could not have stabbed herself, and then have dressed, because death had come to her almost instantly. A knife could not have been inserted through openings in the garments, because their fastenings were along lines far apart.

A knife was on the floor, and blood was on the floor. But it seemed that this blood had not come from the woman's wound. This wound was almost bloodless. Only one of her garments, the innermost, was blood-stained, and only slightly. There had been no robbery. The jury returned an open verdict.

Upon the evening of March 9, 1929 – see the *New York Times* (March 10 and 11, 1929) – Isidore Fink, of 4 East 132nd Street, New York City, was ironing something. He was the proprietor of the Fifth Avenue Laundry. A hot iron was on the gas stove. Because of the hold-ups that were of such frequent occurrence at the time, he was afraid; the windows of his room were closed, and the door was bolted.

A woman, who heard screams, and sounds as if of blows, but no sound of shots, notified the police. Policeman Albert Kattenborn went to the place, but was unable to get in. He lifted a boy through the transom. The boy unbolted the door. On the floor lay Fink, two bullet wounds in his chest, and one in his left wrist, which was powder-marked. He was dead. There was money in his pockets, and the cash register had not been touched. No weapon was found. The man had died instantly, or almost instantly.

There was a theory that the murderer had crawled through the transom. A hinge on the transom was broken, but there was no statement, as to the look of this break, as indicating recency, or not. The transom was so narrow that Policeman Kattenborn had to lift a boy through it. It would have to be thought that, having sneaked noiselessly through this transom, the murderer then, with much difficulty, left the room the same way, instead of simply unbolting the door. It might be thought that the murderer had climbed up, outside, and had fired through the transom. But Fink's wrist was powder-burned, indicating that he had not been fired at from a distance. More than two years later, Police Commissioner Mulrooney, in a radio-talk, called this murder, in a closed room, an "insoluble mystery."

Chapter 13

If a man was scorched, though upon his clothes there was no sign of fire, it could be that the woman of Whitley Bay, who told of having found her sister burned to death on an unscorched bed, reported accurately. If the woman confessed that she had lied, that ends the mystery, or that stimulates interest. The statement that somebody, operated upon by the police, or by a coroner, confessed, has the meaning that has a statement that under pressure an apple produces cider. However, this analogy breaks down. I have never heard of an apple that would, if properly pressed, yield cider, if wanted; or ginger ale, if required; or home brew, all according to what was wanted.

Once upon a time, when mine was an undeveloped suspiciousness, and I'd let dogmatists pull their pedantries over my perceptions, I nevertheless collected occasional notes upon what seemed to me to be unexplained phenomena. I don't do things mildly, and at the same time much enjoy myself in various ways: I act as if trying to make allness out of something. A search for the unexplained became an obsession. I undertook the of job going through all scientific periodicals, at least by way of indexes, published in English and French, from the year 1800, available in the libraries of New York and London. As I went along, with my little suspicions in their infancies, new subjects appeared to me – something queer about some hailstorms – the odd and the unexplained in archaeological discoveries, and in Arctic explorations. By the time I got through with the "grand tour", as I called this search of all available periodicals, to distinguish it from special investigations, I was interested in so many subjects that had cropped up later, or that I had missed earlier, that I made the tour all over again – and then again had the same experience, and had to go touring again – and so on – until now it is my recognition that in every field of phenomena – and in later years I have multiplied my subjects by very much shifting to newspapers – is somewhere the unexplained, or the irreconcilable, or the mysterious – in unformulable motions of all planets, volcanic eruptions, murders, hailstorms, protective colorations of insects, chemical reactions, disappearances of human beings, stars, comets, juries, diseases, cats, lamp posts, newly married couples, cathode rays, hoaxes, impostures, wars, births, deaths.

Everywhere is the tabooed, or the disregarded. The monks of science dwell in smuggeries that are walled away from event-jungles. Or some of them do. Nowadays a good many of them are going native. There are scientific dervishes who whirl amok, brandishing startling statements; but mostly they whirl not far from their origins, and their excitements are exaggerations of old-fashioned complacencies.

Because of several cases that I have noted, the subject of *Fires* attracted my attention. One reads hundreds of accounts of fires, and many of them are mysterious, but one's ruling thought is that the unexplained would be renderable in terms of accidents, carelessness, or arson, if one knew all the circumstances. But keep this subject in mind, and, as in every other field of phenomena, one comes upon cases that are irreconcilable.

Glasgow News (May 20, 1878) – doings in John Shattock's farmhouse, near Bridgwater. Fires had started up unaccountably. A Superintendent of Police investigated and suspected a servant girl, Ann Kidner, aged 14, because he had seen a hayrick flame, while she was passing it. Loud raps were heard. Things in the house, such as dishes and loaves of bread, moved about. The policeman ignored whatever he could not explain and arrested the girl, accusing her of tossing lighted matches. But a magistrate freed her, saying that the evidence was insufficient.

There is a story of "devilish manifestations," in the *Quebec Daily Mercury* (Oct. 6, 1880). For two weeks, in the Hudson Hotel, in the town of Hudson, on the Ottawa River, furniture had been given to disorderly conduct; the beds had been especially excitable. A fire had broken out in a stall in the stable. This fire was quenched, but another fire broke out. A priest was sent for, and he sprinkled the stable with holy water. The stable burned down.

There are several recorded cases of such fires ending with the burning of buildings; but a similarity that runs through the great majority of the stories is of fires localised in special places, and not extending. They are oftenest in the presence of a girl, aged from 12 to 20; but seldom do they occur at night, when they would be most dangerous. It is a peculiarity. See back to the case of the fires in the house in Bedford. It seems that, if those fires had been ordinary fires, the house would have burned down. The cases are of fires, in unscorched surroundings.

New Zealand Times (Dec. 9, 1886) – copying from the *San Francisco Bulletin*, about Oct. 14 – that Willie Brough, 12 years old, who had caused excitement in the town of Turlock, Madison Co., Cal., by settings things afire, "by his glance," had been expelled from the Turlock school, because of his freaks. His parents had cast him off, believing him to be possessed by a devil, but a farmer had taken him in and had sent him to school. "On the first day, there were five fires in the school: one in the centre of the ceiling, one in the teacher's desk, one in her wardrobe, and two on the wall. The boy discovered all, and cried from fright. The trustees met and expelled him, that night." For another account, see the *New York Herald* (Oct. 16, 1886).

Setting fire to teacher's desk, or to her wardrobe, is understandable and would have been more understandable to me, when I was 12 years old; but in terms of no known powers of mischievous youngsters can there be an explanation of setting a ceiling, or walls, afire. It seems to me that no yarn-spinner would have thought of any such particular, or would have made his story look improbable with it, if he had thought of it. I have other accounts in which similar statements occur. This particular of fires on walls is unknown in standardised yarns of uncanny doings. If writers of subsequent accounts probably had never heard of Willie Brough, it is improbable that several of them could invent, or would invent, anything so unlikely. It seems that my reasoning is that, under some circumstances, if something is highly unlikely, it is probable. John Stuart Mill missed that.

Upon the 6th of August, 1887, in a little, two-story frame house, in Victoria Street, Woodstock, New Brunswick, occupied by Reginald C. Hoyt, his wife, five children of his own, and two nieces, fires broke out. See the *New York World* (Aug. 8, 1887). Within a few hours, there were about forty fires. They were fires in unscorched surroundings. They did not extend to their surroundings, because they were immediately put out, or because some unknown condition limited them. "These fires can be traced to no human agency and even the most sceptical are staggered. Without premonition and with no lamps lighted or stoves in use, various articles would burst into flames. Now it would be a curtain high up out of reach, then a bed quilt in another room would begin to smoke and smoulder, and, as if to still further nonplus the theorists, a carpet-covered lounge was found to be all afire underneath, among the jute stretched above the springs. A basket of clothes on the shed burst into flames and the basket itself was partially consumed. A child's dress hanging on a hook, a feather bed, a straw mattress were ignited and would have been consumed but for water poured on them."

New York Herald (Jan. 6, 1895) – fires in the home of Adam Colwell, 84 Guernsey Street, Greenpoint, Brooklyn – that, in twenty hours, preceding noon, Jan. 5th, when Colwell's frame house burned down, there had been many fires. Policemen had been sent to investigate. They had seen furniture burst into flames. Policemen and firemen had reported that the fires were of unknown origin. The Fire Marshal said: "It might be thought that the child Rhoda started two of the fires, but she could not be considered guilty of the others, as she was being questioned, when some of them began." "I do not want

71

to be quoted as a believer in the supernatural, but I have no explanation to give as to the cause of the fires or of the throwing down of the furniture."

Colwell's story was that, upon the afternoon of Jan. 4th, in the presence of his wife and his step-daughter Rhoda, aged 16, a crash was heard. A large, empty, parlour stove had fallen to the floor. Four pictures fell from walls. Colwell had been out. Upon his return, while hearing an account of what had occurred, he smelled smoke. A bed was afire. He called a policeman, Roundsman Daly, who put out the fire, and then, because of unaccountable circumstances, remained in the house. It was said that the Roundsman saw wall paper, near the shoulder of Colwell's son William, start to burn. Detective Sergeant Dunn arrived. There was another fire, and a heavy lamp fell from a hook. The house burned down, and the Colwells, who were in poor circumstances, lost everything but their clothes. They were taken to the police station.

Captain Rhoades, of the Greenpoint Precinct, said: "This is the deepest mystery I have met in my forty years' experience as a policeman. Why, the fires started right under the noses of the men we sent to make an investigation. The more I look into it the deeper the mystery becomes. I cannot say that a supernatural agency has not been at work. How can I? What I can say more than that it is a pretty deep mystery."

Sergeant Dunn – "There were things that happened before my eyes that I did not believe were possible."

New York Herald (Jan. 7, 1895) – "Policemen and firemen artfully tricked by a pretty young girl."

Mr. J.L. Hope, of Flushing, L.I., had called upon Captain Rhoades, telling him that Rhoda had been a housemaid in his home, where, between Nov. 19 and Dec. 19, four mysterious fires had occurred. "Now the Captain was sure of Rhoda's guilt, and he told her so." "She was frightened," and was advised to tell the truth.

And Rhoda told what she was "advised" to tell. She "sobbed" that she had started the fires, because she did not like the neighbourhood in which she lived, and wanted to move away: that she had knocked pictures from the walls, while her mother was in another part of the house, and had dropped burning matches into beds, continuing her trickeries after policemen, detectives, and firemen had arrived.

The Colwells were poor people, and occupied only the top floor of the house that burned down. Colwell, a carpenter, had been out of work two years, and the family was living on the small wages of his son. Insurance was not mentioned.

The police captain's conclusion was that the fires that had seemed "supernatural" to him, were naturally accounted for, because, if when Rhoda was in Flushing, she set things afire, fires in her own home could be so explained. Rather than to start a long investigation into the origin of the fires in Flushing, the police captain gave the girl what was considered sound and wholesome advice. And – though it seems quaint, today – the girl listened to advice. "Pretty young girls" have tricked more than policemen and firemen. Possibly a dozen male susceptibles could have looked right at this pretty, young girl, and not have seen her strike a match, and flip it into furniture; but no flip of a match could set wall paper afire. The case is like the case of Emma Piggot. Only to one person's motives could fires be attributed, but by no known means could she have started some of these fires.

Said Dr. Hastings H. Hart, of the Russell Sage Foundation, as reported in the newspapers, May 10, 1931: "Morons for the most part can be the most useful citizens, and a great deal of the valuable work being done in the United States is being done by such mentally deficient persons."

Dr. Hart was given very good newspaper space for this opinion, which turned out to be popular. One can't offend anybody with any statement that is interpreted as applying to everybody else. Inasmuch as my own usefulness has not been very widely recognised, I am a little flattered, myself. To deny, ridicule, or reasonably explain away occurrences that are the data of this book, is what I call useful. A general acceptance that such things are would be unsettling. I am an evil one, quite as was anybody, in the past, who collected data that were contrary to the orthodoxy of his time. Some of the most useful work is being done in the support of Taboo. The break of Taboo in any savage tribe would bring on perhaps fatal disorders. As to the taboos of savages, my impressions are that it is their taboos that are keeping them from being civilised; that, consequently, one fetish is worth a hundred missionaries.

I shall take an account of "mysterious fires" from the *St. Louis Globe-Democrat* (Dec. 19, 1891). I shall go on to quote from a Canadian newspaper, with idea of supporting Dr. Hart's observations. Reporters, scientists, policemen, spiritualists – all have investigated phenomena of "poltergeist girls" in ways essentially the same as the way of a Canadian newspaper man – and that has been to pick out whatever agreed with their preconceptions, or with their mental deficiencies, or their social usefulness, and to disregard everything else.

According to the story in the *Globe-Democrat,* there had been "extraordinary" occurrences in the home of Robert Dawson, a farmer, at Thorah, near Toronto, Canada. In his household were his wife and an adopted daughter, an

English girl, Jennie Bramwell, aged 14. Adopted daughters, with housemaids, are attracting my attention, in these cases. The girl had been ill. She had gone into a trance and had exclaimed: "Look at that!" pointing to a ceiling. The ceiling was afire. Soon the girl startled Mr. and Mrs Dawson by pointing to another fire. From the next day onwards, many fires broke out. As soon as one was extinguished, another started up. While Mrs. Dawson and the girl were sitting, facing a wall, the wall paper blazed. Jennie Bramwell's dress flamed, and Mrs. Dawson's hands were burned extinguishing the fire. For a week, fires broke out. A kitten flamed. A circumstance that is unlike a particular in the Bedford case is that furniture carried outside and set in the yard, did not burn.

An account, in the *Toronto Globe* (Nov. 9, 1891), was by a reporter, who was a person of usefulness. He told of the charred patches of wall paper, which looked as if a lighted lamp had been held to the places. Conditions were miserable. All furniture had been moved to the yard. The girl had been sent back to the orphan asylum, from which she had been adopted, because the fires had been attributed to her. With her departure, phenomena had stopped. The reporter described her as "a half-witted girl," who "walked about the house with a match, setting light to everything she came across." He was doubtful as to what to think of the reported flaming of a kitten, with a few hairs on its back slightly singed. But the chief difficulty was to explain the fire on the ceiling, and the fires on the walls. I'll not experiment, but I assume that I could flip matches all day at a wall and not set wallpaper afire. The reporter asked Mrs. Dawson whether the girl had any knowledge of chemistry. According to him, the answer was that this little girl, aged 14, who had been brought up in an orphan asylum, was "well versed in the rudiments of the science." Basing upon this outcome of his investigations, and forgetting that he had called the well-versed, little chemist "half-witted," or being more sophisticated than I seem to think, and seeing no inconsistency between scientific knowledge and imbecility, the useful reporter then needed only several data more to solve the mystery. He enquired in the town, and learned that the well-versed and half-witted little chemist was also "an incorrigible little thief." He went to the drug store, and learned that several times the girl had been sent there on errands. The mystery was solved: the girl had stolen "some chemical", which she applied to various parts of Dawson's house.

Occurrences of more recent date. Story in the London *Daily Mail* (Dec. 13, 1921) of a boy, in Budapest, in whose presence furniture moved. The boy was about 13 years of age. Since about his 12th birthday, fires had often broken out, in his presence. Alarmed neighbours, or "superstitious" neighbours, as they were described, in the account, had driven him and his mother from their home. It was said that, when he slept, flames flickered over him and singed his pillow.

In the *New York Times* (Aug. 25, 1929) was published a story of excitement upon the West Indian island of Antigua. This is a story that reverses the particulars of some of the other stories. It is an account of a girl whose clothes flamed, leaving her body unscorched. This girl, a Negress, named Lily White, living in the village of Liberta, flamed, while walking in the streets. However, at home, too, the clothes of this girl often burst into flames. She became dependent upon her neighbours for something to wear. When she was in bed, sheets burned around her, seemingly harmlessly to her, according to the story.

Early in March, 1922, an expedition, composed of newspaper reporters and photographers, headed by Dr. Walter Franklin Prince, arrived at a deserted house that was surrounded by snow banks out of which stuck the blackened backs, legs, and arms of burned furniture. The newspapers had told of doings in this house, near Antigonish, Nova Scotia, and had emphasized the circumstance that, "in the dead of winter," Alexander MacDonald and his family had been driven from their home, by "mysterious fires," unaccountable sounds, and the meanderings of crockery. The phenomena had centred around Mary Ellen, MacDonald's adopted daughter. With the idea that the house was haunted, the expedition entered, and made itself at home, everybody quick on the draw for note paper or camera. Mostly, in poltergeist cases, I see nothing to suggest that the girls – boys sometimes – are mediums, or are operated upon by spirits; the phenomena seem to be occult powers of youngsters. In Macdonald's house, the investigators came upon nothing that suggested the presence of spirits. Mary Ellen and her father, or father by adoption, were induced to return to the house, but nothing occurred. Usually, in cases of poltergeist girls, phenomena are not of long duration. Dr. Prince interviewed neighbours, and recorded their testimony that dozens of fires had broken out, in this girl's presence; but more striking than any testimony by witnesses was the sight, outside this house, of the blackened furniture, sticking out of snow banks (*Journal of the American Society for Psychical Research,* 16, 722).

New York Sun (Feb. 2, 1932) – a dispatch from Bladenboro, North Carolina. "Fires which apparently spring from nowhere, consuming the household effects of C.H. Williamson here, have placed this community in a state of excitement and continue to burn. Saturday a window shade and curtain burned in the Williamson home. Since then fire has burst out in five rooms. Five window shades, bed coverings, table cloths and other effects have suddenly burst into flames under the noses of watchers. Williamson's daughter stood in the middle of the floor, with no fire near. Suddenly her dress ignited. That was too much, and household goods were removed from the house."

In the *New York Sun* (Dec. 1, 1882) is an account of the occult powers of Wm. Underwood, a Negro, aged 27, of Paw Paw, Michigan. The account, copied from the *Michigan Medical News* (5, 263), was written by Dr. L.C. Woodman, of Paw Paw. It was Dr. Woodman's statement that he was convinced that Underwood's phenomena were genuine. "He will take anybody's handkerchief and hold it to his mouth, rub it vigorously with his hands while breathing on it and immediately it bursts into flames and burns until consumed. He will strip and rinse out his mouth thoroughly, wash his hands and submit to the most rigid examination to preclude the possibility of any humbug, and then by his breath blown upon any paper or cloth envelop it in flame. He will, while out gunning and without matches desirous of a fire, lie down after collecting dry leaves and by breathing on them start the fire."

In the *New York Sun* (July 29, 1927) is an account of a visit by Vice-President Dawes, to Memphis, Tennessee. In this city lived a car-repairer, who was also a magician. "He took General Dawes' handkerchief, and breathed upon it, and it caught fire."

Out of the case of the Negro who breathed dry leaves afire, I conceive of the rudiments of a general expression, which I expect to develop later. The phenomena look to me like a survival of a power that may have been common in the times of primitive men. Breathing dry leaves afire would, once upon a time, be a miracle of the highest value. I speculate how that could have come about. Most likely there never has been human intelligence keen enough to conceive of the uses of fire, in times when uses of fire were not of conventional knowledge. But, if we can think of our existence as a whole – perhaps only one of countless existences in the cosmos – as a developing organism, we can think of a fire-inducing power appearing automatically in some human beings, at a time of its need in the development of human phenomena. So fire-geniuses appeared. By a genius I mean one who can't avoid knowledge of fire, because he can't help setting things afire.

I think of these fire-agents as the most valuable members of a savage community, in primitive times; most likely beginning humbly, regarded as freaks; most likely persecuted at first, but becoming established, and then so overcharging for their services that it was learned how, by rubbing sticks, to do without them – so then their fall from importance, and the dwindling of them into their present, rare occurrence – but the preservation of them, as occasionals, by Nature, as an insurance, because there's no knowing when we'll all go back to savagery again, degrading down to an ignorance of even how to start fires – so then a revival of the fire-agents, and civilisation starting up again – only again to be overthrown by wars and grafts, doctors, lawyers, and other racketeers; corrupt judges and cowardly juries – starting down again, perhaps this time not stopping short of worms. Occasionally I contribute to the not very progressive science of biology, and, as I explain atavistic persons in societies, I now make suggestions as to vestigial organs and structures in human bodies – that the vestigial may not be merely a relic, but may be insurance – that the vestigial tail of a human being is no mere functionless retention, but is a provision against times when back to the furry state we may go and need means for wagging our emotions. Conceive of a powerful backward slide, and one conceives of the appearance, by only an accentuation of the existing, of hosts of werewolves and wereskunks and werehyenas in the streets of New York City.

Mostly our data indicate that occasional human beings have the fire-inducing power. But it looks as if it were not merely that, in the presence of the Negress, Lily White, fires started: it looks as if these fires were attacks upon her. Men and women have been found, burned to death, and explanations at inquests have not been satisfactory. There are records of open, and savage, seizures, by flames, of people.

Annual Register (1820, pt. 2, 13) – that Elizabeth Barnes, a girl aged 10, had been taken to court, accused by John Wright, a linen draper, of Foley-place, Mary-le-bone, London, of having repeatedly, and "by some extraordinary means," set fire to the clothing of Wright's mother, by which she had been burned so severely that she was not expected to live. The girl had been a servant in Wright's household. Upon January 5th an unexplained fire had broken out. Upon the 7th, Mrs. Wright and the girl were sitting by the hearth, in the kitchen. Nothing is said, in the account, of relations between these two. Mrs. Wright got up from her chair, and was walking away, when she saw her clothes were afire. Again, upon January 8th, she was, with the girl, in the kitchen, about eight feet from the hearth, where "scarcely any fire" was burning. Suddenly her clothes flamed. The next day, Wright heard screams from the kitchen, where his mother was, and where the girl had been. He ran into the room, and found his mother in flames. Only a moment before had the girl left the kitchen, and this time Wright accused her. But it was Mrs. Wright's belief that the girl had nothing to do with her misfortunes, and that "something supernatural" was assailing her. She sent for her daughter, who arrived, to guard her. She continued to believe that the girl could have had nothing to do with the fires, and went

77

to the kitchen, where the girl was, and again "by some unknown means," she caught fire. "She was injured so dreadfully by the fire that she was put to bed." When she had gone to sleep, her son and daughter left the room – and were immediately brought back by her screams, finding her surrounded by flames. Then the girl was told to leave the house. She left, and there were no more fires. This seemed conclusive, and the Wrights caused her arrest. At the hearing, the magistrate said that he had no doubt that the girl was guilty, but that he could not pronounce sentence, until Mrs. Wright should so recover as to testify.

In *Cosmos: Revue Encyclopédique* (s. 3, 6, 240) is a physician's report upon a case. It is a communication by Dr. Bertholle to the Société Medico-Chirurgicale:

That, upon the 1st of August, 1869, the police of Paris had sent for Dr. Bertholle, in the matter of a woman, who had been found, burned to death. Under the burned body, the floor was burned, but there was nothing to indicate the origin of the fire. Bedclothes, mattresses, curtains, all other things in the room, showed not a trace of fire. But this body was burned, as if it had been in the midst of flames of the intensity of a furnace. Dr. Bertholle's report was technical and detailed: left arm totally consumed, right hand burned to cinders, no trace left of internal organs in the thorax, and organs in the abdomen unrecognisable. The woman had made no outcry, and no other sound had been heard by other dwellers in the house. It is localisation, or specialisation, again – a burned body in an almost unscorched room.

Upon the night of Dec. 23, 1916 – see the *New York Herald* (Dec. 27 and 28, 1916) – Thomas W. Morphey, proprietor of the Lake Denmark Hotel, seven miles from Dover, N.J., was awakened by moaning sounds. He went down the stairs, and found his housekeeper, Lillian Green, burned and dying. On the floor under her was a small, charred place, but nothing else, except her clothes, showed any trace of fire. At a hospital, the woman was able to speak, but it seems that she could not explain. She died without explaining.

One of my methods, when searching for what I call data, is to note in headlines, or in catalogs, or indexes, such clew-words, or clew-phrases, as I call them, as "mystery solved," or an assurance that something has been explained. When I read that common sense has triumphed, and that another superstition has been laid low, that is a stimulus to me to be busy –

Or that story of the drunken woman, of Whitley Bay, near Blyth, who had told of finding her sister burned to death on an unscorched bed, and had recanted. Having read that this mystery had been satisfactorily explained, I got a volume of the *Blyth News & Wansbeck Telegraph* (March 27 and April 3, 1908).

The story in the local newspaper is largely in agreement with the story in the London newspapers: nevertheless there are grounds for doubts that make me think it worth while to re-tell the story.

The account is of two retired schoolteachers, Margaret and Wilhelmina Dewar, who lived in the town of Whitley Bay, near Blyth. In the evening of March 22nd, 1908, Margaret Dewar ran into a neighbour's house, telling that she had found her sister, burned to death. Neighbours went to the house with her. On a bed, which showed no trace of fire, lay the charred body of Wilhelmina Dewar. It was Margaret's statement that so she had found the body, and so she testified, at the inquest. And there was no sign of fire in any other part of the house.

So this woman testified. The coroner said that he did not believe her. He called a policeman, who said that, at the time of the finding of the body, the woman was so drunk that she could not have known what she was saying. The policeman was not called upon to state how he distinguished between signs of excitement and terror, and intoxication. But there was no accusation that, while upon the witness stand, this woman was intoxicated, and here she told the same story. The coroner urged her to recant. She said that she could not change her story.

So preposterous a story as that of a woman who had burned to death on an unscorched bed, if heeded, or if permitted to be told, would be letting "black magic", or witchcraft, into English legal proceedings. The coroner tried persistently to make the woman change it. She persisted in refusing. The coroner abruptly adjourned the inquest until April 1st.

Upon April 1st, Margaret Dewar confessed. Any reason for her telling of a lie, in the first place, is not discoverable. But there were strong reasons for her telling what she was wanted to tell. The local newspaper was against her. Probably the coroner terrified her. Most likely all her neighbours were against her, and hers were the fears of anybody, in a small town, surrounded by hostile neighbours. When the inquest was resumed, Margaret Dewar confessed that she had been inaccurate, and that she had found her sister burned, but alive, in a lower part of the house, and had helped her up to her room, where she had died. In this new story, there was no attempt to account for the fire; but the coroner was satisfied. There was not a sign of fire anywhere in the lower part of this house. But the proper testimony had been recorded. Why Margaret Dewar should have told the story that was called a lie was not inquired into. There are thousands of inquests at which testimonies are proper stories.

Madras Mail (May 13, 1907) – a woman in the village of Manner, near

Dinapore – flames that had consumed her body, but not her clothes – that two constables had found the corpse in a room, in which nothing else showed signs of fire, and had carried the smouldering body, in the unscorched clothes, to the District Magistrate. *Toronto Globe* (Jan. 29, 1907) – dispatch from Pittsburgh, Pa. – that Albert Houck had found the body of his wife, "burned to a crisp", on a table – no sign of fire upon the table, nor anywhere else in the house. *New York Sun* (Jan. 24, 1930) – coroner's inquiry, at Kingston, N.Y., into the death of Mrs. Stanley Lake. "Although her body was severely burned, her clothing was not even scorched."

CHAPTER 14

The story of the "mad bats of Trinidad" is that the discoverer of them had solved a mystery of many deaths of human beings and cattle (*New York Times,* September 29, 1931). "Dr. Pawan, a Trinidad scientist, had discovered that the infection had been caused by mad vampire bats, affected by rabies, which they transmitted in a new form of insidious hydrophobia."

But the existence of hydrophobia is so questionable, or of such rare occurrence, even in dogs, that the story of the "mad bats of Trinidad" looks like some more of the sensationalism in science that is so obtrusive today, and compared with which I am, myself, only a little wild now and then. It is probable that the deaths of human beings and cattle, in Trinidad, have not been accounted for. Once upon a time the explanation would have been "witch-craft." Now it's "rabid vampires." The old hag on her broomstick is of inferior theatrical interest, compared with the insane blood-sucker.

The germ-theory of diseases is probably like all other theories, ranging from those of Moses and Newton and Einstein and Brother Voliva down, or maybe up, or perhaps crosswise, to mine, or anybody else's. Many cases may be correlated under one explanation, but there must be exceptions. No pure, or homogeneous, case of any kind is findable: so every case is variously classifiable. There have been many cases of ailments and deaths of human beings that have not been satisfactorily explained in the medical terms that are just now fashionable, but that will probably be out of style, after a while. Nowadays one is smug with what one takes for progress, thinking of old-time physicians prescribing dried toads for ailments. Here's something for the enjoyment of future smugness. Newspapers of Jan. 14, 1932 – important medical discovery – dried pigs' stomachs, as a cure for anaemia. I now have a theory of what is called evolution, in terms of fashions – that somewhere, perhaps on high, there is a Paris – where, once upon a time, were dictated the modes in bugs and worms, and then the costumes of birds and mammals; grotesquely stretching the necks of giraffes, and then quite as unreasonably reacting with a repentance of hippopotami; passing on to a mental field of alternating extravagances and puritanisms, sometimes neat and tasteful, but often elaborate and rococo, with religions, philosophies, and sciences, imposing upon the fashion-slaves of this earth the latest thing in theories.

In the *New York Sun* (Jan. 17, 1930), Dr. E.S. Godfrey, of the New York State Department of Health, told, in an interview, of mysterious illnesses on a vessel. In a period of four years, twenty-seven officers and men had been stricken by what was called "typhoid fever." Taking his science from the Sunday newspapers, which had full-paged the story of "Typhoid Mary", a scientific detective, with his microscope, boarded this vessel, and of course soon announced that he had "tracked down" one of the sailors, as a "typhoid carrier." Such sleuthing has become a modernised witch-finding. There are, in New York State, today, persecutions that are in some cases as deadly as the witchcraft-persecutions of the past. "There are 188 women and 90 men recorded as typhoid-carriers, in New York State." Why there should be twice as many women as men is plain enough: the carrier-finders, with "Typhoid Mary" in mind, probably went looking for women. It may be a matter of diffi-culty, or it may be impossible, in times of general unemployment, for somebody in the grocery or dairy business, to change into some other occupation: but these 278 "typhoid-carriers", tracked down by medical Sherlock Holmeses, who had read of "typhoid-carriers", are prohibited from working in food-trades and have to report to district health officers once every three months. But this is for the protection of the rest of us. But that is what the witch-finders used to say. Chivalry can't die, so long as there is tyranny: every tyrant has been much given to protecting somebody or something. It is one of the blessings of our era that we are tormented by so many abominations, enormities, and pestiferous, smaller botherations that we can't concentrate upon the germ scares that the medical "finders" would spread, if it were not for so much competition. They did spread, with some success, with their parrot-scare, in the year 1930. Abandoned parrots, in their cages, were found, frozen to death, in parks and doorways. Probably the psittacosis scare, of 1930, did not become the hysteria of former scares, because lay-alarmists were checked by their inability to pronounce the name of it.

There must be something the matter with the germ-theory of diseases, or the nursing and medical professions would not be so over-crowded. There must be something the matter with the germ-theory of diseases, if there is something the matter with every theory.

I looked up the case of "Typhoid Mary." With the preconceptions of everybody who looks up cases, I went looking for something to pick on. It was impossible for me to fail to find what I wanted to consider a case of injustice, if ours is an existence of justice-injustice. I of course found that the case of "Typhoid Mary" as a germ-carrier was not made out so clearly as the "finders" of today suppose.

In the year 1906, it was noted that in several homes, in New York City, where Mary had been employed as a cook, there had been illnesses that were said to be cases of typhoid fever. The matter was investigated, according to what was supposed to be scientific knowledge, in the year 1906. The germ-theory of diseases was the dominant idea. Not a thought was given to relations between this woman and her victims. Had there been quarrels, before illnesses of persons, living in the same house with her, occurred? What was the disposition of the woman? There are millions of men and women, with long hours and little pay, who may, in their states of mind, be more dangerous than germs. There are cooks with grievances, as well as cooks with germs. But Mary's malices were not examined. It was "found" that, though immune herself, she was a distributor of typhoid bacilli. For three years she was "detained" in a hospital, by the public health officials of New York City.

And then what became of Mary's germs? According to one examination, she had them. According to another examination, she hadn't them. At the end of three years, Mary was examined again, and, according to all tests, she hadn't them. She was released, upon promising to report periodically to the Board of Health.

Probably because of lively impressions of "detention", Mary did not keep her promise. Under various aliases, she obtained work as a cook.

About five years later, twenty-five persons, in the Sloane Maternity Hospital, New York City, were stricken with what was said to be typhoid fever. Two of them died. See *Outlook* (109, 803). And Mary was doing the cooking, at the hospital. The Public Health officials "detained" her again, following their conclusion that they said was obvious. I know of hosts of cases that are obvious one way, and just as apparent some other way; conclusive, according to one theorist, and positively established, according to opposing theorists.

She had them, when, to support a theory, she should have them. She hadn't them, when her own support, as "detained," was becoming expensive. She had – she hadn't – But it does seem that in some way this woman was related to the occurrence of illnesses, sometimes fatal.

Of all germ-distributors, the most notorious was Dr. Arthur W. Waite, who, in the year 1916, was an embarrassment to medical science (*New York Sun,* Nov. 29, 1930). In his bacteriological laboratory, he had billions of germs. Waite planned to kill his father-in-law, John E. Peck, 435 Riverside Drive, New York City. He fed the old man germs of diphtheria but got no results. He induced Peck to use a nasal spray, in which he had planted colonies of the germs of tuberculosis. Not a cough. He fed the old man calomel, to weaken his resistance. He turned loose hordes of germs of typhoid and then tried influenza. In desperation, he lost all standing in the annals of distinctive crimes, and went common, or used arsenic. The old-fashioned method was a success. One's impression is that, if anything, diets and inhalations of germs may be healthful.

It is not that I am attacking the germ-theory of diseases, as absolute nonsense. I do not attack this theory, as absolute nonsense, because I conceive of no theory that is more than partly nonsensical. I have some latitude. Let the conventionalists have their theory that germs cause diseases, and let their opponents have their theory that diseases cause germs, or that diseased conditions attract germs. Also there is room for dozens of other theories. Under the heading "Invalidism," I have noted forty-three cases of human beings who were ill, sometimes temporarily, and sometimes dying, at the time of uncanny – though rather common – occurrences in their homes. No conventional theory fits these cases. But the stories, as collected by me, are only fragments.

One day, in July, 1890, in the home of Mr. Piddock, in Hafer-road, Clapham, London – see the London *Echo* (July 16, 1890) – the daughter of the household was dying. Volleys of stones, of origin that could not be found out, were breaking through the glass of the conservatory. It is probable that not a doctor, in London, in the year 1890 – nor in the year 1930 – if what is known as a reputable physician – would admit any possibility of relationship between a dying girl and stones that were breaking windows.

But why should any doctor, in London, in the year 1890, or any other year, accept the existence of any relations between a bombardment of a house and a girl's dying condition? He would be as well-justified in explaining that there was only coincidence, as were early paleontologists in so explaining, when they came upon bones of a huge body, and, some distance away, a relatively small skull – explaining that the skull only happened to be near the other bones. They had never heard of dinosaurs. If many times they came upon similar skulls associating with similar other bones, some of them would at least refuse any longer to believe in mere coincidence; but the more academic ones, affronted by a new thought, would continue in their thought-ruts, decrying all reported instances as yarns, fakery, imposture, nonsense.

The dying girl – showers of stones –

New York Sun (Dec. 22 and 30, 1883) – that, in a closed room in a house in Jordan, New York, in which a man was dying, stones were falling.

In the home of Alexander Urquhart, Aberdeen, Scotland, there was an invalid boy. Stories of doings in this house were told in London newspapers, early in January, 1920 (London *Evening Standard,* January 8, 1920; London *Globe,* January 8 and 12, 1920; London *Daily Chronicle,* January 8 and 9, 1920; London *Daily Express,* January 9, 1920). The boy was simply set down as "an invalid boy," and presumably doctors were not mystified by his ailment. Nobody was recorded as suspecting anything but coincidence between whatever may have been the matter with him, and phenomena that centred around him, as he lay in his bed. It was as if he were bombarded by unseen bombs. Explosive sounds that shook the house occurred over his bed, and, according to reports by policemen, the bed was violently shaken. Policemen reported that objects, in the boy's room, moved –

London *Daily News* (Jan. 10, 1920) – "Aberdeen ghost laid low – prosaic explanation for strange sounds – nothing but a piece of wood that the wind had been knocking against a side of the house."

That probably convinced the London readers who preferred something like the "mice-behind-the-baseboards" conclusion to such stories. But the *Glasgow Herald* (Jan. 13, 1920) continued to tell of "thumping noises, as if a hammer were being used." "The house shook, dishes rattled, and articles of furniture were moved from their positions."

The data are protrusions from burials. The body of a girl – the body of a crow. Somebody dying – and hostile demonstrations that can not convention-ally be explained. But if there were connecting circumstances, they are now undiscoverable. It is said that there is a science of comparative anatomy, by which, given any bone of an animal, the whole skeleton can be reconstructed. So stated, this is one of the tall stories of science. The "father" of the science of comparative anatomy never reconstructed anything except conventionally. The paleontologists have reconstructed crowds of skeletons that are exhibited as evidences of evolution; but Cuvier not only never reconstructed anything new, but now is notorious as a savage persecutor of evolutionists. There can not be reconstruction, unless there be a model. We may have comparative anatomy of our fragmentary circumstances, if we can fit the pieces of a situation-model. And it may be that we are slowly building that. Of course any-thing of the nature of old-fashioned, absolute science is no dream of mine.

From the *Port of Spain Mirror* (Nov. 21, 22, 29, and 30, 1905) and the *Port of Spain Gazette* (Nov. 21 and 22, 1905), I take a story of phenomena that began Nov. 12, 1905, in Mrs. Lorelhei's boarding house, in Queen Street, Port of Spain, Trinidad. The house was pelted with stones. A malicious neighbour was suspected, but then, inside the house, there were occurrences that, at least physically, could be attributed to nobody. Objects were thrown about. Chairs fell over, got up, and whirled. Out of a basket of potatoes, flew the potatoes. Stones fell from unseen points of origin, in rooms. A doctor was quoted as saying that he had seen some of these doings. He had been visiting an invalid, who, in this house, was ill.

In the *Religio-Philosophical Journal* (July 15, 1882), as copied from the *New York Sun,* there is a boarding house story. Mrs. William Swift's boarding house, 52 Willoughby Street, Brooklyn – the occupant of the back parlour was ill. Raps were heard. Several times appeared a floating, vaporous body, shaped like a football. Upon the ailing boarder, the effect of this object was like an electric shock.

In the *Religio-Philosophical Journal* (March 31, 1883) and the *New York Times* (March 12, 1883), there are accounts of the bewitchment of the house, 33 Church Street, Hartford, Conn. Tramping sounds – objects flying about. A woman in this house was ill. While she was preparing medicine in a cup, the spoon flew away. Sounds like *Hey, diddle, diddle!* Then it was as if an occult enemy took a shot at her. An unfindable bullet made a hole in a glass.

In the *Bristol Mercury,* (England; Oct. 12, 1889) and in the *Northern Daily Telegraph* (Blackburn; Oct. 8, 1889) are accounts of loud sounds of unknown origin in a house in the village of Hornington, near Salisbury. Here a child, Lydia Hewlett, aged 9, "was stricken with a mysterious illness, lying in bed, never speaking, never moving, apparently at death's door." It was said that this child had incurred the enmity of a gypsy, whom she had caught stealing vegetables in a neighbour's garden.

One of the cases of "mysterious family maladies," accompanied by poltergeist disturbances, was reported by the *Guernsey Star* (March 7, 1903). In the home of a resident of the island of Guernsey, Mr. B. Collinette, several members of the family were taken ill. Things were flying about.

Early in the year 1893 – as told in the *New York World* (Feb. 17 and 19, 1896) – an elderly man, named Mack, appeared, with his invalid wife, and his daughter Mary, in the town of Bellport, Long Island, N.Y., and made of the ground floor of their house a little candy store. The account in the *World* is of a starting up of persecutions of this family attributed to hostility of other store-keepers, and to dislike "probably because of their thrift." Stones were thrown at the house "by street gamins." Several boys were arrested, but there was no evidence against them. At the time of one of the bombardments, Mary was on the porch of the house. A big dog appeared. He ran against her, knocking her down, injuring her spine, so that she was a cripple the rest of her life. All details of this story are in terms of persecutions by neighbours; in the terms of the telling, there is no suggestion of anything occult. Unidentified persons were throwing stones.

The terrified girl took to her bed. Stones thumped on the roof above her, throwing her into spasms of fright. In one of these convulsions, she died. Missing in this story is anything relating to Mack's experiences before arriving in Bellport. His daughter was crippled, and died of fright. He arrived with an invalid wife.

In his biography of the Bishop of Zanzibar (*Frank, Bishop of Zanzibar,* 112) – I take from a review in the London *Daily Express* (Oct. 27, 1926) – Dr. H. Maynard Smith, Canon of Gloucester, tells of poltergeist persecutions, near the mission station, at Weti (Wete, Pemba Island, Tanzania). Clods of earth of undetectable origin, were bombarding a house in which lived a man and his wife. Clods fell inside the house. The bishop investigated, and he was struck by a clod. Inside the house, he saw a mass of mud appear on a ceiling. The door was open, but this point on the ceiling was in a position that could not be hit by anyone throwing anything from outside. There was no open window.

The bishop came ceremoniously the next morning, and solemnly exorcised the supposed spirit. That these stories indicate the existence of spirits is what I do not think. But it seems that the bishop made an impression. The mud-slinging stopped. But then illness came upon the woman of this house.

Upon the night of August 9, 1920, as told in the London *Daily Mail* (Aug. 19, 1920), a shower of small stones broke the windows in the top floor of Wellington Villa, Grove-road, South Woodford, London, occupied by Mr. H.T. Gaskin, an American, the inventor of the Gaskin Life Boat. There were many showers of stones of undetectable origin. Upon the night of the 13th, policemen took positions in the house, in the street, on roofs, and in trees. The upper floor of the house was bombarded with stones, but where they came from could not be found out. Night of the 14th – a procession. Forty policemen, some of them local, and some of them from Scotland Yard, marched down Grove-road, and went up on roofs, or climbed into trees. Volleys of stones arrived, but the forty policemen learned no more than had the smaller numbers of the preceding investigations. Nevertheless it seems that they made an impression. Phenomena stopped.

The patter of stones – and policemen on roofs, and policemen in trees, and the street packed with sightseers – and this is a spot of excitement – but it has no environment. I can pick up no trace of relations between anybody in this house and anybody outside.

In one of the rooms lay an invalid. Mr. Gaskin was suffering from what was said to be sciatica. In an interview he said that he could not account for the attack upon him, or upon the house: that, so far as he knew, he had no enemy.

In some of these cases, I have tried to dig into blankness. I have shovelled vacancy. I have written to Mr. and Mrs. Gaskin, but have received no answer. I have looked over the index of the London *Times,* before and after August, 1920, with the idea of coming upon something, such as a record of a law case, or some other breeder of enmity, in which Mr. Gaskin might have been involved, but have come upon nothing.

CHAPTER 15

Now I have a theory that our existence is a hermaphrodite –

Or the unproductivity of it, in the sense that the beings, and seas, and houses, and trees, and the fruits of trees, its "immortal truths", and "rocks of ages" that it seems to produce are only flutters that seem to be real productions to us, because we see them very slow-motioned.

My interpretation of theology is that, though mythologically much confused, it is an awareness of the wholeness of one existence – perhaps one of countless existences in the cosmos – and that its distortions are founded upon intuitive knowledge of the unproductive state of this one existence, as a whole – and so its visions of a divine sterility, which are illustrated with figures of blonde hermaphrodites. Of course there are stray legends of male angels, but such stories are symbols of the inconsistency that co-exists with the consistency of all things phenomenal –

Or that parthenogenesis is the essential principle of all things, beings, thoughts, states, phenomenal.

I'd be queried, if I should say, of the consummation of any human romance, that it is parthenogenetic: but humanity, regarded as a whole, is sustained by self-fertilisation. Except for occasional, vague stories of external enrichments, there are no records of invigorations imparted to the human kind from gorillas, hyenas, or swine. Elephants fertilise elephants. I conceive of no bizarre, little love story, with a fruitful outcome, of the attractions of a rhinoceros to a humming bird. Though I have a venerable, little story – account sent to me by Mr. Ernest Doerfler, Bronx, N.Y. – of an eighteenth-century scientist, whose theory it was that human females can be pollinated, and who experimented, by exposing a buxom female to the incidence of the east wind, and of course was successful in establishing his theory, I have no other datum of human and vegetable unions; so this reported occurrence must be considered one of the marvels from which this book of not uncommon events holds aloof.

The parthenogenetic triumphs of the human intellect are circular stupidities. The mathematicians, in their intuitions of the state of a whole, have represented what to the devout is divinity, with the circle, which, to them the "perfect figure," symbolises getting nowhere.

Much of the argument in this book will depend upon our acceptance that nothing in our existence is real. The Whole may be Realness. Out of its phenomena, it may be non-phenomenally producing offspring-realnesses. That is not our present subject. But up comes the question: If nothing phenomenal is real, is everything phenomenal really unreal? But, if I accept that nothing is real, in phenomenal existence, I cannot accept that anything, therein, is really unreal. So my acceptance, in accordance with our general philosophy of the hyphen, is that all things perceptible to us are real-unreal, varying from the direction of one extreme to the other, according to whatever may be the degree of their appearance of individuality. If anybody has the notion that he is a real being – and by realness I mean individuality, or call it entity, or unrelatedness – let him try to tell why he thinks he exists, in a real sense. Recall the most celebrated of the parthenogenetic attempts to make this demonstration:

I think: therefore I am.

We have to accept that in order to think, the thinker must be of existence prior to the thought.

Why do I think?

Because I am.

Why am I?

Because I think.

The noblest triumphs of the human intellect are about as sublime as would be the description of a house in terms of its roof, whereas the description would be equally sublime, if in terms of the cellar, or the bath room. That is Newtonism – or a description of things in terms of one of its aspects, or gravitation. It is Darwinism – a description of all life in terms of selection, one of its aspects. *Gravitation* is only another name for *attraction.* Sir Isaac Newton's contribution to the glories of human knowledge is that an apple falls because it drops. All living things are selected by environment, said Darwin. Then, according to him, when he shifted aspects, all things constituting living environment are selected. Darwinism – that selection selects.

The materialists explain all things, except what they deny, or disregard, in terms of the material. The immaterialists, such as the absolute and the subjective idealists, explain all things in terms of the immaterial. My expression is in terms of the continuity of the material and the immaterial – or that one of these extremes is only an accentuation on one side, and the other only an accentuation on the other side, of the hyphenated state of material-immaterial.

I am a being who thinks: therefore I am a being who thinks. In this circular stupidity there is a simple unity that commends it to conventional lovers of the good, the true, and the beautiful.

I do not think. I have never had a thought. Therefore something or another. I do not think, but thoughts occur in what is said to be "my" mind – though, instead of being "in" it, they are it – just as inhabitants do not occur in a city, but are the city. There is a governing tendency among these thoughts, just as there is among people in any community, or as there is in the movements of the planets, or in the arrangements of cells constituting a plant, or an animal. So far as goes any awareness of "mine," "I" have no soul, no self, no entity, though at times of something like a harmonisation of "my" elements, "I" approximate to a state of unified being.

When I see – as for convenience "I" shall say, even though there is no I that is other than a very imperfectly co-ordinated aggregation of experience-states, sometimes ferociously antagonising one another, but mostly maintaining a kind of civilisation – but when I see that my thoughts are ruled by tendencies, such as to harmonise, organise, or co-ordinate: that they tend to integrate, segregate, nucleate, equilibrate – I am conscious of mere mechanical processes that mean no more in the arrangements of my ideas than they mean in the arrangements of my bones. I'd no more think of offering my ideas as immortal truth than I'd think of publishing X-ray photographs of my bones, as eternal. But the organising tendency implicit in all things – along with the disorganising tendency implicit in all things – has admirably expressed itself in the design that is my skeleton. I think so. I have no reason to think that my skeleton is in any way inferior to anybody else's skeleton. I feel that if I could arrange my ideas with the art that has arranged my bones, I'd have, for writing a book, the justification that all writers feel the need of, trying to excuse themselves for writing books.

But I do not think that mechanism is all that there is in our existence. Only the old-fashioned absolutist conceives, or says he conceives, of our existence as absolutely mechanical. There is an individuality in things that is not of mechanical relations, because individuality is unrelatedness. I conceive of our existence as positive-negative, or as mechanical-immechanical.

But my methods are the largely mechanical methods of everybody, and of everything, that harmonises, or organises. One of these methods is classification. I am impelled to arrange my materials under headings – quite as a wind arranges fallen leaves, of various sizes, into groups – as a magnet makes selections from a pile of various things. So, again, when I see that my thoughts are coerced by conventional processes, I can think of my thoughts as nothing but the products of coercions. I'd not do these slaves the honour of believing them. They impose upon me only to the degree of temporary acceptance of some of them.

Merely thoughtfully, or only intellectually, I have made a collection of notes, under the classification of "Explosions." Some of the occurrences look as if explosive attacks, of an occult order, have been made upon human beings; or as if psychic bombs have been thrown invisibly at people, or at their property.

In the *New York Tribune* (Jan. 7, 1900), there is an account of poltergeist disturbances in a house, in Hyde Park, Chicago. According to the now well-known ways of chairs and tables, at times, these things hopped about, or moved with more dignity. It was if into this house stole an invisible but futile assassin. See back to accounts of visible but futile bullets. Time after time there was a sound like the discharge of a revolver. It was noted that this firing always occurred "at about the height of a man's shoulder." In a booklet, *A Disturbed House and its Relief,* Ada M. Sharpe tells of a seeming psychic bombardment of her home in Tackley, Oxfordshire, England. Beginning upon April 24, 1905, and continuing three years, at times, detonations, as if of exploding bombs, were heard in this house. Upon the first of May, 1911 (*Lloyd's Weekly News,* July 30; *Wandsworth Borough News,* July 21) unaccountable fires broke out in the house of Mr. J.A. Harvey, 356 York-road, Wandsworth, London. Preceding one of these fires, there were three explosions of unknown origin. In January, 1892 (*Peterborough Advertiser,* Jan. 9, 16, and 23, 1892), a house in Peterborough, England, occupied by a family named Rimes, was repeatedly shaken, as if bombed, and as if bombed futilely. Nobody was injured, and there was no damage.

In the *Religio-Philosophical Journal* (Dec. 25, 1880) – copied from the *Owatonna Review* (Minn.) – there is a story maybe of a psychic bomb that was tossed through the wall of a house, in Owatonna, penetrating the wall, without leaving a sign of its passage through the material. It was in a house occupied by a family named Dimant. There had been petty persecutions by an uncatchable: such as persistent ringing of the doorbell. One evening members of this family were in one of the rooms, when something exploded. Mrs. Dimant was knocked insensible. Fragments of a cylindrical glass object were found. But no window had been open, and there had been no other way by which, by known means, this object could have entered this house.

I note something of agreement between notions that are now developing – notions that will be called various names, one of which is not "practical" – and experiments by inventors that are attempts to be very practical. It is said that by means of "rays" inventors have been able to set off distant explosives. If by other means, or by subtler "rays," explosions at a distance can be made to occur, whatever the practical ones are trying to do may be far more effectively accomplished – if the data of this chapter do mean that there have been explosions that were the products of means, or powers, that are at present mysterious.

There are stories of brilliantly luminous things that are called "globe lightning" that have appeared in houses, and have moved about, before exploding, as if guided by intelligence of their own, or as if directed by a distant control. These stories are easily findable in books treating of lightning and the freaks of lightning. I pick out an account from a periodical. There seems to be no relation with lightning. In the *English Mechanic* (90, 140), Col. G.T. Plunket tells of an experience, in July, 1909, in his home, in Wimbledon, London. He and his wife were sitting in one of their rooms, when his wife saw a luminous thing moving toward them. It went to a chair, upon the back of which it seemed to rest, for a moment. It exploded. Col. Plunket did not see this thing, but he heard the explosion. As to the lightning-explanation, he writes that it was a fine evening.

London *Daily Mail* (July 23, 1925) – "Explosion riddle – mystery of a boy's wounds." "Injured by a mysterious explosion, which occurred in his mother's house, at Riverhall-street, South Lambeth, S.W., yesterday morning, Charley Orchard, 5, was conveyed to hospital in a serious condition. He was hurt on the face and chest, and some of his fingers were blown away.

"His mother had just called him to breakfast when the explosion occurred.

"Neighbours who heard the report of the explosion thought there was an outbreak of fire and summoned the fire brigade.

"An all-day search failed to discover the cause of the explosion."

The London newspapers, Sept. 26, 1910, told of a tremendous, unexplained explosion in a house in Willesden, London. I take from the local newspaper, the *Willesden Chronicle* (Sept. 30) – "A fire of a most mysterious character ... Absolutely no cause can be assigned for the outbreak, which was followed by a terrific explosion, completely wrecking the premises." But in no account is it made clear that first there was a fire, and that the explosion followed. A policeman, standing on a nearby corner, saw this house, 71 Walm-lane, Willesden, flame and burst apart. "Windows and doors at the back of the house were blown across the lawn to the rear fence, a distance of about 60 feet." "On examination of the premises, it was found that the two gas meters under the stairs were shut off, so that it was evident that the explosion was not caused by gas." Representatives of the Salvage Corps and of the Home Office investigated, but could conclude nothing except that chemicals, or petrol, might have exploded.

The occupants of this house, named Reece, were out of town, week-ending. Mr. Reece was communicated with, and it was his statement that there had been nothing in the house that could have exploded.

Willesden Chronicle (Oct. 7) – "The mystery of the fire and explosion which occurred last Sunday week at the corner of Walm-lane and Grosvenor-gardens, Willesden Green, has now been cleared up." "A charred sofa in the drawing-room and other evidence revealed the cause of the outbreak." Before leaving the house, Saturday morning (Sept. 24th), Mr. Reece, while smoking a pipe, had leaned over this sofa, and sparks from his pipe had fallen upon it. For thirty-six hours a fire, so caused, had smouldered, before bursting into flames. There were two standard spirit lamps in the room. In the fire, they must have exploded simultaneously.

The writer of this explanation picked the remains of a sofa out of a wreck of charred furniture. He leaned Reece over the sofa, because that would make his explanation work out as it should work out. Reece made no such statement, and he was not quoted. The explosion of two spirit lamps could do much damage, but this explosion was tremendous. The house was wrecked. The walls that remained standing were in such a toppling condition that the ruins were roped off.

The jagged walls of this wrecked house are more of our protrusions from vacancy. We visualise them in an environment of blankness. Somewhere there may have been a witch or a wizard.

Upon June 13, 1885, a resident of Pondicherry, Madras, India, was sitting in a closed room, when a mist appeared near him. At the same time there was a violent explosion. This man, C. André, sent an account to the French Academy (*Comptes Rendus,* 101, 899). I take from a report, in *L'Astronomie* (5, 311) M. André tried to explain in conventional terms, mentioning that at the time the weather was semi-stormy, and that an hour later rain fell heavily.

In times still farther back, the mist would have been told of, as the partly materialised form of an enemy, who had expressed his malices explosively. In times, still somewhere in the future, this may seem the most likely explanation.

Or the mist was something like the partly visible smoking fuse of an invisible bomb that had been discharged by a distant witch or wizard. And that does not seem to me to be much more of a marvel than would be somebody's ability to blow up a quantity of dynamite, though at a distance, and with no connecting wires.

In the *New York Herald Tribune* (Nov. 29, 1931), there is an account of the doings of Kurt Schimkus, of Berlin, who had arrived, in Chicago, to demonstrate his ability to discharge, from a distance, explosives, by means of what he called his "anti-war rays." According to reports from Germany, Schimkus had so exploded submarine mines and stores of buried cartridges. Herr Schimkus will have success and renown, I think: he knows that nothing great and noble and of benefit to mankind has ever been accomplished without much lubrication. He announced that slaughter was far-removed from his visions: that he was an agency for peace on earth and good will to man, because by exploding an enemy's munitions, with his "anti-war rays," he would make war impossible. Innocently, myself, I speculate upon the possible use of "psychic bombs," in blowing up tree stumps, in the cause of new pastures.

In the *New York Herald Tribune* (March 25, 1931), there is a story of an explosion that may have been set off by "rays" that at present are not understood. It is the story of the explosion that wrecked the sealing ship, *Viking,* off Horse Island, north of Newfoundland. It reminds me of the woman, who, in the New York hotel, feared fire. This ship was upon a moving picture expedition. Varrick Frissell, film producer, aboard this vessel, started to think of the kegs of powder aboard, and he became apprehensive. He started to make a warning sign to hang on the door of the powder room. Just then the ship blew up.

New York Herald Tribune (Dec. 13, 1931) – an account of disasters to two wives of a man – not a datum of his relations, or former relations, with anybody else. In the year 1924, illness was upon the wife of W.A. Baker, an oil man, who lived in Pasadena, California. It was said that her affliction was cancer. She was found, hanged, in her home. It was said that despondency had driven her to suicide. In the year 1926, Baker married again. Upon the night of Dec. 12, 1931, there was an explosion, somewhere under the bed of the second Mrs. Baker, or in the room underneath. The bed was hurled to the ceiling, and Mrs. Baker was killed. It was a tremendous explosion, but nobody else in the house was harmed.

Bomb experts investigated. They concluded that no known explosive had been used. They said that there had been no escape of gas. "The full force of the explosion seemed concentrated almost beneath Mrs. Baker's room."

In the years 1921-22, and early in the year 1923, there were, in England and other countries, explosions of coal such as had never occurred before. There was a violent explosion in a grate in a house in Guildford, near London, which killed a woman, and knocked down walls of the house (London *Daily News,* Sept. 16, 1921). There were other explosions of coal, during this year, but in 1922 attention was attracted by many instances.

In this period there was much disaffection among British coal miners. There was a suspicion that miners were mixing dynamite into coal. But, whether we think that the miners had anything to do with these explosions, or not, suspicions against them, in England, were checked by the circumstances that no case of the finding of dynamite in coal was reported, and that there were no explosions of coal in the rough processes of shipments.

There came reports from France. Then stoves, in which was burned British coal, were blowing up in France, Belgium, and Switzerland. The climax came about the first of January, 1923, when in one day there were several of these explosions in Paris, and explosions in three towns in England.

About the first of January, 1921, Mr. J.S. Frost, of 8 Ferristone-road, Hornsey, London, bought a load of coal. In his home were three children, Gordon, Bertie, and Muriel. I take data from the London newspapers, but especially from the local newspapers, the *Hornsey Journal* (Feb. 18; March 11, 25; April 8, 15; May 13, 20) and the *North Middlesex Chronicle* (Feb. 12, 19, 26; March 12, 19, 26; April 2, 16; May 14). In the grates of this house, coal exploded. Also, coal in buckets exploded. A policeman was called in. He made his report upon coal that not only exploded, but hopped out of grates, and sauntered along floors, so remarkable that an Inspector of Police investigated. According to a newspaper, it was this Inspector's statement that he had picked up a piece of coal, which had broken into three parts, and had then vanished from his hands. It was said that burning coals leaped from grates, and fell in showers in other rooms, having passed through walls, without leaving signs of this passage. Flat irons, coal buckets, other objects "danced." Ornaments were dislodged, but fell to the floor, without breaking. A pot on a tripod swung, though nobody was near it. The phenomena occurred in the presence of one of the boys, especially, and sometimes in the presence of the other boy.

There has been no poltergeist case better investigated. I know of no denial of the phenomena by any investigator. One of the witnesses was the Rev. A.L. Gardiner, vicar of St. Gabriel's, Wood Green, London. "There can be no doubt of the phenomena. I have seen them, myself." Another witness was Dr. Herbert Lemerle, of Hornsey. Dr. Lemerle told of a clock that mysteriously vanished. Upon the 8th of May, a public meeting was held in Hornsey, to discuss the phenomena.

In the newspapers there was a tendency to explain it all as mischief by the children of this household.

The child, Muriel, terrified by the doings, died upon April 1st (London *Daily Express,* April 2, 1921). The boy, Gordon, frightened into a nervous breakdown, was taken to Lewisham Hospital.

The coal in all these cases was coal from British coal mines. The newspaper that told of these explosions told of the bitterness and vengefulness of British coal miners, enraged by hardships and reduced wages, uncommon in even their harsh experiences –

Or see back –

There's a shout of vengefulness, in Hyde Park, London – far away, in Gloucestershire, an ancient mansion bursts into flames.

CHAPTER 16

But why this everlasting attempt to solve something? – whereas it is our acceptance that, in a final sense, there is, in phenomenal affairs, nothing – or that there is only the state of something-nothing – so that all problems are only soluble-insoluble – or that most of the social problems we have, today, were at one time conceived of as solutions of preceding problems – or that every Moses leads his people out of Egypt into perhaps a damn sight worse – Promised Lands of watered milk and much-adulterated honey – so why these everlasting attempts to solve something?

But to take surgical operations upon warders of Sing Sing Prison, and the loss of rectitude by lace curtains, and the vanishing man of Berlin; "Typhoid Mary", and a Chinese hair-clipper, and explosions of coal, and bodies on benches in a Harlem Park –

Robert Browning's conception was to take three sounds, and make, not a fourth, but a star ("Abt Vogler," verse 7).

Out of seven colours, not to lay on daubs, but to paint a picture.

Out of seven million Americans, Russians, Germans, Irishmen, Italians, and on, or so long as geography holds out, not to pile a population, but to organise – more or less – into New York City.

Sulphur and lava in a barren plain, and a salty block of stone, shaped roughly like a woman – signs of erosion on rocks far above water-level – a meteor that had set a bush afire – the differences of languages of peoples – and all the other elements that organised into *Genesis*.

Data of variations and heredity and adaptations; of multiplications and of checks and of the doctrine of Malthus; of acquired characters and of transmissions – and they organised into *The Origin of Species* –

Just as, once upon a time, minerals that had affinity for one another came together and took on geometrical appearances.

But a crystal is not supposed to be either a prohibition or an anti-prohibition argument. I know of a crystal of quartz that weighs several hundred pounds. But it has not been mistaken for propaganda –

Or all theories – theological, scientific, philosophical – and that they represent the same organising process – but that self-conscious theorists, instead of recognising that thought- forms were appearing in their minds, as in wider existence have appeared crystalline constructions, have believed that it was immortal Truth that they were conceiving.

Oxygen and sulphur and carbon –

Or Emma Piggot and Ambrose Small and Rose Smith –

Or let's have just a little, minor expression, or organisation, a small composition, arranging the data of poltergeist girls. The elements of this synthesis are moving objects, fires, girls in strange surroundings, youth and the atavism of youth.

Case of Jennie Bramwell – she was an adopted daughter. The Antigonish girl was an adopted daughter. See the Dagg case – adopted daughter. "Adoption" is a good deal of a disguise for getting little girls to work for not much more than nothing. It is not so much that so many poltergeist girls have been housemaids and "adopted daughters", as that so many of them have been not in their own homes; lost and helpless youngsters, under hard task-masters, in strange surroundings –

Or the first uncertain and precarious appearances of human beings upon this earth – and a need for them, and a fostering, a nurturing, a protection, far different from conditions in these swarming times, when the need is for eliminations –

A lost child in primordial woods – and the value of her, which no genius, king, or leveller of kings, has today –

That objects moved in her presence – fruits of trees that came down from the trees and set themselves beside her – the shaking of bushes that cast, to her, berries – then night and coldness – faggots joining twigs, and dancing around her – heaping – the crackling of flames to warm her –

Or that, to this day, grotesque capers of chairs, the antics of sofas, and the seeming wantonness of flames are survivals of co-operations that once upon a time moved even the trees, when a child was lost in the forest.

The old mathematicians has this aesthetic appraisal of their thoughts: they wrought theorems and calculi "for elegance," and were scornful of uses. But virtually everything that they produced "for elegance" was put to work by astronomers, navigators, surveyors. I assemble, compositionally, what I call data; but I am much depressed, perhaps, fearing that they have meaning outside themselves, or may be useful.

There is, upon this earth, today, at least one artist. Prof. Albert Einstein put together, into what he called one organic whole, such a diversity of elements as electromagnetic waves and irregularities in the motions of the planet Mercury; the fall of a stone from a train to an embankment, the geometry of hyper-space, and accelerated co-ordinate systems, and Lorentz transformations, and the displacement of stars during eclipses –

And the exploitation of everything by something, or, more or less remotely, by everything else – the need of astronomers for Einsteinism, because it was so encouragingly unintelligible, whereas schoolboys were beginning to pick Newtonism to pieces – and in the year 1918 it was announced that the useful Einstein had predicted displacements of stars, according to his theory, and that his predictions had been confirmed.

For purposes of renewed confirmation – or maybe in innocence of trying to confirm anything, or at least not consciously intending to observe whatever was wanted – an expedition was sent by Lick Observatory to report upon the displacement of stars during the solar eclipse of October, 1922. The astronomers of this expedition agreed that the displacements of stars confirmed Einstein, the Prophet. Einstein was said to be useful, and, in California, school children, dressed in white, sang unto him kindred unintelligibilities. In New York, mounted policemen roughly held back crowds from him, just as he, to make his system of thoughts, had clubbed many astronomical data into insensibility. He had taken into his system of thoughts irregularities of the planet Mercury, but had left out irregularities of the planet Venus. Crowds took him into their holiday-making, but omitted asking what it was all about.

Upon June 12, 1931, Prof. Erwin Freundlich reported to the Physics Association of Berlin that, according to his observations, during the eclipse of May 9, 1929, stars were not displaced, as, according to Einstein, they should be – or that, outside itself, Einsteinism is meaningless.

There was no excitement over this tragedy, or comedy, because this earth's intellectuals, mostly, take notice only when they're told to take notice; and to orthodoxy it seemed wisest that this earth's thinkers should not think about this. Prof. Freundlich explained the astronomers of the Lick expedition, quite as I explain all astronomers. He gave his opinion that they had confirmed Einstein; because, "the American astronomers had committed an error of prime importance by leaving out of consideration observations that did not fit in with the results they wanted to obtain." If there be much more of such agreements with me, I shall have to hunt me some new heresies. For an account of Prof. Freundlich's report, see the *New York Herald Tribune* (June 14, 1931).

Outside itself Einsteinism has no meaning.

As a worthless thing – As an unrelated thing its state is that of which artists have dreamed, in their quest for absoluteness – the dream of "art for art's sake."

Up to Dec. 6, 1931, I thought of Prof. Einstein's theories as almost alone, or as representing almost sublime worthlessness. But *New York Times* (Dec. 6, 1931) – scientists of the University of California, experimenting upon an admixture of phosphorus in the food of swine, were developing luminous pigs. "Just what they will be good for has not been announced."

Mine is a dream of being not worth a displaced star to anybody. I protest that with the elements of this book my only motive is compositional – but comes the suspicion that I protest too much.

There has been a gathering of suggestions – that there are subtler "rays" than anything that is known in radioactivity, and that they may be developed into usefulness. The Ascot Cup and the Dublin jewels – and, if they were switched away by a means of transportation now not commonly known, a common knowledge may be developed to enormous advantage in commercial and recreational and explorative transportations.

In the period of my writing of this book, Californian scientists were trying to make pigs shine at night. Another scientist, who could not yet announce much usefulness, was feeding skimmed milk to huckleberries. For all I know one of us may revolutionise something or another.

Chapter 17

London *Daily Chronicle* (March 30, 1922) – "It is incredible, but nothing has been heard of Holding."

For three weeks a search had been going on – cyclists, police, farmers, people from villages.

At half past ten o'clock, morning of the 7th of March, 1922, Flying Officer B. Holding had set out from an aerodrome, near Chester, England, upon what was intended by him to be a short flight in Wales. About eleven o'clock, he was seen, near Llangollen, Wales, turning back, heading back to Chester –

Holding disappeared far from the sea, and he disappeared over a densely populated land. One of my jobs was that of looking over six London newspapers for the years 1919-1926, and it is improbable that anything was learned of what became of Holding, later, without my knowing of it. I haven't a datum upon which to speculate, in the Holding mystery; but now I have a story of two men, whose track on land stopped as abruptly as stopped Holding's track in the sky; and this time I note an additional circumstance. The story of these men is laid in a surrounding of hates of the intensity of oriental fanaticism.

Upon July 24th, 1924, at a time of Arab-hostility, Flight-Lieutenant W.T. Day and Pilot Officer D.R. Stewart were sent from British headquarters, upon an ordinary reconnaissance over a desert in Mesopotamia. According to schedule, they would not be absent more than several hours. I take this account from the London *Sunday Express* (Sept. 21 and 28, 1924).

The men did not return, and they were searched for. The plane was soon found, in the desert. Why it should have landed was a problem. "There was some petrol left in the tank. There was nothing wrong with the craft. It was, in fact, flown back to the aerodrome." But the men were missing. "So far as can be ascertained, they encountered no meteorological conditions that might have forced them to land." There were no marks to indicate that the plane had been shot at. There may be some way, at present very exclusively known, of picking an aeroplane out of the sky. According to the rest of this story, there may be some such way of picking men out of a desert.

In the sand, around the plane, were seen the footprints of Day and Stewart. "They were traced, side by side, for some forty yards from the machine. Then, as suddenly as if they had come to the brink of a cliff, the marks ended."

The landing of the plane was unaccountable. But, accepting that as a minor mystery, the suggested explanation of the abrupt ending of the footprints was that Day and Stewart had been captured by hostile Bedouins, who had brushed away all trails in the sand, starting at the point forty yards from the plane. But hostile Bedouins could not be thought of as keeping on brushing indefinitely, and a search was made for a renewal of traces.

Aeroplanes, armoured cars, and mounted police searched. Rewards were offered. Tribal patrols searched unceasingly for four days. Nowhere beyond the point where the tracks in the sand ended abruptly, were other tracks found. The latest account of which I have record is from the London *Sunday News* (March 15, 1925) – mystery of the missing British airmen still unsolved.

London *Evening News* (Sept. 28, 1923) – "Second-Lieut. Morand, while at shooting practice, at Gadaux, France – himself firing at a target on the ground, while a sergeant piloted the machine – suddenly fell back, calling for the pilot to land, as he had been wounded. It was found that he had a serious wound in his shoulder, and he was taken to Bordeaux, by the hospital aeroplane." It was said that he had been shot. "But no clue has been found, as to the origin of the shot."

I especially notice this case, because it was at a time of other "accidents" to French fliers. The other "accidents" were different, in that they did not occur in France, and in that they were not shootings. I know of no case that in all particulars I can match with the disappearance of Day and Stewart; but there are records of airmen who, flying over a land where the sight of them directed hate upon them, were unaccountably picked out of the sky.

In this summer of 1923, French aviators told of inexplicable mishaps and forced landings, while flying over German territory. The instances were so frequent that there arose the belief that, with "secret rays", the Germans were practising upon French aeroplanes. From a general impression of an existence of rationality-irrationality, we can conceive that the Germans were practising upon French aeroplanes something that they were most particularly endeavouring to keep secret from France – if they had any such powers. But I think that they had not – or officially they had not. There may have been a hidden experimenter, unknown to the German authorities.

An article upon this subject was published in the London *Daily Mail* (Sept. 10, 1923). "Two theories have been put forward. One is that by a concentration of wireless rays the magneto of the aeroplane may be affected; and another is that a new ray, which will melt certain metals, has been discovered. In this connection it is notable that most of the forced landings of the French aeroplanes, when flying from Strasbourg to Prague, have taken place in the vicinity of the German aerodrome, near Furth." It was said that for some time, at the German wireless station at Nauen, there had been experiments upon directional wireless, with the object of sending out rays, concentrated along a certain path, as the beams of a searchlight are directed. The authorities at Nauen denied that they had knowledge of anything that could have affected the French aeroplanes, in ways reported, or supposed. Automobiles can be stopped, by wireless control, if they be provided with special magnetos: otherwise not. Sir Oliver Lodge was quoted, by the *Daily Mail,* as saying that he knew of no rays that could stop a motor, unless specially equipped. Professor A.M. Low's opinion was that some day distant motors may be stopped – "I feel confident that, in 50 or 60 years' time, such a thing will be possible." Prof. Low said that he knew of laboratory experiments in which, over a distance of two feet, rays of sufficient power to melt a small coil of wire had been transmitted. But, as to the reported "accidents" in Germany, Prof. Low said: "There is a wide difference between transmitting such a power over a distance of a foot or two, and a distance of one or two thousand yards."

In the *Daily Mail* (April 5, 1924) was an account of invisible rays, which had been discovered by Mr. H. Grindell-Mathews, powerful enough, under laboratory-conditions, to stop the engine of a motor-cycle, at a distance of fifty feet.

Of course high among virtues are the honourable lies of governments. Whether virtuously said, or accurately reported, I don't know: but it is said, or reported, that, in the year 1929, the British government spent $500,000 investigating alleged long-distance "death-rays", and developed nothing that was effective. It is said, or reported, that the Italian navy gave opportunity to an inventor to demonstrate what he could do with "death-rays", but that his demonstrations came to nothing. We have no data for thinking that, in the year 1929, any government was in possession of a secret of long-distance "death-rays." The forced landings of the French aeroplanes, in the summer of 1923, remain unexplained.

There may be powerful rays that are not electromagnetic. French aviators may have been brought to earth by no power that is called "physical" – though I know of no real demarcation between what is called physical and what is called mental. See back to the series of "mysterious attacks", in England, in April and May, 1927. Three times, as if acted upon by an unknown influence, automobiles behaved unaccountably.

Our data are upon "accidents" that have not been satisfactorily explained. There have been occurrences that were similar to effects that inventors are, by mechanical means, striving for, in the cause of military efficiencies. And these experimenters are practical persons. It may be that we are on the track of a subtler slaughter. It looks as if a lonely possessor of a secret, such as is called "occult," operated wantonly, or in the malicious exercise of a power, upon automobiles, in England, in the months of April and May, 1927. He was a criminal. But I am a practical thinker, and a useful citizen, on the track of much efficiency, which will be at the disposal of God's second choice of people – which I think we must be, judging by the afflictions that are upon us, at this time of writing – a power that would, by this great nation, be used only righteously, if anybody could ever distinguish between righteousness and exploitation and tyranny. One of the engaging paradoxes of our existence – which strip mathematics of meaning – is that a million times a crime is patriotism. I am unable to conceive that a power to pick planes out of the sky would be so terrible as to stop war, because up comes the notion that counter-operations would pick the pickers. If we could have new abominations, so unmistakably abominable as to hush the lubricators, who plan murder to stop slaughter – but that is only dreamery, here in our existence of the hyphen, which is the symbol of hypocrisy.

New York Times (Oct. 25, 1930) – that about forty automobiles had been stalled, for an hour, on the road, in Saxony, between Risa and Wurzen.

About forty chauffeurs were probably not voiceless, in this matter; and, if the German Government were experimenting with "secret rays", that was some more of its public secrecy. In the *New York Times* (Oct. 27) was quoted a mathematician and former Premier of France, Paul Painlevé – "No experiment thus far conducted would permit us to credit such a report nor give any prospect of seeing it accomplished in the near future."

Upon May 26, 1925 – see the London *Daily Mail* (May 28, 1925) – at Andover, Hampshire, England, a corporal of the R.A.F., making a parachute practice jump, was killed by a fall of 1,900 feet from an aeroplane. There is not a datum for thinking that there was anything to this occurrence that aligns it with other occurrences told of in this chapter. But there is association. About the time of the accident, or whatever it was that befell this man, and at the same place, Flight Sergeant Frank Lowry, and Flying Officer John Kenneth Smith, pilot, were in an aeroplane, making wireless tests. They had been in the air about fifteen minutes, when Smith, having called to his companion, without hearing from him, looked around, and saw smoke coming from the back cockpit, and saw Lowry in a state of collapse.

Lowry was dead. "Flight-Lieut. Cyril Norman Ellen said that there was nothing in the machine likely to kill a man, and that Lowry must have come in contact with an electric current in the air. No similar case has been reported."

In the *Daily Mail* (Oct. 14, 1921), a writer (T. Gifford) tells of a scene of "accidents", at a point on a road in Dartmoor. This story is like an account of the series of "accidents" to automobiles, in England, in April and May, 1927, except that the "accidents" were strictly localised.

The story told by Gifford is that one day in June, 1921, a doctor, riding on his motor-cycle, with his two children in a side-car, suddenly, at this point, on the Dartmoor road, called to his children to jump. The machine swerved, and the doctor was killed. Several weeks later, at this place, a motor coach suddenly swerved, and several passengers were thrown out. Upon August 26, 1921, a Captain M. – for whom I apologise – it is not often that a Mr. X. or a Captain M. appears in these records – was, at this point on the road, thrown from his motor-cycle. Interviewed by Gifford, he told, after evasions, that something described by him as "invisible hands" had seized upon his hands, forcing the machine into the turf.

More details were published in the *Daily Mail* (Oct. 17, 1921). The scene of the "accidents" was on the road, near the Dartmoor village of Post Bridge. In the first instance, the victim was Dr. E.H. Helby, Medical Officer of Princetown Prison.

In *Light* of August 26, 1922 (42, 540), a correspondent noted another "accident" at this point. Details of the fourth "accident" were told, in the London *Sunday Express* (Sept. 12, 1926). The victim was travelling on his motor-cycle. "He was suddenly and violently unseated from his mount, and knew no more until he regained consciousness in a cottage, to which he had been carried, after a collapse." The injured man could not explain.

CHAPTER 18

I record that, once upon a time, down from the sky came a shower of virgins.

Of course they weren't really virgins. I can't accept the reality of anything, in such an indeterminate existence as ours.

See the *English Mechanic* (87, 436) – a shower of large hailstones, at Remiremont, France, May 26, 1907. Definitely upon some of these objects were printed representations of the Virgin of the Hermits.

It used to be the fashion, simply and brusquely to deny such a story, and call it a device of priestcraft; but the tendency of disbelievers, today, is not to be so free and monotonous with accusations, and to think that very likely unusual hailstones did fall, at Remiremont, and that out of irregularities or discolorations upon them, pious inhabitants imagined pictorial representations. I think, myself, that the imprints upon these hailstones were of imaginative origin, but in the sense that illustrations in a book are; and were not simply imagined by the inhabitants of Remiremont, any more than are some of the illustrations of some books only smudges that are so imaginatively interpreted by readers that they are taken as pictures.

The story of the hailstones of Remiremont is unique in my records. And a statement of mine has been that our data are of the not extremely uncommon. But, early in this book, I pointed out that any two discordant colours may be harmonised by means of others colours; and there are no data, thinkable by me, that can not be more or less suavely co-ordinated, if smoothly doctored; or that can not be aligned with the ordinary, if that be desirable.

I am a Jesuit. I shift aspects from hailstones with pictures on them, to pictures on hailstones – and go on with stories of pictures on other unlikely materials.

According to accounts – copied from newspapers – in the *Spiritual Magazine* (n.s., 7, 360) and in the *Religio-Philosophical Journal* (March 29, 1873), there was more excitement in Baden-Baden, upon March 12th, 1872, than at Remiremont. Upon the morning of this day, people saw pictures that in some unaccountable way had been printed upon window panes of houses, with no knowledge by occupants as to how they got there. At first the representations were crosses, but then other figures appeared. The authorities of Baden ordered the windows to be washed, but the pictures were indelible. Acids were used, without effect. Two days later, crosses and death's heads appeared upon window glass, at Rastadt.

The epidemic broke out at Boulley, five leagues form Metz. Here, because of feeling, still intense from the Franco-Prussian War, the authorities were alarmed. Crosses and other religious emblems appeared upon window panes – pictures of many kinds – death's heads, eagles, rainbows. A detail of Prussian soldiers was sent to one house to smash a window, upon which was pictured a band of French zouaves and their flags. It was said that at night the pictures were invisible. But the soldiers did not miss their chance: they smashed a lot of windows, anyway. Next morning it looked as if there had been a battle. In the midst of havoc, the zouaves were still flying their colours.

This story, I should say, then became a standardised newspaper yarn. I have a collection of stories of pictures appearing upon window glass, that were almost busily told in American newspapers, after March, 1872, not petering out until about the year 1890.

But it can not be said that all stories told in the United States, of this phenomenon, or alleged phenomenon, were echoes of the reported European occurrences, because stories, though in no such profusion as subsequently, had been told in the United States before March, 1872. *New York Herald* (Aug. 20, 1870) – a representation of a woman's face, appearing upon window glass, in a house in Lawrence, Mass. The occupant of the house was so pestered by crowds of sightseers that, not succeeding in washing off the picture, he removed the window sash. *Human Nature*, June 1871 (5, 328) – copied from the *Chicago Times* – house in Milan, Ohio, occupied by two tenants, named Horner and Ashley. On window panes appeared blotches, as if of water mixed with tar, or crude oil – likenesses of human faces taking form in these places. *New York Times* (Jan. 18, 1871) – that, in Sandusky and Cinncinnati, Ohio, pictures of women had appeared upon window panes.

Still, it might be thought that there was one origin for all the stories, and that that was the spirit-photograph controversy, which, in the early eighteen-seventies, was a subject of intense beliefs and disbeliefs, in both Europe and America. A point that has not been taken up, in this controversy, which continues to this day, even after the fateful spread of knowledge of double exposure, is whether the human imagination can affect a photographic plate. I incline to the idea that almost all spirit-photographs have been frauds, but that a few may not have been – that no spirits were present, but that, occasionally, or very rarely, a quite spookless medium has, in a profound belief in spirits, engendered, out of visualisations, something wraith-like that has been recorded by a camera. Against the explanation that stories of pictures on window panes probably had origin in the spirit-photograph craze, I mention that similar stories were told centuries before photography was invented. For an account of representations of crosses that appeared, not upon window glass, but upon people's clothes, as told by Joseph Grünpech, in his book, *Speculum Naturalis Coelestis,* published in the year 1508, see *Notes and Queries* (s. 8, 1, 283).

"A remarkable instance of this *lusus naturæ* occurred a few days after the death of the late Dean Vaughan, of Llandaff. There suddenly appeared on the wall of Llandaff Cathedral, a large blotch of dampness or some minute fungus, forming a lifelike outline of the dean's head and face." (*Notes and Queries,* Feb. 2, 1908, s. 9, 9, 115).

Throughout this book, my views, or preconceptions, or bigotries, are against spiritual interpretations, or assertions of the existence of spirits, as independent very long from human bodies. However, I do think of the temporary detachability of mentalities from bodies, and that is much like an acceptance of the existence of spirits. My notion is that Dean Vaughan departed, going where any iceberg goes when it melts, or where any flame goes when it is extinguished: that intense visualisations of him, by a member of his congregation, may have pictorially marked the wall of the church.

According to reports in the London *Daily Express* (July 17 and 30, 1923) and in the *Sunday Express* (Aug. 12, 1923), it may be thought, by anybody so inclined to think, that, in England, in the summer of 1923, an artistic magician was travelling, and exercising his talents. Somebody, or something, was perhaps impressing pictures upon wall and pillars of churches. The first report was that, on the wall of Christ Church, Oxford, had appeared a portrait of the famous Oxford cleric, Dean Liddell, long dead. Other reports came from Bath, Bristol, and Uphill, Somerset. At Bath – in the old abbey of Bath – the picture was of a soldier, carrying a pack. The Abbey authorities scraped off this picture, but the portrait, at Oxford, was not touched.

There is a description, in *T.P.'s and Cassell's Weekly* (London; Sept. 11, 1926), of the portrait on the wall of Christ Church, Oxford, as seen three years later. It is described as "a faithful and unmistakable likeness of the late Dean Liddell, who died in the year 1898." "One does not need to call in play any imaginative faculty to reconstruct the head. It is set perfectly straight upon the wall, as it might have been drawn by the hand of a master artist. Yet it is not etched; neither is it sketched, not sculptured, but it is there plain for all eyes to see."

And it is beginning to look as if, having started somewhat eccentrically with a story of virgins, we are making our way out of the marvellous. Now accept that there is a very ordinary witchcraft, by which, under the name *telepathy,* pictures can be transferred from one mind to another, and there is reduction of the preposterousness of stories of representations on hailstones, window glass, and other materials. We are conceiving that human beings may have learned an extension of the telepathic process, so as to transfer pictures to various materials. So far as go my own experiences, I do not know that telepathy exists. I think so, according to many notes that I have taken upon vagrant impressions that come and go, when my mind is upon something else. I have often experimented. When I incline to think that there is telepathy, the experiments are convincing that there is. When I think over the same experiments, and incline against them, they indicate that there isn't.

New York Sun (Jan. 16, 1929) – hundreds of persons standing, or kneeling, at night, before the door of St. Ann's Roman Catholic Church, in Keansburg, N.J. They saw, or thought they saw, on the dark, oak door, the figure of a woman, in trailing, white robes, emitting a glow. The pastor of the church, the Rev. Thomas A. Kearney, was interviewed. "I don't believe that it is a miracle or that it has to do with the supernatural. As I see it, it is unquestionably in the outline of a human figure, white-robed and emitting light. It is rather like a very thin motion picture negative that was underexposed, and in which human outlines and detail are extremely dim. Yet it seems to be there."

Or pictures on hailstones – and wounds that appeared on the bodies of people. In the name of the everlasting *If,* which mocks the severity of every theorem in every text book, and is not so very remote from every datum of mine, we can think that, by imaginative means, at present not understood, wounds appeared upon people in Japan, and Germany, and in a turning, off Coventry Street, London, if we can accept that in some such way, pictures have ever appeared upon hailstones, window panes, and other places. And we can think that pictures have appeared upon hailstones, window panes, and other places, if we can think that wounds have appeared upon people in Japan and other places. *Ave* the earthworm!

It is my method not to try to solve problems – so far as the solubility-insolubility of problems permits – in whatever narrow specialisations of thought I find them stated: but, if, for instance, I come upon a mystery that the spiritualists have taken over, to have an eye for data that may have bearing, from chemical, zoological, sociological, or entomological sources – being unable to fail, of course, because the analogue of anything electrical, or planetary, is findable in biological, ethical, or political phenomena. We shall travel far, even to unborn infants, to make hailstones reasonable.

I have so many heresies – along with my almost incredible credulities –

or pseudo-credulities, seeing that I have freed my mind of beliefs – that, mostly, I can not trace my infidelities, or enlightenments, back to their sources. But I do remember when I first doubted the denial by conventional science of the existence of pre-natal markings. I read Dr. August Weismann's book upon this subject, and his arguments against the possibility of pre-natal markings convinced me that they are quite possible. And this conversion cost me something. Before reading Dr. Weismann, I had felt superior to peasants, or the "man in the street", as philosophers call him, whose belief is that pregnant women, if frightened, mark their offsprings with representations of rats, spiders, or whatever; or, if having a longing for strawberries, fruitfully illustrate their progeny, and were at one time of much service to melodrama. I don't know about the rats and strawberries, but Dr. Weismann told of such cases as that of a woman with a remarkable and distinctive disfigurement of an ear, and of her similarly marked offspring. His argument was that thousands of women are disfigured in various ways, and that thousands of offsprings are disfigured, and that it is not strange that in one case the disfigurement of an offspring should correspond to the disfigurement of a parent. But so he argued about other remarkable cases and left me in a state of mind that has often repeated: and that is with the idea that much mental development is in rising down to the peasants again.

If there can be pre-natal markings of bodies, and, as I interpret Dr. Weismann's denials, there can be, and, if they be of mental origin, my mind is open to the idea that other – and still more profoundly damned stories of strange markings – may be similarly explained. If a conventional physician is scornful, hearing of a human infant, pre-natally marked, I'd like to hear his opinion of a story I take from the London *Daily Express* (May 14, 1921). Kitten, born at Nice, France – white belly distinctly marked with the grey figures, *1921* – the mother cat had probably been looking at something, such as a calendar, so dated. "Or reading a newspaper?" said scornful doctor would ask, pointing out that, if I think there are talking dogs, it is only a small "extension", as I'd call it, to think of educated cats keeping themselves informed upon current events.

London *Sunday News* (Aug. 3, 1924) – "Dorothy Parrot, 4-year-old child of R.S. Parrot, of Winglet Mill, Georgia, was marked by a red spot on her body. Out of this spot formed three letters, *R.I.C.* Doctors cannot explain."

London *Daily Express,* Nov. 17, 1913 – phenomena of a girl, aged 12, of the village of Bussus-Bussuel, near Abbeville, France. If asked questions, answers appeared in letterings on her arms, legs, and shoulders. Also, upon her body appeared pictures, such as of a ladder, a dog, a horse.

In September, 1926, a Rumanian girl, Eleonore Zegun, was taken to London, for observation by the National Laboratory for Psychical Research. Countess Wassilko-Serecki, who had taken the girl to London, said in an interview (London *Evening Standard,* Oct. 1, 1926) that she had seen the word *Dracu* form upon the girl's arm. This word is the Rumanian word for the Devil.

Or the *Handwriting on the Wall* – and why don't I come out frankly in favour of all, or anyway a goodly number of, the yarns, or the data, of the Bible? *The Defender of Some of the Faith* is clearly becoming my title.

In recent years I have noted much that has impressed upon my mind the thought that religionists have taken over many phenomena, as exclusively their own – have coloured and discredited with their emotional explanations – but that someday some of these occurrences will be rescued from theological interpretations and exploitations, and will be the subject-matter of –

New enlightenments and new dogmas, new progresses, delusions, freedoms, and tyrannies.

I incline to the acceptance of many stories of miracles, but think that these miracles would have occurred, if this earth had been inhabited by atheists.

To me, the Bible is folklore, and therefore is not pure fantasy, but comprises much that will be rehabilitated. But also to me the Bible is non-existent. This is in the sense that, except in my earlier writings, I have drawn a dead-line, for data, at the year 1800. I may, upon rare occasions, dip farther back, but my notes start in the year 1800. I shall probably raise this limit to 1850, or maybe 1900. I take for a principle that our concern is not in marvels. It is in repetitions, or sometimes in almost the commonplace. There is no desirability in going back to antiquity for data, because, unless phenomena be appearing now, they are of only historical interest. At present, there is too much history.

Handwriting on walls – I have several accounts; but, if anybody should be interested enough to look up this phenomenon for himself, he will find the most nearly acceptable record in the case of Esther Cox, of Amherst, Nova Scotia. This case was of wide notoriety, and, of it, it could be said that it was well-investigated, if it can be supposed that there ever has been a case of anything that has been more than glanced at, or more than painstakingly and profoundly studied, simply to confirm somebody's theory.

If I should tell of a woman, who, by mental picturings, not only marked the body of her unborn infant, but transformed herself into the appearance of a tiger, or a lamp post, or became a weretiger, or a were-lamp-post – or of a magician, who, beginning with depicting forest scenes on window glass, had learned to transform himself into a weredeer, or a weretree – I'd tell of a kind of sorcery that used to be of somewhat common occurrence.

I have a specimen. It is a Ceylon leaf insect. It is a wereleaf. The leaf insect's likeness to a leaf is too strikingly detailed to permit any explanation of accidental resemblance.

There are butterflies, which, with wings closed, look so much like dried leaves that at a distance of a few feet they are indistinguishable from dried leaves. There are tree hoppers with the appearance of thorns; stick insects, cinder beetles, spiders that look like buds of flowers. In all instances these are highly realistic portraitures, such as the writer, who described the portrait of Dean Liddell, on the church wall, would call the handiwork of a master artist.

There have been so many instances of this miracle that I now have a theory that, of themselves, men never did evolve from lower animals; but that, in early and plastic times, a human being from somewhere else appeared upon this earth, and that many kinds of animals took him for a model, and rudely and grotesquely imitated his appearance, so that, today, though the gorillas of the Congo, and of Chicago, are only caricatures, some of the rest of us are somewhat passable imitations of human beings.

The conventional explanation of the leaf insect, for instance, is that once upon a time a species of insects somewhat resembled leaves of trees, and that individuals that most closely approximated to this appearance had the best chance to survive, and that in succeeding generations, still higher approximations were still better protected from their deceived enemies.

An intelligence from somewhere else, not well-acquainted with human beings – or whatever we are – but knowing of the picture galleries of this earth, might, in Darwinian terms, just as logically explain the origin of those pictures – that canvasses that were daubed on, without purpose, appeared; and that the daubs that more clearly represented something recognisable were protected, and that still higher approximations had a still better chance, and that so appeared, finally, highly realistic pictures, though the painters had been purposeless, and with no consciousness of what they were doing –

Which contrasts with anybody's experience with painters, who are not only conscious of what they are doing, but are likely to make everybody else conscious of what they're so conscious of.

It is not merely that hands of artists have painted pictures upon canvas: it is that, upon canvas, artists have realised their imaginings. But, without hands of artists, strikingly realistic pictures and exquisite modellings have appeared. It may be that for crosses on window panes, emblems on hailstones, faces on church walls, pre-natal markings, stigmata, telepathic transferences of pictures, and leaf insects we shall conceive of one expression.

To the clergyman who told the story of the hailstones of Remiremont, the most important circumstance was that, a few days before the occurrence, the town council had forbidden a religious procession, and that, at the time of the fall of the hailstones, there was much religious excitement in Remiremont.

English Mechanic (87, 435) – story told by Abbé Gueniot, of Remiremont:

That, upon the afternoon of the 26th of May, 1907, the Abbé was in his library, aware of a hailstorm, but paying no attention to it, when a woman of his household called to him to see the extraordinary hailstones that were falling. She told him that images of "Our Lady of the Treasure" were printed on them.

"In order to satisfy her, I glanced carelessly at two hailstones which she held in her hand. But, since I did not want to see anything, and, moreover, could not do so without spectacles, I turned to go back to my book. She urged: 'I beg of you to put on your glasses.' I did so, and saw very distinctly on the front of the hailstones, which were slightly convex in the centre, although the edges were somewhat worn, the bust of a woman, with a robe turned up at the bottom like a priest's cope. I should, perhaps, describe it still more exactly by saying that it was like the Virgin of the Hermits. The outlines of the image were slightly hollow, as though they had been formed with a punch, but were very boldly drawn. Mlle. André asked me to notice certain details of the costume, but I refused to look at it any longer. I was ashamed of my credulity, feeling sure that the Blessed Virgin would hardly concern herself with instantaneous photographs on hailstones. I said: 'But do you not see that these hailstones have fallen on vegetables, and thus received these impressions? Take them away; they are no good to me.' I returned to my book, without giving further attention to what had happened. But my mind was disturbed by the singular formation of these hailstones. I picked up three in order to weigh them, without looking at them closely. They weighed between six and seven ounces. One of them was perfectly round, like balls with which children play, and had a seam around it, as though it had been cast in a mould."

Then the Abbé's conclusions:

"Savants, though you may try your hardest to explain these facts by natural causes, you will not succeed." He thinks that the artillery of heaven had been directed against the impious town council. However people with cabbages suffered more than people with impieties.

"What appeared most worthy of notice was that the hailstones, which ought to have been violently precipitated to the ground in accordance with the laws of acceleration of the speed of falling bodies, appeared to have fallen from the height of but a few yards." But other, or unmarked hailstones, in this storm, did considerable damage. The Abbé says that many persons had seen the images. He collected the signatures of fifty persons who asserted that they had been witnesses.

I notice several details. One is the matter of a hailstone with a seam around it, as if it had been cast in a mould. This looks as if some hoaxer, or pietist – who was all prepared, having prophetic knowledge that an extraordinary shower of big hailstones was coming – had cast printed lumps of ice in a mould. But accounts of big hailstones, ridged and seamed, are common. Another detail is something that I should say the Abbé Gueniot had never before heard of. The detail of slow-falling objects is common in stories of occult occurrences, but, though for more than ten years I have had an eye for such reports, in reading of hundreds, or thousands, of hailstorms, I know of only half a dozen records of slow-falling hailstones.

In the *English Mechanic* (87, 507), there is more upon this subject. It is said that, according to the newspapers of Remiremont, these "prints" were inside the hailstones, and were found on surfaces of hailstones that had been split: that 107 persons had given testimony to the Bishop of Sainte-Dié; and that several scientists, one of whom was M. de Lapparent, the Secretary of the French Academy, had been consulted. The opinion of M. de Lapparent was that lightning might have struck a medal of the Virgin, and might have reproduced its image upon the hailstones.

I have never come upon any other supposition that there can be manifold reproductions of images, or prints, by lightning. The stories of lightning-pictures are mostly unsatisfactory, because most of them are of alleged pictures of leaves of trees, and, when investigated, turn out to be simply forked veinings, not very leaf-like. There is no other record, findable by me, of hailstones said to be pictorially marked by lightning, or by anything else. It would be much of coincidence, if, at a time of religious excitement in Remiremont, lightning should make its only known, or reported, pictures on hailstones, and make those pictures religious emblems. But that religious excitement did have much to do with the religious pictures on hailstones, is thinkable by me.

CHAPTER 19

The astronomers are issuing pronouncements upon what can't be seen with telescopes. The physicists are announcing discoveries that can't be seen with microscopes. I wonder whether anybody can see any meaning in an accusation that my stories are about invisibles.

I am a sensationalist.

And it is supposed that modern science, which is supposed to be my chief opposition, is remote from me and my methods.

In December, 1931, Dr. Humason, of the Mount Wilson Observatory, announced his discovery of two nebulae that are speeding away from this earth, at a rate of 15,000 miles a second. There was a race. Prof. Hubble started it in the year 1930, with announced discoveries of nebulae rushing away at – oh, a mere two or three thousand miles a second. In March, 1931, somebody held the record with an 8,000-mile-a-second nebula. At this time of writing, Dr. Humason is ahead.

When a tabloid newspaper reporter announces speedy doings by more or less nebulous citizens, as "ascertained" by him, by methods that did not necessarily indicate anything of the kind, his performance is called sensationalism.

It is my statement that Dr. Hubble and Dr. Humason are making their announcements, as inferences from a method that does not necessarily indicate anything of the kind.

In the *New York Herald Tribune* (Jan. 6, 1932), Dr. Charles B. Davenport, of the department of genetics, in Carnegie Institution, received only four inches of space for one of those scares that used to be spread-headed – unknown disease that may wipe out humanity. "Some time in the future our boasted skyscrapers might become inhabited by bats, and the safe deposit vaults of our cities become the caves of wild animals." The unknown disease is antiquated sensationalism. I look back at my own notion of the appearance of were-things in the streets of New York –

I now have a little story that pleases me, not so much because I think that I at least hold my own with my professorial rivals, but because, with it, I exercise some of those detective abilities that all of us, even professional detectives, possibly, are so sure we have. I reconstruct, according to my abilities, an incident that occurred somewhere near Wolverhampton, England, about the first of December, 1890. The part of the story of which I have no record – that is the hypothetical part – is that, at this time, somewhere near Wolverhampton, lived

116

a tormented young man. He was a good young man. Not really, of course, if nothing's real. But he approximated. Though for months he had not gone travelling, he was obsessed with a vividly detailed scene of himself, behaving in an unseemly manner to a female, in a railway compartment. There was another mystery. Somebody had asked him to account for his absence, somewhere, about the first of December, whereas he was convinced that he had not been absent – and yet – but he could make nothing of these two mysteries.

Upon the Thursday before the 6th of December, 1890 – see the *Birmingham Daily Post* (Dec. 6) – a woman was travelling alone, in a compartment of a train from Wolverhampton to Snow Hill. According to my reconstruction, she began to think of stories of reprehensible conduct by predatory males to females travelling alone in railway compartments.

The part of the story that I take from the *Birmingham Post* is that when a train went past Soho Station, a woman fell from it. She gave her name as Matilda Crawford, and said that a young man had insulted her. An odd detail is that it was not her statement that she had leaped from the train, but that the insulting young man had pushed her through a window.

In the next compartment had sat a detective. At an inquiry, he testified that – at least so far as went his observations upon visible entrances and exits – there had been nobody but this woman in this compartment.

In the *New York Herald Tribune* (Jan. 23, 1932) was published an explanation, by Dr. Frederick B. Robinson, president of the College of the City of New York, of some of us sensationalists:

"'Professors have not scored so well in making good appearances from the publicity standpoint', Dr. Robinson said. 'Living sheltered lives', he added, 'they yearn for public notice and sometimes get it at the expense of their college. Surely a great New England institution was not elevated in public esteem when one of its professors of English engaged in a series of publicity-stunts, the first of which was to give solemn advice to young men to be snobs.'"

At a meeting of the American Chemical Society, at Buffalo, N.Y., Sept. 3, 1931, Dr. William Engleback told of cases in which, by use of glandular extracts, the height of dwarfed children had been increased an inch or two. For the announcement of this mild little miracle, he received several inches of newspaper space. *New York Times* (Dec. 16, 1931) – meeting of the Institute of Advanced Education, at the Roerich Museum, New York – something more like a miracle. I measured. Dr. Louis Berman got nine inches of newspaper space. Dr. Berman's announcement was that sorcerers of his cult – the endocrinologists – would breed human beings sixteen feet high.

117

Meeting of the American Association for the Advancement of Science, in New Orleans, December, 1931 – report upon the work of Dr. Richard P. Strong, of the Harvard Medical School, in the matter of *filaria* worms that infest human bodies – and an attempt to make it more interesting. That an ancient mystery had been solved – Biblical story of the fiery serpents at last explained. There's no more resemblance between these tiny worms and the big fiery things that – we are told – grabbed people, than between any caterpillar and a red-hot elephant. But that the *filaria* worms had been "identified" as the fiery monsters of antiquity was considered a good story and was given much space in the newspapers. However, see an editorial, not altogether admiring, in the *New York Herald Tribune* (Jan. 5, 1932).

Still, I do, after a fashion, hold my own. *New York Sun* (Oct. 9, 1931) -- that, shortly after the Civil War, Captain Neil Curry sailed from Liverpool to San Francisco. The vessel caught fire, about 1500 miles off the west coast of Mexico. The Captain, his wife, and two children, and thirty-two members of the crew took to three small boats, and headed for the mainland. Then details of suffering for water.

"Talk of miracles!" In the midst of the ocean, they found themselves in a volume of fresh water.

I note the statement that Capt. Curry discovered fresh water around the boats, not by disturbance of any kind, but because of the green colour of it, contrasting with the blue of the salt water.

I wrote to Capt. Curry, who at the time of my writing was living in Emporia, Kansas, and received an answer from him, dated Oct. 21, 1931, saying that the story in the *Sun* was accurate except as to the time, that the occurrence had been in the year 1881.

Here is something, both very different and strikingly similar, which I take from Dr. Richardson's *Journal,* as quoted by Sir John Franklin, in his *Narrative of a Journey to the Shores of a Polar Sea* (157) – a story of a young Chipewyan Indian. His wife had died, and he was trying to save his new-born child. "To still its cries, he applied it to his breast, praying earnestly to the great Master of Life, to assist him. The force of the powerful passion by which he was actuated produced the same effect in his case, as it has done in some others, which are recorded: a flow of milk actually took place from his breast."

Intensest of need of water – and it may be that, to persons so suffering, water has been responsively transported. But there have been cases of extremest need for water to die by. One can think of situations in which more frenziedly have there been prayers for water, for death, than ever for water to live by.

New York Sun (Feb. 4, 1892) – that, after the burial of Frances Burke, of Dunkirk, N.Y., her relatives, suspecting that she had been in a trance, had her body exhumed. The girl was found dead in a coffin that was full of water. It was the coroner's opinion that she had been buried alive, and had been drowned in her coffin. No opinion at to the origin of the water was published.

CHAPTER 20

The importance of the invisible –

That I'd starve to death, in the midst of eatables, were it not for the invisible means of locomotion by which I go and get them, and the untouchable and unseeable processes by which I digest them –

That every stout and determined materialist, arguing his rejection of the unseeable and the untouchable, lives in a phantom-existence, from which he would fade away were it not for his support by invisibles –

The heat of his body – and the heat has never been seen.

His own unseeable thoughts, by which he argues against the existence of the invisible.

Nobody has ever seen steam. Electricity is invisible. The science of physics is occultism. Experts in the uses of steam and electricity are sorcerers. Mostly we do not think of their practices as witchcraft, but we have an opinion upon what would have been thought of them, in earlier stages of the Dark Age we're living in.

Or by the "occult", or by what is called the "supernatural", I mean something like an experience that I once saw occur to some acquaintances of mine.

A neighbour had pigeons, and the pigeons loafed on my window sill. They were tempted to come in, but for weeks, stretched necks, fearing to enter. I wished they would come in. I went four blocks to get them sunflower seeds. Though I will go thousands of miles for data, it is most unusual for me to go four blocks – it's eight blocks, counting both ways – for anybody. One time I found three of them, who had flown through an open window, and were upon the frame of a closed window. I went to them slowly, so as not to alarm them. It seems that I am of a romantic disposition, and, if I take a liking to anybody, who seems female, like almost all birds, I want her to perch on my finger. So I put out a finger. But all three birds tried to fly through the glass. They could not learn by rebuffs but kept on trying to escape through the glass. If, back in the coop, these pigeons could have told their story, it would have been that they were perched somewhere, when suddenly the air hardened. Everything in front was as clearly visible as before, but the air had suddenly turned impenetrable. Most likely the other pigeons would have said: "Oh, go tell that to the sparrows!"

There is a moral in this, and it applies to a great deal in this book, which is upon the realisation of wishes. I had wished for pigeons. I got them. After the investigation by the three pioneers all of them came in. There were nine of them. It was the unusually warm summer of 1931, and the windows had to be kept open. Pigeons on the backs of chairs. They came up on the table and inspected what I had for dinner. Other times they spent on the rug, in stately groups and processions, except every now and then, when they were not so dignified. I could not shoo them out, because I had invited them. Finally, I did get screens, but it takes weeks to be so intelligent. So the moral is in the observation that, if you wish for something, you had better look out, because you may be so unfortunate as to get it. It is better to be humble and contented with almost nothing, because there's no knowing what something may do to you. Much is said of the "cruelty of Nature": but, when a man is denied his "heart's desire", that is mercy.

But I am suspicious of all this wisdom, because it makes for humility and contentment. These thoughts are community-thoughts, and tend to suppress the individual. They are corollaries of mechanistic philosophy, and I represent revolt against mechanistic philosophy, not as applying to a great deal, but as absolute.

Nevertheless, by the "occult," or the "supernatural," I do not mean that I think that it is altogether exemplified by the experience of the pigeons. In our existence of law-lawlessness, I conceive of two magics: one is representing unknown law, and the other as expressing lawlessness – or that a man may fall from a roof, and alight unharmed, because of anti-gravitational law; and that another man may fall from a roof, and alight unharmed, as an expression of the exceptional, of the defiance of gravitation, of universal inconsistency, of defiance of everything.

London *Times,* Oct. –

Oh, well, just as an exception of our own – never mind the data, this time – take my word for it that I could cite many instances of remarkable falls, if I wanted to.

It looks to me as if, for instance, some fishes climb trees, as an expression of lawlessness, by which there is somewhere an exception to the generalisation that fishes must be aquatic. I think that *Thou Shalt Not* was written on high, addressed to fishes. Whereupon a fish climbed a tree. Or that it is law that hybrids shall be sterile – and that, not two, but three animals went into a conspiracy, out of which came the okapi. There is a "law" of specialisation. Evolutionists make much of it. Stores specialise, so that dealers in pants do not sell prunes. But then appear drugstores, which sell drugs, books, soups, and mouse traps.

I have had what I think is about the average experience with magic. But, except in several periods, I have taken notes upon my experiences; and most persons do not do this, and forget. We forget so easily that I have looked over notes and have come upon details of which I had no remembrance. From records of my own experiences, I take an account of a series of small occurrences, several particulars of which are of importance to our general argument.

I was living in London – 39 Marchmont Street, W.C.1. I was gathering data, in the British Museum Library. In my searches, I had noted instances of pictures falling from walls, at times of poltergeist disturbances; but I note here that my data upon physical subjects, such as earthquakes and auroral beams and lights on dark parts of the moon were about five to one, as compared with numbers of data upon matters of psychic research. Later, the preponderance shifted the other way. The subject of pictures falling from walls was in my mind, but it was much submerged by other subjects and aspects of subjects. It was so inactive in my mind that, when I was told of several pictures that had fallen in our house, I put that down to household insecurities and paid no more attention.

The abbreviations in the notes are *A*, for my wife; *Mrs. M.,* for the landlady; *E*, the landlady's daughter; the *C's,* the tenants upstairs. According to me, this is not the unsatisfactoriness of so many stories about a *Mr. X,* or a *Mrs. Y.,* because according to me, only two of us, whom I identify, were more than minor figures; also we may suspect that, of these two, one was rather more central than the other – according to me. However, also, I suspect that, if *E* should tell this story, I'd be put down, much minored, as *Mr. F. A* and I occupied the middle floor, which was of two rooms, one of them used by us as a kitchen, though it was furnished to rent as a furnished room.

March 11, 1924 – see Charles Fort's *Notes,* Letter E, Box 27 – "I was reading last night, in the kitchen, when I heard a thump. Sometimes I am not easily startled, and I looked around in a leisurely manner, seeing that a picture had fallen, glass not breaking, having fallen upon a pile of magazines in a corner. Two lace curtains at sides of window. Picture fell at foot of left curtain. Now, according to my impression, the bottom of the right-hand curtain was vigorously shaken, for several seconds, an appreciable length of time after the fall of the picture.

"Morning of the 12th – find that one of the brass rings, on the back of the picture frame, to which the cord was attached, had been broken in two places – metal bright at the fractures.

"*A* reminded me that, in the *C's* room, two pictures had fallen recently."

I have kept this little brass ring, broken through in one place, and the segment between the breaks, hanging by a metal shard at the point of the other break. The picture was not heavy. The look is that there had been a sharp, strong pull on the picture cord, so doubly to break this ring.

"March 18, 1924 – about 5 P.M., I was sitting in the corner, where the picture fell. There was a startling, crackling sound, as if of glass breaking. It was so sharp and loud that for hours afterward I had a sense of alertness to dodge missiles. It was so loud that Mrs. *C.*, upstairs, heard it."

But nothing had broken a window pane. I found one small crack in a corner, but the edges were grimy, indicating that it had been made long before.

"March 28, 1924 – This morning, I found a second picture – or the fourth, including the falls in the rooms upstairs – on the floor, in the same corner. It had fallen from a place about three feet above a bureau, upon which are piled my boxes of notes. It seems clear that the picture did not ordinarily fall, or it would have hit the notes, and there would have been a heartbreaking mess of notes all over the floor."

Oh, very. Sometimes I knock over a box of notes, and it's a job of hours to get them back in their places. I don't know whether it has any meaning, but I think about this: the accounts of pictures falling from walls, which were among these notes.

"The glass in the picture was not broken. This time, the cord, and not a ring, was broken. I quickly tied the broken cord, and put the picture back. I suppose I should have had *A* for a witness. Partly I did not want to alarm her, and partly I did not want her to tell, and start a ghost-scare centering around me."

I would have it that, in some unknown way, I was the one who was doing this. I'd like to meet *Mrs. C.,* sometime, and perhaps listen to her hint that she has psychic powers, and hint that she was the one who went around psychically, knocking down pictures in our house.

The cord of this second, or fourth, picture was heavy and strong. It was beyond my strength to break a length of it. But something had broken this strong cord. I looked at the small nail in the wall. It showed no sign of strain.

Of course I was reasoning about all this. Said I: "If, when this house was furnished, all the pictures were put up about the same time, their cords may all weaken about the same time." But a ring broke, one of the times. Upstairs, one of the pictures had fallen in a kitchen, and the other in a living room, where conditions were different. Smoke in a kitchen has chemical effects upon picture cords.

"April 18, 1924 – *A* took a picture down from the kitchen wall, to wash the glass – London smoke. The picture seemed to fall from the wall into her hands. *A* said: 'Another picture cord rotten.' Then: 'No: the nail came out.' But the cord had not broken, and the nail was in the wall. Later, that day, *A* said: 'I don't understand how that picture came down.'"

There was nothing resembling a "scare" in the house. There were no discussions. I think that there was an occasional laughing suggestion – "Must be spooks around." I had three or four reasons for saying nothing about the matter to anybody.

"July 26, 1924 – Heard a sound downstairs. Then Fannie called up: 'Mrs. Fort, did you hear that? A picture fell right off the wall.'"

I go on with my account, or with the mistake that I am making. Just so long as I gave the *New York Something or Another,* or the *Tasmanian Whatever,* for reference, that was all very well. But now I tell a story of my own, and everybody who hasn't had pictures drop from walls, in his presence, will resent pictures falling from walls, because of my occult powers.

There are several notes that may indicate a relation between my thoughts upon falling pictures, and then, later, a falling picture.

"Oct. 22, 1924 – Yesterday, I was in the front room, thinking casually of the pictures that fell from the walls. This evening, my eyes bad. Unable to read. Was sitting, staring at the kitchen wall, fiddling with a piece of string. Anything to pass away time. I was staring right at a picture above corner of bureau, where the notes are, but having no consciousness of the picture. It fell. It hit boxes of notes, dropped to floor, frame at a corner broken, glass broken."

There was another circumstance. I remember nothing about it. The notes upon it are as brief as if I had not been especially impressed by something that I now think was one of the strangest particulars – that is, if by indicating that I had searched for something, I meant that I had searched thoroughly.

"The cord was broken several inches from one of the fastenings on back of picture. But there should have been this fastening, a dangling piece of cord, several inches long. This missing. I can't find it."

"Night of Sept. 28-29, 1925 – a picture fell in *Mrs. M's* room."

Note the lapse of time.

I am sorry to record that a note, dated Nov. 3, 1926, is missing. As I remember it, and according to allusions, in notes of Nov. 4th, it was only a remark of mine that for more than a year no picture had fallen.

"Nov. 4, 1926 – This is worth noting. Last night, I noted about the pictures, because earlier in the evening, talking over psychic experiences with France and others, I had mentioned falling pictures in our house. Tonight, when I came home, *A* told me of a loud sound that had been heard, and how welcome it was to her, because it had interrupted *E,* in a long, tiresome account of the plot of a moving picture. Later, *A* exclaimed: 'Here's what made the noise!' She turned on the light, in the front room, and on the floor was a large picture. I had mentioned to *A* that yesterday my mind was upon falling pictures. I took that note after she had gone to bed. I looked at the picture – cord broken, with frayed ends. I have kept a loop of this cord. The break is under a knot in it. Nov. 5 – I have not strongly enough emphasized *A's* state of mind, at the time of the fall of the picture. *E's* long account of a movie had annoyed her almost beyond endurance, and probably her hope for an interruption was keen." Here is an admission that I did not think, or suspect, that it was I, who was the magician, this time.

In October, 1929, we were living in New York, or, anyway, in the Bronx. I do not have pictures on walls, in places of my own. I can't get the pictures I'd like to have; so I don't have any. I haven't been able to get around to painting my own pictures, but, if I ever do, maybe I'll have the right kind to put up.

"October 15, 1929 – I was looking over these notes, and I called *A* from the kitchen to discuss them. I note that *A* had been doing nothing in the kitchen. She had just come in: had gone to the kitchen to see what the birds were doing. While discussing those falling pictures, we heard a loud sound. Ran back, and found on the kitchen floor a pan that had fallen from a pile of utensils in a closet."

"Oct. 18, 1930 – I made an experiment. I read these notes aloud to *A,* to see whether there would be a repetition of the experience of Oct. 15, 1929. Nothing fell."

"Nov. 19, 1931 – tried that again. Nothing moved. Well, then, if I'm not a wizard, I'm not going to let anybody else tell me that he's a wizard."

CHAPTER 21

I looked at a picture, and it fell from a wall.

The diabolical thought of Usefulness rises in my mind.

If ever I can make up my mind to declare myself the enemy of all mankind, then shall I turn altruist, and devote my life to being of use and of benefit to my fellow-beings.

Everything that is of slavery, ancient and modern, is a phenomenon of usefulness. The prisons are filled with unconventional interpreters of uses. If it were not for uses, we'd be free of lawyers. Give up the idea of improvements, and that is an escape from politicians.

Do unto others as you would that others should do unto you, and you may make the litter of their circumstances that you have made of your own. The good Samaritan binds up wounds with poison ivy. If I give anybody a coin, I hand him good and evil, just as truly as I hand him head and tail. Whoever discovered the uses of coal was a benefactor of all mankind, and most damnably something else. Automobiles, and their seeming indispensable services – but automobiles and crime and a million exasperations. There are persons who think they see clear advantages in the use of a telephone – then the telephone rings.

If, by looking at it, a picture can be taken down from a wall, why could not a house be pulled down, by still more intently staring at it?

If, occultly, mentally, physically, however, a house could be pulled down, why could not a house be put up, by concentrating upon its materials?

Now visions of the Era of Witchcraft – miracles of invisible brick-laying, and marvels of masonry without masons – subtle uses and advantages that will merge both *A. D.* and *B. C.* into one period of barbarism, known as *B.W.* –

But the factories and labours and labourers – everything else that is now employed in our primitive ways of building houses. Unemployment and starvation and charity – political disturbances – the outcry against putting the machines out of work. There is no understanding any messiah, inventor, discoverer, or anybody else who is working for betterment, except by recognising him as partly a fiend.

And yet, in one respect, I am suspicious of all this wisdom. The only reason that it is not conventional mechanistic philosophy is that the conventionalist is more subdued. But, if in every action there is a reaction that is equal and opposite, there is to every advantage, or betterment, an equal disadvantage, or worsement. This view – except as quantitatively expressed – seems to me to be

in full agreement with my experiences with advantages and uses and better-
ments; but, as quantitatively expressed, it is without authority to me, because I
can not accept that ever has any action-reaction been cut in two, its parts sepa-
rate, and isolated, so that it could be determined what either part was equal to.

I looked at a picture, and it fell from a wall.

Once upon a time, Dr. Gilbert waved a wand that he had rubbed with
the skin of a cat, and bits of paper rose from a table. This was in the year 1, of
Our Lord, Electricity, who was born as a parlour stunt.

And yet there are many persons who have read widely, who think that
witchcraft, or the idea of witchcraft, has passed away.

They have not read widely enough. They have not thought widely enough. What idea has ever passed away? Witchcraft, instead of being a "superstition of the past," is of common report. I look over my data for the year 1924,
for instance, and note the number of cases, most of them called "poltergeist
disturbances," that were reported in England. Probably in the United States
more numerously were cases reported, but, because of library facilities, I have
especially noted phenomena in England. Cases of witchcraft and other uncanny occurrences, in England, in the year 1924, were reported from East Barnet,
Monkton, Lymm, Bradford, Chiswick, Mountsorrel, Dudley, Hayes, Maidstone, Minster Thanet, Epping, Grimsby, Keighley, and Clyst St. Lawrence.

New York newspapers reported three cases, close together, in the year
1927. *New York Herald Tribune* (Aug. 12, 1927) – Fred Koett and his wife compelled to move from their home, near Ellinwood, Kansas. For months this
house had been bewitched – pictures turned to the wall – other objects moving
about – their pet dog stabbed with a pitch fork, by an invisible. *New York Herald
Tribune* (Sept. 12, 1927) – Frank Decker's barn, near Fredon, N.J., destroyed by
fire. For five years there had been unaccountable noises, opening and shutting
doors, and pictures on walls swinging back and forth. *Home News* (Bronx; Nov.
27, 1927) – belief of William Blair, County Tyrone, Ireland, that his cattle were
bewitched. He accused a neighbour, Isabella Hazelton, of being a witch --
"witch" sued him for slander – $25 and costs.

My general expression is against the existence of poltergeists as spirits –
but that the doings are the phenomena of undeveloped magicians, mostly
youngsters, who have no awareness of their powers as their own – or, in cases
of mischievous, or malicious, persecutions, are more or less consciously directed influences by enemies – or that, in this aspect, "poltergeist disturbances"
are witchcraft under a new name. The change of name came about probably for
two reasons: such a reaction against the atrocities of witchcraft-trials that the

existence of witches was sweepingly denied, so that continuing phenomena had to be called something else; and the endeavour of the spiritualists to take over witchcraft, as evidence of the existence of "spirits of the departed."

If witches there be, there must of course be some humorous witches. The trail of the joke crosses our accounts of the most deadly occurrences. In many accounts of poltergeist disturbances, the look is more of mischief than of hate of victims. The London *Daily Mail* (May 1, 1907) is responsible for what is coming now:

An elderly woman, Mme. Blerotti, had called upon the Magistrate of the Ste. Marguerite district of Paris, and had told him that, at the risk of being thought a madwoman, she had a complaint to make against somebody unknown. She lived in a flat, in the Rue Montreuil, with her son and her brother. Every time she entered the flat, she was compelled by some unseen force to walk on her hands, with her legs in the air. The woman was detained by the magistrate, who sent a policeman to the address given. The policeman returned with Mme. Blerotti's son, a clerk, aged 27. "What my mother has told you, is true," he said. "I do not pretend to explain it. I only know that when my mother, my uncle, and myself enter the flat, we are immediately impelled to walk on our hands." M. Paul Reiss, aged fifty, the third occupant of the flat, was sent for. "It is perfectly true," he said. "Everytime I go in, I am irresistibly impelled to walk around on my hands." The concierge of the house was brought to the magistrate. "To tell the truth," he said, "I thought that my tenants had gone mad, but as soon as I entered the rooms occupied by them, I found myself on all fours, endeavoring to throw my feet in the air."

The magistrate concluded that here was an unknown malady. He ordered that the apartments should be disinfected.

There used to be a newspaper story of the "travelling needle." People perhaps sat on needles, though they thought it more dignified to report that needles had entered their bodies by way of their elbows. Then, five, ten, twenty years later, the needles came out by way of distant parts. We seldom hear of the "travelling needle," nowadays: so I think that most – not all – of these old stories were newspaper yarns. I was interested in these stories, as told back in the eighteen-eighties and nineties, but never came upon one that seemed to me to be authentic or to offer material much to speculate upon. I took suggestion from the method of "black magic," of piercing, with a needle, the heart, or some other part, of an image of a proposed victim, and, according to beliefs, succeeded in affecting a corresponding part of a human being –

An inquest, in the Shoreditch (London) Coroner's court, Nov. 14, 1919 –

a child, Rosina Newton, aged thirteen months, had died. A needle was found in her heart. "There was no skin-wound to show where it had entered the body." It was the short life of this child that attracted my attention. The parents had no remembrance of any injury to her, such as that of a needle entering her body.

It seems unlikely that anybody so intensely hated this infant as to concentrate upon a desire for her death, but I have gotten stories that may indicate the doing of harm to children, as vengeance upon parents.

And in the annals of "black magic" often appears the sorcerer, who obtains something of the belongings, or of the body, of a victim, to secure a contact, or a sense of contact. Parings of fingernails are recommended, but the procuring of a lock of the victim's hair is supposed to be most effective. There may be psychic hounds, who, from a belonging, pick up a scent, and then maintain, and operate along, a path, or a current, between themselves and their victims. In such terms, of harm, or of possession, may be understandable the hair-clippers of our records.

There is a strange story in the *Times of India* (Bombay; Aug. 30, 1928). A part of this story that does not seem so very strange to me is that three times a new-born infant of a Muslim woman, of Bhongir, had been mysteriously and supernaturally snatched away from her. The strange part is that the police, though they had explained that these disappearances were only ordinary, or natural, kidnappings, had gone to the trouble of taking this woman, who for the fourth time was in a state of expectation, to the Victoria Zenana Hospital, at Secunderabad; and that the hospital authorities had gone to the trouble and expense of assigning her to a special ward, where special nurses watched her, night and day. The fourth infant arrived, and this one, so surrounded by test-conditions, did not mysteriously vanish; so it was supposed to be demonstrated that the three disappearances were ordinary kidnappings. The explanation that occurs to one is that, though it was not mentioned in the *Times of India,* there was probably a scare, at Bhongir, and that this demonstration was made to allay it.

Just how, by ordinary, or "natural," means, anybody could, time after time, without being seen, snatch a new-born infant from a woman, was not inquired into. All such "demonstrations" start with the implied assumption that there is no witchcraft, and then show that there is not witchcraft. That is, there is no consideration for the thought that a witch might exist, and might fear to practice so publicly, as in a hospital ward. The "demonstration" was that there was not witchcraft in a hospital ward, and that therefore there is not witchcraft. Many of our data are of most public, or daring, or defiant occurrences; but it is notable that they stop – mostly, thought not invariably – when public attention is aroused. Sometimes they stop, and then renew periodically.

About the first of May, 1922, Pauline Picard, a Breton child, aged 12, disappeared from her home on a farm, near, Brest, France. I take this account from various issues of the *Journal des Debats* (Paris; May and June, 1922). Upon May 26th, a cyclist, passing Picard's farm, saw something in a field, not far from the road. He investigated. He came upon Pauline's naked and headless body. At the roadside were found her clothes. It was noted that they were "neatly folded."

The body was decomposed. Hands and feet, as well as head, were missing. This body, visible from the road, was found at a point half a mile from the Picard farmhouse.

It seems most likely that, if it was seen by a passing cyclist, it could not long have been lying, so conspicuous, but unseen, by members of the Picard family. Nevertheless, that it had so lain was the opinion that was accepted at the inquest. It was said that the child must have wandered from home, and, returning, must have died of exhaustion; and that the body had been defaced by rats and foxes. This story of the wandering child, dying of exhaustion, half a mile from her home, was given plausibility by the circumstances that once before Pauline had wandered far and that she had been affected mentally. At least, she had disappeared and had been found far away.

Upon April 6th, of this year, 1922, Pauline disappeared. Several days later, a child was found wandering in the streets of Cherbourg. The Picards were notified, and, going to Cherbourg, identified this child as Pauline, who, however, did not recognise them, being in a state of lapsed consciousness, or amnesia. If Pauline Picard, aged 12, had made this journey afoot, or by means that are called "natural," between a farm near Brest, and Cherbourg, in a state of amnesia, which it seems would somewhere be noted, but had not been reported, she had gone, unreported, a distance by land, of about 230 miles.

Twice Pauline Picard disappeared. The first disappearance was not an ordinary runaway, or was not an ordinary kidnapping, because something had profoundly affected this child mentally. I have notes upon more than a few cases of persons who have appeared, as if they had been occultly transported, or at any rate have appeared in places so far from their homes that they were untraceable, and were amnesiatics. An expression for which I should like to find material is that, three times, in distant parts of India, "wolf children" were reported, after the times of disappearance of the infants of Bhongir. The official explanation of the second disappearance and the death of Pauline

Picard bears the marks of dictation by Taboo. If the body of this child had been also otherwise mutilated, the explanation of defacement by rats and foxes would be more nearly convincing; but something, or somebody, had, as if to prevent identification, removed, without other mutilations, hands and feet and head – and also, contradictorily, had placed the body in a conspicuous position, as if planning to have it found. The verdict at the inquest required belief that this decomposed body had lain, conspicuous, but unseen, for several weeks, in this field. There is a small particular that adds to the improbability. It seems that the clothes – also conspicuous by the roadside – had not been lying there, for several weeks, subject to the disturbing effects of rains and wind. They were "neatly folded."

It is as if somebody had removed head, hands, and feet from this body, and had stripped the clothes from it, so that it could not be identified; and had placed the clothes near by, so that it could be identified.

A field – the dismembered body of a child – a farmhouse nearby. But I can pick up no knowledge of relations with environment. Friendly neighbours – or a neighbour with a grudge – all around is vacancy. A case that was called "unparalleled" was told of, in the New York newspapers (*New York Times,* April 30, 1931). Here, too, the surroundings are blankness: in the usual way the story was told, as an unrelated thing. Perhaps, somewhere near by, brooding over a crystal globe, or some other concentration-device, was the origin of a series of misfortunes.

Early in April, 1931, Valentine Minder, of Hauppauge, Long Island, N.Y., was suffering with what was said to be mastoiditis. His eight children were stricken with what was said to be measles, and then, one after another, in a period of six days, the eight children were taken ill with mastoiditis, and were removed to a hospital. The circumstance, because of which these cases were called "unparalleled", is that mastoiditis was supposed to be not contagious.

These cases, which, if "unparalleled," were mysterious, were a culmination of a series of misfortunes. About two years before, Minder's home had burned down. Then came his illness, a loss of vitality, the loss of his job, and a state of destitution. Toward the end of 1930, Mrs. Minder was stricken with an indefinable illness and became an invalid.

So far as was known, mastoiditis is not contagious. Out of many cases of family maladies, misfortunes, and fatalities, I pick one in which it seems that even more decidedly there is no place for the idea of contagion. Of course there is a place for the idea of coincidence. That is one square peg that fits into round holes and octagonal holes, dodecagonal holes, cracks, slits, gaps – or seems to, so long as whether it does or doesn't is not enquired into. London *Daily Chronicle* (Nov. 3, 1926) – that Mr. A.C. Peckover, the well-known violinist, one of the examiners to the Royal College of Music, had at the home of his sister, in Skipton, awakened one morning, to find himself blind. He was taken to the Bradford Eye and Ear Hospital. Here was his father, who, almost simultaneously, had been stricken with blindness.

In the matter of the deaths that followed the opening of Tut-Ankh-Amen's tomb, it is my notion that, if "curses" there be, they lose their vitality, anyway after several thousand years –

Or that a tomb was violated, and that funerals followed – by the deadly magic of no mummy, but of a living Egyptian – that, somewhere in Egypt, a sense of desecration became an obsession, from which came "rays," or a more personal and searching vengeance.

I wonder why the "wealthy farmer" appears in so many records of more or less uncanny doings. Perhaps any farmer who becomes wealthy, so becomes by sharp practices, and has enemies, whose malices against him demonstrate. In November, 1890, the household of Stephen Haven, a wealthy farmer, living near Fowlerville, Michigan, was startled by cries, one night. Haven was found at the bottom of a deep well. He had walked in his sleep. Two months later, he was again missing from his bed room, was searched for, and was found, standing, with the water up to his neck, in Silver Lake. Other members of the family were alarmed and alert. They heard slight sounds, one night – Haven was found, fast asleep, trying to set the house afire. Another time – and a thud was heard. The man, asleep, had tried to hang himself. According to the story, as told in the *Brooklyn Eagle* (Nov. 18, 1892), Haven had finally been found dead, at night. He had fallen from the upper-story doorway of his barn.

See back to occurrences in Sing Sing Prison, in December, 1930. *New York Herald Tribune* (Jan. 18, 1932) – "Warden Lewis E. Lawes fell this evening on the sleet-covered steps of his home at the prison and his right arm was broken in three places."

In matters of witchcraft, my general expression – as I say, to signify that neither as to anything in this book, nor anywhere else, have I beliefs – my general expression upon poltergeist girls is not that they are mediums, controlled by spirits, but that effects in their presence are phenomena of their own powers, or talents, or whatever; but that there are cases in which it seems to me that youngsters were mediums, or factors, not to spirits, but to living human beings, who had become witches, or wizards, by their hates – or that, in some cases, sorcery, unless so involuntarily accompliced, can not operate. See back to the Dagg case – here there seemed to be a girl's own phenomena, and also the presence of another being, who was invisible. The story was probably largely a distortion. The story was that there was a feud – that a "voice" accused a neighbour, Mrs. Wallace, of having sent it into the Dagg home. If this woman could invisibly transport herself, into somebody else's home, for purposes of malice and persecution, we'd not expect her to accuse herself – but there is such an element in a hate, as a sense of dissatisfaction with injuring an enemy, unless the victim knows who's doing it. Also the accusation was soon confused into an acquittal.

I have noted a case of occurrences in a shop, in London, which I tell of, mostly because it has highly the look of authenticity. Not a girl, but a boy, was present. I'd think that the doings were his own phenomena, were it not for the circumstance of "timing." By "timing", in this case, I mean the occurrence of phenomena upon the same days of the weeks. The phenomena of "timing", or the occurrence of doings, about the same time each day, appears in many accounts of persecutions by invisibles, for which I have found no room, in this book.

London *Weekly Dispatch* (Aug. 18, 1907) – disturbances in the stationary shop of Arthur Herbert George, 20 Butte Street, South Kensington, London, according to Mr. George's sworn statement before the Commissioner of Oathes, at 85 Gloucester-road, South Kensington. George and his assistant, a boy, or a young man, aged 17, saw books and piles of stationary slide unaccountably from shelves. Everything that they had replaced fell again, so that they could make no progress, trying to restore order. No vibration, no force of any kind, was felt. Two electric lamps in the window toppled over. Then there was livelier action: packages of note paper flew around, striking George and his assistant several times. George shut the door, so that customers should not come in and be injured. The next day boxes of stationary and bottles of ink were flying around, and four persons were struck. To this statement was appended an affidavit by an antique dealer, Sidney Guy Adams, 23 Butte Street, testifying that he had seen heavy packages of note paper flying around and that he had been struck by one of them. In the *Weekly Dispatch* (Sept. 1), it was said that there had been a repetition of the disturbances, upon the same days of the week (Wednesday, Thursday, and Friday) as the days of former phenomena. The damage to goods amounted to about £10.

Upon May 31st, Englishmen – in a land where reported witchcraft is of common occurrence – were startled. This tabooed subject had been brought up in Parliament. A member of the House of Commons had told of a case of witchcraft, and had asked for an investigation.

See back to "mysterious thefts." Accept data and implications of almost any of the succeeding groups of stories, and "cat burglars", and other larcenous practitioners, become thinkable as adepts in skills that are not describable as "physical."

Dean Forest Mercury (May 26, 1905) – that £50 had been stolen from a drawer in the home of John Markey near Blakeney (Dean Forest). The disappearance of this money was considered unaccountable. Just why, I could not find out, because the influence of Taboo smothered much, in this case. The members of this household could not explain how this money could have vanished, and brooding over the mystery made them "superstitious." They asked a woman, who, according to her reputation, had much knowledge of witchcraft, to investigate. Then came occurrences that made them extremely, hysterically, insanely "superstitious." It was as if an invisible resented the interference. Soon after the arrival of this woman – Ellen Haywood – something went through this house, smashing windows, crockery, and other breakables.

That is about all that I can pick up from the local newspaper, and from other newspapers published in the neighbourhood.

Markey's daughter broke down, with terror. There is only this record: no particulars of her experiences. Without detail, or comment, it is told that Markey's grand-daughter became insane. Both women were removed: one to a hospital, and the other to an asylum. Markey's wife ran screaming from the house and hid in the forest. A Police Inspector came from Gloucester and organized a search for her; but she was not found. For three days, without food or shelter, she hid. Then she returned, telling that she had seen the searchers, but had been in such a state of terror – by whatever was censored out of the records – that she had been afraid to come out of hiding. Markey's son became violently insane, smashing furniture, and seriously injuring himself, crying out that the whole family was bewitched. He, too, was taken to an asylum.

There was a demand for an inquiry into this case, and it was voiced in the House of Commons. It was voiced against Taboo. There is no more to tell.

I have notes upon another case that looks like resentment against an intrusion – if a woman died, but not in an epileptic fit, as alleged. There were accounts in the London newspapers, but I take from a local newspaper, the *Isle of Ely and Wisbech Advertiser* (Feb. 21, 1923), details of what occurred in the home of Mr. Joseph Scrimshaw, at Gorefield, near Wisbech. Other members of Scrimshaw's household were his mother, aged 82, and his daughter, Olive, aged 16. The phenomena were in the presence of this girl. First, Mrs. Scrimshaw's lace cap rose from her head. Then a wash stand crashed to the floor. Objects, such as books, dishes, a water filter, fell to the floor. There was much smashing of furniture and crockery. Names of neighbours, who witnessed these unconventionalities, are John Fennelow, T. Marrick, W. Maxey, and G.T. Ward. A piano that weighed 400 pounds moved from place to place. Police-constable Hudson was a witness of some of the phenomena. As to a suggestion that, for any reason of notoriety, or hoaxing, Scrimshaw could be implicated, it was noted that the damage to furniture amounted to about £140.

A woman – Mrs. J.T. Holmes – who, sometime before, had been accused of witchcraft, went to this house, and practised various incantations to exorcise the witch, or the evil spirit, or whatever. She suddenly died. It was said that she was subject to fits and had died in one of her convulsions. Whether his decision related to Taboo, or not, the coroner decided not to hold an inquest.

Upon Dec. 12, 1930 – see the *Home News* (Bronx; Dec. 22, 1930) – a resident of the Bronx, Elisha Shamray – who had changed his name from Rayevsky – opened a pharmaceutical laboratory, in Jackson Street, lower East Side, New York. During the night he died. His brother, Dr. Charles Rayevsky, came from Liberty, N.Y., to arrange for the funeral. He died a week later. The next night, the third of these brothers, Michael Shamray, Tremont Ave., Bronx, was on his way to arrange for the second funeral. He was struck by an automobile and was killed.

In August, 1927, Wayne B. Wheeler was the general counsel of the Anti-Saloon League of America. Upon August 13th, an oil stove exploded, in his home, and his wife was killed. Later, his father-in-law dropped dead. Upon the 5th of September, Wheeler died (*New York Times,* Sept. 6, 1927).

New York Sun (Feb. 3, 1932) – Mount Vernon, Ohio, Feb. 3 – "Fear that the mysterious illness which has killed three young brothers may strike again in the same family gripped surviving members of the household today."

Upon the 24th of January, Stanley Paazig, aged 9, died in the home of his parents, on a farm, near Mount Vernon. Upon the 31st, Raymond, aged 8, died. Marion, aged 6, died, Feb. 2nd.

The State Health Department had been unable to identify the malady. "Chemists spent twenty-four hours making tests of the youngest victim's blood without finding a trace of poison."

CHAPTER 22

Belief in God – in Nothing – in Einstein – a matter of fashion –

Or that college professors are mannequins, who doll up in the latest proper things to believe, and guide their young customers modishly.

Fashions often revert, but to be popular they modify. It could be that a re-dressed doctrine of witchcraft will be the proper acceptance. Come unto me, and maybe I'll make you stylish. It is quite possible to touch up beliefs that are now considered dowdy, and restore them to fashionableness. I conceive of nothing, in religion, science, or philosophy, that is more than the proper thing to wear, for a while.

"Typhoid Mary" – I doubt her germs – or I suspect that she was more malicious than germy. But nobody else – at least so far as go the published accounts – which could not be expected to go very far back in the years 1906-14 – thought of ignoring her germs, and of bottling her "rays." For my own suspicion that this was a case of witchcraft, I shall, for a while, probably be persecuted, by an amused tolerance, but, if back in the year 1906, anybody had given his opinion that "Typhoid Mary" was a witch, he'd have been laughed at outright.

Nobody accused "Typhoid Mary", except properly. According to the demonology of her era, she was distributing billions of little devils. Her case is framed with the unrecorded. As to her relations with her victims, I have nothing upon which to speculate.

The homes of dying men and women have been bombarded with stones of undetectable origin. Nobody was accused. We have had data of unexplained explosions, and data of seeming effects of "rays", not physical, upon motors. To me it is thinkable that a distant enemy could, invisibly, make an oil stove explode, and kill a woman, and then – if by means other than any known radioactivity, aeroplanes ever have been picked from the sky – pick from existence other members of her family. The explosion of the oil stove is simply a bang, such as cartoonists sometimes draw, with a margin of vacancy.

But there have been cases of persons who were accused of witchcraft.

This statement – like every other statement, issuing from the Supreme Court of the United States of America, from a nursery, from a meeting of the American Association for the Advancement of Science, or from the gossip of imbeciles – means whatever anybody wants it to mean. One interpretation is that superstitious people have attributed various misfortunes, which were probably due to their own ignorance and incompetence, to the malice of neighbours. At any rate, these cases are sketches of relations with environment, and so far we have been in a garden of evil, in which blossomed deaths and destructions, without visible stems, and without signs of the existence of roots.

New York Evening World (Sept. 14, 1928) – Michael Drouse, a farmer, living near Bruce, Wisconsin, who shot and fatally wounded John Wierzba, told Sheriff Dobson that he did it because Wierzba had bewitched his cows. *New York Times* (Sept. 8, 1929) – action by the Rye (N.Y.) National Bank against Leland Waterbury, of Poundridge, for recovery of properties, which the bank alleged had been taken from its client, Howard I. Salres, by "evil eye" methods. "The case has come to be known as 'the Westchester witchcraft case.'" *New York Times* (Oct. 9, 1930) – charges of sorcery brought against Henry Dorn, at Janesville, Wisconsin. "After a member of the State Board of Medical Examiners listened today to the charges of sorcery against Henry Dorn, a 64-year-old farmer, he said he was convinced that they were unfounded." Dorn's sister had accused him of casting "spells of sickness" upon members of her household.

So that case was disposed of.

I am not given to fortune-telling. I dislike the idea of fortune-telling, so called, or termed more pretentiously. But I do think that anybody could tell the fortune of any member of any State Board of Medical Examiners, who would say, of any charge of sorcery, that he was convinced that it was well-founded.

There were other charges against Dorn. They remind one of accusations in old-time witchcraft trials –

That Dorn had caused apples to rot on trees, cows to go dry, and hens to cease laying.

Opponents to the idea of witchcraft are much influenced by their inability to conceive how anybody could make apples rot, inability to visualise the process of drying a cow, or entering into the organism of a hen, and stopping her productions. And science does not tell them how this could be done. So.

And they can not conceive how something makes apples grow, or why they don't rot on trees; how the milk of a cow is secreted, or why she shouldn't be dry; how the egg of a hen develops. And science does not tell them.

It's every man for himself, and save who can – and damnation is in accepting any messiah's offers of salvation. We're told too much, and we're told too little. We rely. And for two pins – having had experiences by which I am pretty well assured that nobody ever has two pins, when they're called for – I'd finish this book, as a personal philosophy, or for myself, alone, and then burn it. It's everybody for himself, or he isn't anybody.

It's every thinker for himself. He can be told of nothing but surfaces. Theological fundamentalists say, rootily, they think, that all things have makers – that God made all things. Then what made God? even little boys ask. Space is curved, and behind space, or space-time, there is nothing, says Prof. Einstein. Also may he be construed as saying that it is only relatively to something else that anything can be curved.

Throughout this book there is a permeation that may be interpreted as helplessness and hopelessness – absence of anything in science more than approximately to rely on – solaces and reassurances of religion, but any other religion would do as well – all progresses returning to their points of origin – philosophies only intellectual dress-making –

But, if it's every man for himself, it is my expression that out of his illusion that he has a self, he may develop one.

In records of witchcraft trials, often appears the statement that the accused person was seen, at the time of the doings, in a partly visible, or semi-substantial state. In June, 1880, at High Easter, Essex, England, (London *Times,* June 24, 1880), there were poltergeist disturbances in the home of a family named Brewster. Furniture wandered. A bed rocked. Brewster saw, or thought he saw, a shadowy shape, which he recognized as that of his neighbour, Susan Sharpe. He and his son went to the home of the woman and dragged her to a pond. They threw her into the pond, to see whether she would sink or float. But, though once upon a time, this was the scientific thing to do, fashions in science had changed. Brewster and his son were arrested and were bound over to keep the peace – just as should be any woman, who, during rush hours in the subway, should appear in a hoop skirt.

A case that was a blend of ancient accusations and modern explanation was reported in the London *Evening News* (July 14, 1921) – that is, "mysterious illnesses" attributed to the doings of an enemy, but an attempt to explain materialistically. Residents of a house in Putney had, in the London South Western Court, accused their neighbour, Frank Gordon Hatton, of "administering poisonous fumes down their chimney." Saying that the complainants had failed to prove their case, the magistrate dismissed the charge.

If anybody could have a sane idea as to what he means by insanity, he might know what he is thinking about, by bringing in this convenient way of explaining unconventional human conduct. Whatever insanity is supposed to be, it can not so satisfactorily be applied as the explanation of two persons' beliefs relatively to one set of circumstances. According to newspaper accounts of a murder, in July 1929, Eugene Burgess, and his wife, Pearl, went insane together, upon the same subject. It was their belief that, when Burgess's mother died, in the year 1927, she had been willed to death by a neighbour, Mrs. Etta Fairchild. It was their belief that this woman had cast illness upon their daughter. They killed Mrs. Fairchild. In an account, in the *New York Sun* (Oct. 16, 1929), Mrs. Burgess is described: "Belying the comparison to the ignorant peasant women who have stood trial for similar crimes for hundreds of years, Mrs. Burgess looked like a prosperous clubwoman."

These are accounts of accusations of witchcraft, by persons, against other persons, according to their superstitions, or perceptions. Now there will be accounts of cases in which there are suggestions of witchcraft to me, according to my ignorance, or enlightenment.

Chicago Tribune (Oct. 23, 1892) – marvellous – though not at all extraordinary – doings in the home of Jerry Meyers, a farmer, living near Hazelwood, Ohio. Meyers had been absent from his home. When he returned, he heard a hysterical story from his niece, Ann Avey, of Middletown, Ohio, who was visiting him. Soon after he had left the house stones were thrown at her, or fell around her. Objects in the house moved toward her. Mr. Meyers was probably astonished to hear this, but what he wanted was his dinner. The girl went to the barn to gather eggs. On her way back, stones fell around her. Whether Meyers got his dinner, or not, he got a gun. Neighbours had heard of the doings. Stationed around the house were men with shot guns: but stones of unknown origin continued to bombard the house. Ann Avey fled back to her home in Middletown. Phenomena stopped.

In this case of the girl who was driven from her uncle's home, the circumstance that I pick out as significant is that assailments by stones began after Mrs. Meyers left the house. It was said that she had gone to visit friends, in the village of Lockland. Of course hospitalities are queer, but there is a good deal of queerness in the hospitality of somebody who would go visiting somewhere else, while her husband's niece was visiting in her home.

About the last of November, 1892, in the town of Hamilton, Ontario, a man was on his way to a railroad station. In a cell, in a prison, in Fall River, Massachusetts, sat a woman.

Henry G. Trickey was, in Hamilton, on his way to a railroad station. In the Fall River jail was Lizzie Borden, who was accused of having murdered her parents.

In August, 1892, Trickey, a reporter of the *Boston Globe,* had written what was described as a "scandalous article" about Lizzie Borden. The *Globe* learned that the story was false and apologised. Trickey was indicted.

He went to Canada. This looks as if he fled from prosecution.

Lizzie Borden sat in her cell. There may have been something more deadly than an indictment, from which there was no escape for Trickey. While boarding a train, at Hamilton, he fell and was killed.

In the town of Eastbourne, Sussex, England, in April, 1922, John Blackman, a well-known labour leader, was committed to prison, under a maintenance order, for arrears due to his wife. The judge who committed him died suddenly. When Blackman was released, he still refused to pay so back he went to prison. The judge who sent him back "died suddenly." He continued to refuse to pay, and twice again was re-committed to prison, and each time the judge in his case "died suddenly." See *Lloyd's Sunday News* (Oct. 14, 1923).

Upon November 29, 1931, there was an amateur theatrical performance in the home of Miss Phoebe Bradshaw, 106 Bedford Street, New York City. *Villain* – Clarence Hitchcock, 23 Grove Street, New York. *Wronged husband* -- John L. Tilker, 1976 Belmont Avenue, Bronx. Tilker was given a cap pistol. Also he carried a loaded revolver of his own, for which he had a permit. When the time came, Tilker, with his own revolver, fired at Hitchcock, shooting him in the neck. "He was apparently new at play-acting, and in his excitement fired his own revolver, instead of the dummy."

Hitchcock lay dying in St. Vincent's Hospital. Soon something occurred to Tilker. He was taken to the Willard Parker Hospital, suffering from what was said to be scarlet fever. Hitchcock died, Jan. 17, 1932. See the *New York Herald Tribune* (Jan. 18, 1932).

New York Evening Journal (Feb. 6, 1930) – "Two bitter women enemies are teetering on the verge of death today, one 'doing satisfactorily', while the other is 'weaker, and in a highly critical condition.' Both are sufferers from cancer. They are Mrs. Frances Stevens Hall and her most hated opponent in the famed Hall-Mills murder trial, Jane Gibson, the pig woman, whose testimony was used in an effort to send Mrs. Hall to the electric chair four years ago."

Upon the 8th of February, Jane Gibson died.

In the Fall of 1922, Mrs. Jane Gibson was a sturdy woman-farmer. It was her accusation that, upon the night of the murder of Dr. Edward Hall and Elinor Mills, Sept. 14, 1922, she had seen Mrs. Hall bending over the bodies. So she testified. She returned to her home, and soon afterward was stricken. At the re-trial, in November, 1926, she repeated the accusation, though she had to be carried on a cot into the court room. "Most of her days since that time were spent in the hospital."

CHAPTER 23

Dead men in a Harlem park – and houses are torn by explosions, of unknown origin – the sneak of an invisible clipper of hair – vampires and murder – theatrically a girl is stabbed, on a staircase, in the presence of a large audience – the internal organs of a woman are burned into unrecognisability –

And the stoutest opponents of witchcraft, one with persecutions, and the other with denials, have been religion and science –

And more power to them, for it –

Except that witchcraft is appalling.

In our existence of the hyphen, the appalling can be only one view of a state that combines the direst and the most desirable.

Religion is belief in a supreme being. Science is belief in a supreme generalisation. Essentially they are the same. Both are the suppressors of witchcraft, and I shall take up these oppositions together. But, in a state of realness-unrealness, there can not be real opposition. In our existence of the hyphen, what is called opposition is only one view of the state of opposition-stimulation.

There is no way of judging anything, except by its manifestations. Just as much as it has been light, religion has been darkness. Today it is twilight. In the past it was mercy and charity and persecution and bloody, maniacal, sadistic hatred – hymns from chapels and screams from holy slaughter houses – aspirations going up from this earth, with smoke from burning bodies. I can say that from religion we have never had opposition, because there has never been religion – that is that religion never has existed, as apart from all other virtues and vices and blessings and scourges – that, like all other alleged things, beings, or institutions, religion never has, in a final sense, had identity. An atheist, of zeal, may be thought of as religious. Or I can take the unmonistic view, and accept that there is, or used to be, religion, just as, practically, I ignore that all things and beings of my daily experiences are so bound up with one another that they have not identities, and go about my daily affairs as if things and beings really were entities.

New York Sun (March 26, 1910) – eruption of Mt. Etna – people of Borelli praying – the oncoming lava. The molten flood moved onward toward a shrine. Here the praying ones concentrated. The lava reached the shrine, and suddenly changed its course.

New York Times (July 27, 1931) – "A revival of the ancient rain dance of Northern Saskatchewan Indians, despite the ban by government agents, is reported to have occurred recently. Fields were parched and cattle were suffering, when Chief Buffalo Bow, head of the File Hills Reserve, decided to invoke the Great Spirit. The forty-eight-hour dance, led by six singers in relays, centred about a great tree, on the bark of which a petition for aid had been carved. The Great Spirit seemed to answer, for soon after the mystic rites had been performed, the rain began and continued for two days, July 14 and 15, bringing relief all over Saskatchewan."

If, according to the views of the majority of the inhabitants of this earth, both Jehovah and the Great Spirit are myths, lava, if it would not have changed its course anyway, and rain, if it would not have fallen anyway, were influenced by witchcraft, if there be witchcraft. My general situation is that of any mathematician. Consider any of his theorems. The parallelogram of forces. In the text books, this demonstration works out – if the incident forces be without irregularities – if resistances be unchanging – if the body acted upon be changeless – if the student has no awareness of the changes and the irregularities that are everywhere.

In the London *Daily Chronicle* (July 7, 1924) was reported a case of an English girl, who had come back from Lourdes, cured, she thought. It is not often that the doctors will have anything to do with one of these cases; but it was arranged to investigate this case. At the Hospital of St. John and St. Elizabeth, St. John's Wood, London, the girl was examined by fifty doctors. She had gone, with a nurse, to Lourdes. The nurse was questioned, and testified that the girl's hand had been covered with sores, from blood poisoning, and that she had been cured, at Lourdes. The diseased condition of the girl, when she arrived in Lourdes, was certified by three doctors, of Lourdes. The sores had disappeared, but some contraction of the hand remained. The official decision of the fifty doctors, who were not of Lourdes, was: "On the evidence submitted, the cure is not proven."

I should like to come upon a record of the opinions of fifty drivers of hansom cabs, as to automobiles, when automobiles were new and uncertain, but were of some slight menace to the incomes of hansom cabbies.

In the *New York World-Telegram* (July 24, 1931), there is a story of a boy, who, at the Medical Center Hospital, New York, was cured of paralysis by the touch of a bit of bone of St. Anne, taken to the hospital from the Church of St. Anne, 110 East 12th Street, New York City. The boy was the son of Hugh F. Gaffney, 348 East 18th Street, New York City.

If, according to the views of the majority of the inhabitants of this earth, there is no more divinity at Lourdes, or at 110 East 12th Street, than anywhere else, there are reasons for thinking that it is witchcraft that is practised at these places.

The function of God is the focus. An intense mental state is impossible, unless there be something, or the illusion of something, to centre upon. Given any other equally serviceable concentration-device, prayers are unnecessary. I conceive of the magic of prayers. I conceive of the magic of blasphemies. There is witchcraft in religion: there may be witchcraft in atheism.

In the *New York Evening World* (Sept. 19, 1930) is an account of joy in Naples: the shouts of crowds, and the ringing of church bells. In the Cappella del Tesoro Cathedral had been displayed the phial containing the "blood of St. Januarius." It had boiled.

It is my notion that, if intenser than the faith in Naples, had been a desire for a frustration of this miracle, the "blood of St. Januarius" might have frozen.

Upon the 5th of March, 1931 – see the *New York Herald Tribune,* March 6th – 15,000 worshippers were kneeling, at a pontifical high mass, in the Military Plaza, at San Antonio, Texas. Considering the intense antagonism to Catholicism in Mexico, at this time, one thinks of the presence of some of this feeling in San Antonio. From a palm tree, the topmost tuft fell into the kneeling congregation. Six persons were injured.

My general expression is that some of the reported phenomena that are called "miracles" probably have occurred, but have been arbitrarily taken over by the religionists, though they are the exclusive properties of priests no more than of travelling salesmen – that scientists have been repelled by the reported phenomena, because of a fear of contamination from priestcraft – but that any scientist who preaches the "ideals of science", and also lets fears of contaminations influence him, is as false to his preachments as ever any priest has been.

See the *New York Herald Tribune* (Dec. 6, 1931) – an account of the opening, in Goa, Portuguese India, of the coffin of Saint Francis Xavier.

"A special emissary sent by Pope Pius XI led the ceremonial procession, in which marched three archbishops, fifteen bishops and hundreds of other members of the clergy. A throng of 10,000 persons heard the papal mass and benediction in the Church of Dom Jesus. The congregation passed before the coffin and kissed the dead saint's feet."

But there have been scientists, especially medical scientists, who, in spite of contaminations, have not been held back from investigations.

In January, 1932, the New York newspapers told that many miracles had been reported in Goa.

There is no opposition, as sheer, to witchcraft, by religionists. It is competition.

CHAPTER 24

Our only important opposition is, not science, but a belief that we are in conflict with science.

This is an old-fashioned belief.

There is nothing told of in this book that is more of an affront to old-time dogmas than is the theory of the Nobel Prize-winner, Dr. Bohr, that the sun is deriving its energy from nowhere (*New York Times,* Jan. 17, 1932).

The quantum theory is a doctrine of magic. The idea of playing leapfrog, without having to leap over the other frog, is simply another representation of the idea of entering a closed room without passing through the walls. But there is a big difference between "authoritative pronouncements" and my expressions. It is the difference between sub-atomic events and occurrences in boarding houses. The difference is in many minds – unlike my mind, to which all things are phenomena, and to which all records are, or may be, data – in which electrons and protons are dignified little things, whereas boarders and tramps on park benches can't be taken solemnly. Charles Darwin was similarly received when, in the place of academic speculations upon evolutions, he treated of bugs and bones and insides of animals. Not, of course, that I mean anything by anything.

Quantum-magic is a doctrine of discontinuity. So it seems to be opposed to my expressions upon hyphenation, which seem to be altogether a philosophy of continuity. But I have indicated that also I hyphenate in another "dimension." I conceive of all phenomena as representing continuity in one "dimension", and as representing discontinuity in another "dimension" – that is, all phenomena as inter-dependent and bound up with one another, or continuous, and at the same time so individualised that nothing is exactly like anything else, or that everything is alone, or discontinuous. I conceive of our existence as one organic state, or being, that is an individual, or that is unrelated to anything else, such as other existences, in the cosmos, its state of oneness expressing in the continuity of its internal phenomena, and its state of individuality, or apartness from everything else in the cosmos, expressing in a permeation of that individuality, or discontinuity, throughout its phenomena. Of course, if the word *cosmos* means *organised universality,* I misuse the word here. For various reasons I let it stand.

There are hosts of persons, who consider themselves up-to-date, or ahead of that; who bandy arguments in the latest, scientific lingo, and believe anything that they're told to believe of electrons, but would be incapable of extending an idea from electrons to boarders – even though they argue that every boarder is only a composition of electrons – and go right on thinking of affairs, in general, in old-fashioned, materialistic terms.

Well, then, in old-fashioned terms, what had I this morning for breakfast?

I think: therefore I had breakfast.

If no line of demarcation can be drawn between one's breakfasts and one's thoughts, or between a cereal and a cerebration, this is the continuity of the material and the immaterial. If there is no material, as absolutely differentiated from the immaterial, what becomes of any opposition from what may still survive of what is called *materialistic science?*

"Science is systematised and formulated knowledge."

Then anybody who has systematised and formulated knowledge enough to appear, on time, at the breakfast table, is, to that degree, a scientist. There are scientific dogs. Most of them have a great deal of systematised and formulated knowledge. Cats and rabbits and all those irritating South American rodents that were discovered by cross-word puzzle-makers are scientists. A magnet scientifically picks out and classifies iron filings from a mass of various materials. Science does not exist, as a distinguished entity.

Our data have been upon witchcraft in love affairs, in small-town malices, and occasional murders of no importance. According to the phantom, *materialistic science,* there is no witchcraft. In the monistic sense, I agree. Witchcraft is so bound up with other "natural forces", that it can not be picked out, as having independent existence. But, in terms of common illusions, I accept that there is witchcraft; and, just for the sake of seeming to have opposition, which makes for more interest, I pretend that there is science.

Stars and planets and ultra-violet radiations from the sun – palaeolithic and neolithic inter-relationships, and zymotic multiplications, and tetrahedronic equilaterality –

And the little Colwell girl, who kept the firemen busy – and a kid named "Rena"got a haircut – there was a house in which a pan of soft soap wandered from room to room – a woman alone in a compartment of a railway train, and then maybe she wasn't alone –

The disdain of any academic scientist – if among the sensationalists of today, there survive an academic scientist – for what I call the data of witchcraft –

And now my subject is the witchcraft of science.

In the year 1913, the German scientist, Emil Abderhalden, announced his discovery of the synthesis of inorganic materials into edible substances. It was said that to avoid all uncertainties – this back in those supreme old days when all scientists were certain – this announcement had been long-delayed. But experiments had been successes. Dogs fed upon synthetic foods had gained weight astonishingly, as compared to dogs that had been fed ordinary meals. Reports were much tabulated. Statistics – very statistical. Then came the War. If Dr. Abderhalden, or anybody else in Germany, could out of muds of various kinds have produced those alleged meals, perhaps we'd all be fighting to this day. As it is, we have had a rest and can do the necessary breeding, before again starting up atrocities. So, at least for the sake of vigorous new abominations, it seems to be just as well that some of the widely advertised scientific successes aren't so successful.

But the dogs got fat.

There is scarcely an annual meeting of any prominent scientific association, at which are not made, by eminent doctors and professors, announcements of great discoveries that, by long and careful experimentation, constructive and eliminative tests, and guards against all possible sources of error, had been established. A year or so later, these boons to suffering humanity are forgotten.

Almost always these announcements are not especially questioned and bring no confusion upon their sponsors. There is much "scientific caution." A scientist doesn't know but that he may make an announcement, himself, someday. But about the middle of July, 1931, Professor Wilhelm Gluud, of the Westphalian University of Münster, was not received with the usual "caution." Prof. Gluud announced – these Professors never merely say anything – that synthetic albumen could be produced from coal. This dreamery was attacked, and later, in July, Prof. Gluud admitted that he had been "premature" in his announcement (*New York Herald Tribune,* July 26, 1931).

But something had convinced a scientist, of international reputation, so that he had risked that reputation by making his announcement.

So one inclines to think.

If he had made no experiments, and had simply and irresponsibly squawked into publicity, we have some more monism, and can draw no line between a Westphalian Professor and any Coney Island "barker." But, if he did make experiments, and, if, in spite of later developments, which showed that, according to chemical principles, success was impossible, he nevertheless had reasons to believe that some of his experiments were successes, these successes that agreed with his theory were realisations of his imaginings.

About the same time (July, 1931) another scientist was embarrassed. The Russian physiologist, Pavlov, had announced that he had taught white mice to respond to a bell, at meal time –

But now see here!

Just how disdainful should persons who put in their time ringing dinner bells for mice be of others who collect accounts of meandering pans of soft soap?

It was Pavlov's statement, or "announcement", that he had taught white mice to respond to a bell, at meal time, and that a second generation of white mice had been keener in so responding. This improvement was supposed to represent cumulative hereditary influences.

But Sir Arthur Thompson, of Aberdeen, Scotland, made an announcement.

And now see here, again! I should like to hear Sir Arthur's opinion upon the dignity of such subjects as "the vanishing man", and stones that were pegged at a farmer's niece. He, too, had been ringing dinner bells for animals.

Thompson's announcement was that he had noted no improved teachableness in a second generation of white mice. Whereupon Pavlov withdrew his announcement, saying that he must have been deceived by his assistant (*New York Times,* August 15, 1931).

This is becoming a stock-retreat. Before he shot himself, in August, 1925, Prof. Kammerer, accused of having faked, with India ink, what he called acquired characters in the feet of toads, explained that he had been betrayed by an assistant.

I conceive that, though Pavlov retreated before a "higher authority", his white mice may have been keener in a second generation, though nobody else's white mice would have been of any improved discernment in a fifteenth generation – and that, though biologically, nuptial pads could not appear upon the feet of Prof. Kammerer's toads –

Pictures on hailstones – a face on a cathedral wall – and an insect takes on the appearance of a leaf –

That it may be that a man did not altogether deceive himself and others, but that faint markings did appear upon the feet of toads, as responses to his theory – but in all the uncertainty and the evanescence of the incipient – that, convinced that he was right, Prof. Kammerer may have supplemented faint markings with India ink, just to tide over, at a time of enquiry – then exposure – suicide.

The story of cancer-cure announcements is a record of abounding successes in the treatment of cancerous dogs, cats, chickens, rats, mice, and guinea pigs – followed by appeals to the public for funds for the study of the unknown causes, and the still undiscovered cure for cancer. Look over the records of cancerous growths that, according to triumphant announcements have been absorbed, or stopped, in mice and guinea pigs, and try to think that all were only deliberate deceptions. My good-bad opinion of human nature won't stand it. But, if some of these experiments were the successes they were said to be, and if the treatments are now repudiated or forgotten, these successes were realised imaginings. I know of nothing in science that has the look of better establishment than that there have been some cures of cancer, under radium-treatment. But, in the year 1930, the British Radium Commission issued a warning that the use of radium had not been established as a cancer-cure (*New York Times,* Oct. 9, 1930). The look to me is that, in all the earnestness and charlatanry; devotion to ideals, and fakery, and insincerity; exploitations and duperies of this cult, some cures, as if by the use of radium, have occurred; but that applications of soft soap, if subject to an equal intensity of thought, would have done just as well –

Which brings us to the appalling unnecessity of vivisection, if experiments upon the animals of a toy Noah's Ark, to cure them of their splinters, would be just as enlightening, if anything can be construed into meaning anything that anybody wants it to mean – in an existence in which there is not meaning, but meaning-meaninglessness.

And – not wanting to write three or four hundred pages upon this subject – I shall not go much into records of professional rascals, or faithful and devoted scientists, who have exploited, or have tried to minister unto, the desire of old codgers to caper. I take from the *New York Evening Post* (April 12, 1928) an account of "discoveries of major importance to the science of rejuvenation", as announced, in Berlin, by Professor Steinach, to the annual congress of German surgeons. Professor Steinach's announcement was that he had discovered the secret of rejuvenation in uses of the pituitary gland. If any reader isn't quite sure where the pituitary is, I remind him that it is connected with the fundibulum. It is in a part of the body that is most profoundly engaged in sex-relations. It is in the brain.

Dr. Steinach announced that, with twelve injections of pituitary serum, in senile rats, he had "restored their failing appetite, induced a new growth of hair, rejuvenated all bodily functions and generally transformed ailing or half-dead creatures into youthful animals."

There is witchcraft in science –

If bald old rats have turned young and hairy – if dogs, fed on coal-products, have astonishingly fattened – if tens of thousands of mice and guinea pigs have magically gone fat, or gone thin, in the presence of experimenters –

If, in not all these cases has the treacherous, or perhaps kind-hearted, assistant slipped, say, a brisk and hairy young rat into the place of a decrepit old codger; or has not, in secret rascality, or benevolence, meatily supplemented the fare of dogs supposed to be thriving upon coal-products –

If not in all these cases have eminent trappers laid snares for dollars.

My pseudo-conclusion, or acceptance – which is as far as I can go, in the fiction that we're living – is that some of these announcements have been pretty nearly faithful report of occurrences; and that, by witchcraft, or in response to intense desires of experimenters, senile rats have lost the compensations of old age and have suffered again the tormenting restlessness of youth – all this by witchcraft, and not by injections that in themselves could have no more of a rejuvenating effect upon either rats or humans, than upon mummies.

But, if Prof. Steinach, by witchcraft, or by the effects of belief, did grow hair upon the bald skin of a rat – to say nothing of the more frolicsome effects of his practices – how comes it that he was not equally successful with the human subjects of his sorcery? Today the Steinach treatment stands discredited. Especially destructive have been Dr. Alexis Carrel's attacks upon it. It may be that the Professor's own greed defeated him. It may be that he failed, because he dissipated his sorcery among many customers.

Chapter 25

If I can bridge a gap –

Then that, in a moment of religious excitation, an inhabitant of Remiremont, focusing upon a point in the sky, transferred a pictorial representation from his mind to hailstones –

The turning off Coventry Street – streets in Japan, Kiel, Berlin, New York City – other places – and that wounds, as imagined by haters of people, have appeared upon the bodies of people –

Or the story of the sailor aboard the steamship *Brechsee*, in December, 1931 – and that it was during a storm – and that in the mind of somebody else aboard this vessel a hate pictured this man, as struck by lightning, and that upon his head appeared a wound, as pictured.

The gap, or the supposed gap, is the difference, or the supposed, absolute difference, between the imagined and the physical.

Or, for instance, the disappearance of Ambrose Small, of Toronto – and it was just about what his secretary, who had embezzled from him, probably wished for, probably unaware that an inventory would betray him. A picturisation, in the secretary's mind, of his employer, shooting away to Patagonia, to Franz Josef Land, or to the moon – so far away that he could never get back – but could the imagined realise? Or why didn't I keep track, in the newspapers of December, 1919, for mention of the body of a man, washed up on a beach of Java, scarcely decipherable papers in his pockets indicating that the man was a Canadian? Are the so-called asteroids bodies of people who have been witched away into outer space?

Rose Smith – that when she was released from prison, her visualisations crept up behind her former employer, and killed him? According to some viewpoints, I might as well try to think of a villain, in a moving picture, suddenly jumping from the screen, and attacking people in the audience. I haven't tried that, yet.

Case of Emma Piggot – and the fires in the home of her employers were just about what the girl, alarmed by the greediness of her thefts, may have wished for. Also there are data that may mean that, because of experiences unknown to anybody else, this girl knew that, from a distance, she could start fires.

There is an appearance of affinity between the Piggot case and the fires in the house in Bedford. There was a sulphur fire that was ordinary. It was followed by a series of fires that were, at least according to the impressions in Bedford, extraordinary. In no terms of physics, nor of chemistry, was an explanation possible; yet investigators felt that a relationship of some kind did exist. The relationship may have existed in the mind of Anne Fennemore. After the sulphur fire had been put out, she may have started fearing fires, especially in the absence of the only male member of the household. Her fear may have been realised.

Story of the Colwell girl – here, too, fires in a house seem to have related to a girl's mental state – or that the fires were related to her desire to move to another house. Having the not uncommon experience of learning how persuasive are police captains, she "listened to advice", and confessed to effects, in terms of ordinary incendiarism, though, according to reports by firemen and policemen, some of the fires could not have been produced by flipping lighted matches.

In the case of Jennie Bramwell, there is no knowing what were the feelings of this girl, who had been "adopted", probably to do hard farm-work. If she, too, had nascently the fire-inducing power, which manifested under the influence of desire, or emotion, I think of her, in the midst of drudgery, wishing destruction upon the property of her exploiters, and fires following. At any rate, the story of the little Barnes girl, which quite equals anything from the annals of demonology, is very suggestive – or the smoulder of hate, in the mind of a child, for an exploiter – and flames leaped upon a woman.

There is a particular in the case of Emma Piggot that makes it different from the other cases. In the other cases, fires broke out in the presence of girls. But, according to evidence, Emma Piggot was not in the house wherein started the fires for which she was accused. Then this seems to be a case of distance-ignition, or of distance-witchcraft. I'd not say that invisibly starting a fire, at a distance, by means of mental rays, is any more mysterious than is the shooting-off of distant explosives by means of rays called physical, which nobody understands.

I am bringing out:

That, as a "natural force", there is a fire-inducing power;

That, mostly, it appears independently of wishes, or of the knowledge, of the subjects, but that sometimes, conformably to wishes, it is used –

That everything that I call witchcraft is only some special manifestation of transformations, or transportations, that, in various manifestations, are general throughout "Nature."

The "accidents" on the Dartmoor road – or that somewhere near this road lived a cripple. That his mind had shaped to his body – or that somewhere near this road lived somebody who had been injured by a motor car, and lay on his bed, or sat in his invalid's chair, and radiated against the nearby road a hate for all motorists, sometimes with a ferocity, or with a directness, that knocked cars to destruction.

Or Brooklyn, April 10, 1893 – see back to the supposed series of coincidences – man after man injured by falling from a high place, or being struck by a falling object – or that somewhere in Brooklyn was somebody who had been crippled by a fall, and, brooding over what he considered a monstrous injustice that had so singled him out, radiated influences that similarly injured others.

See back to the account of what occurred to French aeroplanes, flying over German territory. Tracks in the sand of a desert. Occurrences, about Christmas Day, 1930, in Sing Sing and Dannemora Prisons – or a prisoner in a punishment-cell – and nothing to do in the dark, except to concentrate upon vengefulness. I think that sometimes, coming from dungeons, there are stinks of hates that can be smelled. It was a time that for almost everybody else was a holiday.

Tracks that stopped, in a desert – or the tracks of a child that stopped, on a farm, in Brittany – the story of Pauline Picard:

Or the hate of a neighbour for the Picards, and vengeance by teleporting their offspring – the finding of Pauline in Cherbourg – again her disappearance –

That this time the body of the child was mutilated and stripped, so that it could not be identified, and was transported to some lonely place, where it decomposed –

But a change of purpose, or a vengefulness that required that the parents should know – transportation to the field, of this body, which probably could not be identified – transportation of the "neatly folded" clothes, so that it could be identified.

In the matter of the two bodies on benches in a Harlem park, I have another datum. I think I have. The dates of June 14 and June 16 are close together, and Mt. Morris Park and Morningside Park are not far apart –

Or a man who lived in Harlem, in June, 1931 – and that he was a park bencher – about whom I can say nothing except that his trousers were blue, and that his hat was grey. Something may have sapped him, pursued him, driven him into vagrancy –

But that he probably had the sense of localisation, as to benches, that everybody has in so many ways, such as going to the same seat, or as near as possible to the same seat, upon every visit to a moving picture theatre – that every morning he had sat on a particular bench, in Mt. Morris Park –

But that, upon the morning of June 14th, because of a whim, suspicion, or intuitive fear, he went to Morningside Park instead –

That somebody else sat on his particular bench – that there occurred something that was an intensification of the experiences of John Harding and another man, when crossing Fifth Avenue, at Thirty-third Street – to the man who was sitting on this particular bench, and to another man upon a nearby bench –

But that, two days later, the trail of the intended victim was picked up –

Home News (Bronx; June 17, 1931) – that, in Morningside Park, morning of the 16th, a policeman noticed a man – blue trousers and grey hat – seemingly asleep on a bench. The man was dead. "Heart trouble."

At a time of intensely bitter revolts by coal miners against their hardships, there were many coal explosions, but in grates and stoves, and not in shipments. No finding of dynamite in coal was reported. If in coal there is storage of radiations from the sun, coal may be absorbent to other kinds of radiations – or a savagely vengeful miner's hope for future harm in every lump he handled. If, in the house in Hornsey, there were not only coal-explosions, but also poltergeist doings, we note that these phenomena occurred only in the presence of two boys of the household – or especially one of these boys. Between the occultism of adolescence and the occultism of lumps of coal, surcharged with hatreds, there may have been rapport.

That, somewhere near the town of Saltdean, Sussex, Sept., 1924, somebody hated a shepherd, and stopped the life of him, as have been stopped the motions of motors – and that the place remained surcharged with malign vibrations that affected somebody else, who came along, in a sidecar. The wedding party at Bradford – and the gaiety of weddings is sometimes the bubbling of vitriol – or that, from a witch, or a wizard, so made by jealousy, mental fumes played upon this house, and spread to other houses. At the same time, there are data that make me think that volumes of deadly gases may be occultly transported. And a young couple, walking along a shore of the Isle of Man – that, from a state of jealousy, witchery flung them into the harbour, and that somebody who stepped into the area of influence was knocked after them. See back to the story of a room in a house in Newton, Massachusetts. See other cases of "mass psychology." See a general clearing up –

If I can bridge the gap between the subjective and the objective, between what is called the *real* and what is called the *unreal,* or between the imaginary and the physical.

When, in our philosophy of the hyphen, we think of neither the material nor the immaterial, but of the material-immaterial, accentuated one way or the other in all phenomena; when we think of the imaginary, as deriving from material sustenance, or, instead of transforming absolutely, only shifting accentuation, we accept that there is continuity between what is called the *real* and what is called the *unreal,* so that a passage from one state to the other is across no real gap, or is no absolute jump. If there is no realness that can be finally set apart from unrealness – in phenomenal being – my term of the "realisation of the imaginary", though a convenience is a misnomer. Maybe the word *transmediumisation,* meaning the passage of phenomena from one medium of existence to another, is not altogether too awkward, and is long and important-enough-looking to give me the appearance of really saying something. I mean the imposition of the imaginary upon the physical. I mean, not the action of mind upon matter, but the action of mind-matter upon matter-mind.

Theoretically there is no gap. But very much mine are inductive methods. We shall have data. Not that I can more than really-unreally mean anything by that. The interpretations will be mine, but the data will be for anybody to form his own opinions upon.

Granting that the gap has not been disposed of, inductively, I reduce it to two questions:

Can one's mind, as I shall call it, affect one's own body, as I shall call it?

If so, that is *personal witchcraft,* or *internal witchcraft.*

Can one's mind affect the bodies of other persons, and other things outside?

If so, that is what I shall call *external witchcraft.*

CHAPTER 26

Hates and malices – murderous radiations from human minds –

Or the flashes and roars of a thunder storm –

And there has been the equivalence of picking strokes of lightning out of the sky, and harnessing them to a job.

A house afire – or somebody boils an egg.

Devastation or convenience –

Or what of it, if I bridge a gap?

I take it that the story of Marjorie Quirk is only an extreme instance of cases of internal, or personal, witchcraft that, today, are commonly accepted. London *Daily Express* (Oct. 3, 1911) – inquest upon the body of Marjorie Quirk, daughter of the Bishop of Sheffield. The girl had been ill of melancholia. In a suicidal impulse she drank, from a cup, what she believed to be paraffin. She was violently sick. She died. "It was stated yesterday that the cup was found perfectly clean near the paraffin drum, and Dr. Borman said that he could not find the slightest trace of paraffin in the mouth or throat."

New York Herald Tribune (Jan. 30, 1932) – Boston, Jan. 29 – "Nearly half a hundred students and physicians living in Vanderbilt Hall of the Harvard Medical School have experienced mild cases of what apparently was paratyphoid, it was learned today.

"The first thirty of the group fell ill two weeks ago following a fraternity dinner at which Dr. George H. Bigelow, state health commissioner, discussed 'food poisoning.' A few days later twenty more men reported themselves ill. The food was prepared at the hall.

"Today state health officers started an examination of kitchen help in the belief that one of the employees may be a typhoid carrier. College authorities said they did not believe the food itself was at fault, but were inclined to think the subject of Dr. Bigelow's address may have influenced some of the diners to diagnose mere gastronomic disturbances more seriously. All of the students have recovered."

To say that fifty young men had gastronomic disturbances is to say much against conditions of health in the Harvard Medical School. To say that the subject of illness may have induced illness is to say that there was personal, or internal, witchcraft, usually called auto-suggestion. See back to "Typhoid Mary" and other probable victims of carrier-finders. To say that there may have been a carrier among the kitchen help is to attribute to him, and is to say that it was only coincidence that illnesses occurred after a talk upon illnesses. It's a hell of a way, anyway, to have dinner with a lot of young men, and talk to them about food-poisoning. Hereafter Dr. Bigelow may have to buy his own dinners. If he tells shark-stories, while bathing, he'll do lonesome swimming.

Physiologists deny that fright can turn one's hair white. They argue that they can not conceive how a fright could withdraw the pigmentation from hairs, so they conclude that all alleged records of this phenomenon are yarns. Say it's a black-haired person. The physiologists, except very sketchily, can not tell us how that hair became black, in the first place. Somewhere, all the opposition to the data of this book is because the data are not in agreement with something that is not known.

There have been many alleged instances. See the indexes of *Notes and Queries* (s. 6: 1, 444; 6: 85, 134, 329; 7, 37; 8, 97; 9, 378; s. 7: 2: 6, 93, 150, 239, 298, 412, 518; 3, 95; 4: 195, 415; 7, 344; s. 10: 9, 445; 10: 33, 75; 11, 433). I used to argue that Queen Marie Antoinette's deprivation of cosmetics, in prison, probably accounted for her case. Now that my notions have shifted, that cynicism has lost its force to me. Mostly the instances of hair turning white, because of fright, are antiques, and can't be investigated now. But see the *New York Times* (Feb. 8, 1932):

Story of the sinking of a fishing schooner, by the Belgian steamship, *Jean Jadot* – twenty-one members of the crew drowned – six of them saved, among them Arthur Burke, aged 52.

"Arthur Burke's hair was streaked with gray before the collision but was quite gray when Burke landed yesterday at Pier 2, Erie Basin."

It may be that there have been thousands, or hundreds of thousands, of cases in which human beings have died in violent convulsions that were the products of beliefs – and that, also, merciful, but expensive, science has saved a multitude of lives, with a serum that has induced contrary beliefs – just as that serum, if injected into the veins of somebody, suffering under the pronouncement that twice two are four, could be his salvation by inducing a belief that twice two are purple, if he should want to be so affected –

Or what has become of hydrophobia?

In the *New York Telegram* (Nov. 26, 1929) was published a letter from Gustave Stryker, quoting Dr. Mathew Woods, of Philadelphia, a member of the Philadelphia County Medical Society. Dr. Woods had better look out, unless he's aiming at cutting down expenses, such as dues to societies. Said Dr. Woods:

"We have observed with regret numerous sensational stories concerning alleged mad dogs and the terrible results to human beings bitten by them which are published from time to time in the newspapers.

"Such accounts frighten people into various disorders and cause brutal treatment of animals suspected of madness, and yet there is upon record a great mass of testimony from physicians asserting the extreme rarity of hydrophobia even in the dog, while many medical men of wide experience are of the opinion that if it develops in human beings at all it is only on extremely rare occasions and that the condition of hysterical excitement in man described by newspapers as 'hydrophobia' is merely a series of symptoms due usually to a dread of the disease, such dread being caused by realistic newspaper and other reports acting upon the imaginations of persons scratched or bitten by animals suspected of rabies.

"At the Philadelphia dog pound where on an average more than 6,000 vagrant dogs are taken annually and where the catchers and keepers are frequently bitten while handling them, not one case of hydrophobia has occurred during its entire history of twenty-five years, in which time, about 150,000 have been handled."

My own attention was first attracted, long ago, when I noticed, going over files of newspapers, the frequency of reported cases of hydrophobia, a generation or so ago, and the fewness of such reports in the newspapers of later times. Dogs are muzzled, now – in streets; in houses they're not. Vaccines, or powdered toads, caught at midnight, in graveyards, would probably cure many cases, but would not reduce the number of cases in dogs, if there ever have been cases of hydrophobia in dogs.

In the *New York Times* (July 4, 1931) was published a report by M. Roéland, of the Municipal Council of Paris:

"It will be noticed that rabies has almost entirely disappeared, although the number of dogs has increased. From 166,917 dogs in Paris, in 1924, the number has risen, in 1929, to 230,674. In spite of this marked increase, only ten cases of rabies in animals were observed. There were no cases of rabies in man."

Sometimes it is my notion that there never has been a case of hydrophobia, as anything but an instance of personal witchcraft; but there are so very many data for thinking that a disease in general is very much like an individual case of the disease, in that it runs its course and then disappears – quite independently of treatment, whether by the poisoned teat of a cow, or the dried sore of a mummy – that I suspect that once upon a time there was, to some degree, hydrophobia. When I was a boy, pitted faces were common. What has become of smallpox? Where are yellow fever and cholera? I'm not supposed to answer my own questions, am I? But serums, say the doctors. But there are enormous areas in the Americas and Europe, where vaccines have never penetrated. But they did it, say the doctors.

Eclipses occur, and savages are frightened. The medicine men wave wands – the sun is cured – they did it.

The story of diseases reads like human history – the rise and fall of Black Death – and the appearance and rule of Smallpox – the Tubercular Empire – and the United Afflictions of Yellow Fever and Cholera. Some of them passed away before serums were thought of, and in times when sanitation was unpopular. Several hundred years ago there was a lepers' house in every good-sized city in England. A hundred years ago there had not been much of what is called improvement in medicine and sanitation, but leprosy had virtually disappeared, in England. Possibly the origin of leprosy in England was in personal witchcraft – or that if the Bible had never devastated England, nobody there would have had the idea of leprosy – that when wicked doubts arose, the nasty suspicions of people made them clean.

So it may be that once upon a time there was hydrophobia, but the indications are that most of the cases that are reported in these times are sorceries wrought by the minds of victims upon their bodies.

A case, the details of which suggest that occasionally a dog may be rabid, but that his bites are dangerous only to a most imaginatively excited victim, is told of, in the *New York Herald Tribune* (Nov. 16, 1931). Ten men were bitten by a dog. "The dog was killed and was found to have the rabies." The men were sailors aboard the United States destroyer, *J.D. Edwards,* at Cheefoo (Yantai), China. One of these sailors died of hydrophobia. The nine others showed no sign of the disease.

In such a matter as a fright turning hair grey, it is probable that conventional scientists mechanically, unintelligently, or with little consciousness of the whyness of their opposition, deny the occurrences, as unquestioning obediences to Taboo. My own concatenation of thoughts is – that, if one's mental state can affect the colour of one's hair, a mental state may in other ways affect one's body – and then that one's mental state may affect the bodies of others – and this is the path to witchcraft. It is not so much that conventional scientists disregard, or deny, what they can not explain – if, in anything like a final sense, nothing ever has been, or can be, explained. It is that they disregard, or deny, to clip concatenations that would lead them from concealed ignorance into obvious bewilderment.

Every science is a mutilated octopus. If its tentacles were not clipped to stumps, it would feel its way into disturbing contacts. To a believer, the effect of the contemplation of a science is of being in the presence of the good, the true, and the beautiful. But what he is awed by is Mutilation. To our crippled intellects, only the maimed is what we call understandable, because the unclipped ramifies away into all other things. According to my aesthetics, what is meant by the beautiful is symmetrical deformation. By Justice – in phenomenal being – I mean the appearance of balance, by which a reaction is made to look equal and opposite to an action – so arbitrarily wrought by the clip and disregard of all ramifications of the action – expressing in the supposed condign punishment of a man, regardless of effects upon other persons. This is the arbitrary basis of the mechanical theory of existence – the idea that an action can be picked out of a maze of interrelationships, as if it were a thing in itself. Some wisdom of mine is that if a man is dying of starvation he can not commit a crime. He is good. The god of all idealists is *Malnutrition*. If all crimes are expressions of energy, it is unjust to pick on men for their crimes. A higher jurisprudence would indict their breakfasts. A good cook is responsible for more evil than ever the Demon Rum has been: and, if we'd all sit down and starve to death, at last would be realised Utopia.

My expression is that, if illnesses, physical contortions, and deaths can be imposed by the imaginations of persons upon their own bodies, we may develop the subject-matter of a preceding chapter, with more striking data –

Or the phenomenon of the stigmata –

Which, considered sacred by pietists, is aligned by me with hydrophobia.

This phenomenon is as profoundly damned, in the views of all properly trained thinkers, as are crucifixes, sacraments, and priestly vestments. As to its occurrences, I can quote dozens of churchmen, of the "highest authority", but not one scientist, except a few Catholic scientists.

Over and over and over – science and its system – and theology and its system – and the fights between interpretations by both – and my thought that the freeing of data from the coercions of both, may, or may not, be of value. Once upon a time the religionists denied, or disregarded much that the scientists announced. They have given in so disastrously, or have been licked so to a frazzle, that, in my general impression of controversies that end up in compromises, this is defeat too nearly complete to be lasting. I conceive of a return-movement – open to free-thinkers and atheists – in which many of the data of religionists – scrubbed clean of holiness – will be accepted.

As to the records of stigmatics, I omit the best-known, and most convincingly reported, of all the cases, the case of the French girl, Louise Lateau, because much has been published upon her phenomena, and because accounts are easily available.

In the newspapers of July, 1922 – I take from the London *Daily Express* (July 10) – was reported the case of Mary Reilly, aged 20, in the Home of the Sisters of the Good Shepherd, Peekskill, N.Y. It was said intermittently, upon her side, appeared a manifestation in the form of a cross of blood. Mostly the appearances are of the "five wounds of Christ," or six, including marks on the forehead. For an account of the case of Rose Ferron, see the *New York Herald Tribune* (March 25, 1928). According to this story, Rose Ferron, aged 25, of 86 Asylum Street, Woonsocket, R.I., had, since March 17, 1916, been a stigmatic, wounds appearing upon her hands, feet, and forehead. The hysterical condition of this girl – in both the common and the medical meaning of the term -- is indicated by the circumstance that for three years she had been strapped to her bed, with only her right arm free.

At this time of writing, I have, for four years, been keeping track of the case of Theresa Neumann, the stigmatic girl of Konnersreuth, Germany: and, up to this time, there has been no exposure of imposture. See the *New York Times* (April 8, 1928) – roads leading to her home jammed with automobiles, carriages, motor cycles, vans, and pilgrims on foot. Considering the facilities – or the facilities, if nothing goes wrong – of modern travel, it is probable that no other miracle has been so multitudinously witnessed. A girl in bed – and all day long, the tramp of thousands past her. Whether admission is charged, I do not know. The story of this girl agrees with the stories of other stigmatics: flows of blood, from quick-healing wounds, and phenomena on Fridays. It was said that medical men had become interested, and had "demanded" Theresa's removal to a clinic, where she could be subjected to a prolonged examination, but that the Church authorities had objected. This is about what would be expected of Church authorities, and that the medical men, unable to have their own way, then disregarded the case, is something else that is about what would be expected.

My expression is that, upon stigmatic girls have appeared wounds, similar to the alleged wounds of a historical, and therefore doubtful, character, because this melodrama is most strikingly stimulative to the imagination – but that an atheistic girl – if there could be anything for an atheistic girl to be equally imaginatively hysterical about – might reproduce other representations upon her body. In the *Month* (134, 248) is an account of Marie-Julie Jahenny, of the village of La Fraudais (Loire-Inférieure) France, who, upon

March 21, 1873, became a stigmatic. Upon her body appeared the "five wounds." Then upon her breast appeared the picture of a flower. It is said that for twenty years this picture of a flower remained visible. According to the story, it was in the mind of the girl before it appeared upon her body, because she predicted that it would appear. One has notions of the possible use of indelible ink, or of tattooing. That is very good. One should have notions.

If a girl drinks a liquid that would harm nobody else, and dies, can a man inflict upon himself injuries that would kill anybody else, and be unharmed?

There is a kind of stigmatism that differs from the foregoing cases, in that weapons are used to bring on effects; but the wounds are similar to the wounds of stigmatic girls, or simply are not wounds, in an ordinary, physical sense. There is an account, in the *Sphinx* (Leipzig) of March 1893 (16, 81), of a fakir, Soliman Ben Aissa, who was exhibiting in Germany, who stabbed daggers into his cheeks and tongue, and into his abdomen, harmlessly, and with quick-healing wounds.

Such magicians are of rare occurrence, anyway in the United States and Europe; but the minor ones who eat glass and swallow nails are not uncommon.

But, if in Germany, or anywhere else, in countries that are said to be Christian, any man ever did savagely stab himself in the abdomen, and be unhurt, and repeat his performances, how is it that the phenomenon is not well-known and generally accepted?

The question is like another:

If, in the Theological Era, a man went around blaspheming, during thunderstorms, and was unhurt, though churches were struck by lightning, how long would he remain well-known?

In March, 1920, a band of Arab dervishes exhibited in the London music halls. In the London *Daily News* (March 12, 1920) are reproduced photographs of these magicians, showing them with skewers that they had thrust through their flesh, painlessly and bloodlessly.

Taboo. The censor stopped the show.

For an account of phenomena, or alleged phenomena, of the Silesian cobbler, Paul Diebel, who exhibited in Berlin, in December, 1927, see the *New York Times* (Dec. 18, 1927). "Blood flows from his eyes, and open wounds appear on his chest, after he has concentrated mentally for six minutes, it is declared. He drives daggers through his arms and legs and even permits himself to be nailed to a cross without any suffering, whatever, it is said. His manager asserts that he can remain thus for ten hours. His self-inflicted wounds, it is declared, bleed or not as he wishes, and a few minutes after the knife or nails are withdrawn all evidence of incisions vanishes."

The only thing that can be said against this story is that it is unbelievable. *New York Herald Tribune* (Feb. 6, 1928) – that, in Vienna, the police had interfered with Diebel and had forbidden him to perform. It was explained that this was because he would not give them a free exhibition, to prove the genuineness of his exhibitions. "In Munich, recently, he remained nailed to a cross several hours, smoking cigarettes and joking with his audience."

After April 8, 1928 – see the *New York Times* of this date – I lost track of Paul Diebel. The story ends with an explanation. Nothing is said of the alleged crucifixions. The explanation is a retreat to statements that are supposed to be understandable in commonplace terms. I do not think that they are so understandable. Diebel "has disclosed his secret to the public, saying that shortly before his appearance, he scratched his flesh with his fingernails or a sharp instrument, being careful not to cut it. On the stage, by contracting his muscles, these formerly invisible lines assumed blood-red hue and often bled."

I have heard of other persons, who have "disclosed" trade secrets.

Upon March 2, 1931, a man lay, most publicly, upon a bed of nails. See the *New York Herald Tribune* (March 3, 1931). In Union Square, New York City, an unoriental magician, named Brawman, from the unmystical region of Pelham Bay, in the Bronx, gave an exhibition that was staged by the magazine, *Science and Invention*. This fakir from the Bronx lay upon a bed of 1200 nails. In response to his invitation, ten men walked on his body, pressing the points of the nails into his back. He stood up, showing deep, red marks made by the nails. These marks soon faded away.

I have thought of leaf insects as pictorial representations wrought in the bodies of insects, by their imaginations, or by the imaginative qualities of the substances of their bodies – back in plastic times, when insects were probably not so set in their ways as they now are. The conventional explanation of protective colorations and formations has, as to some of these insects, considerable reasonableness. But there is one of these creatures – the Tasmanian leaf insect – that represents an artistry that so transcends utility that I considered the specimen I saw, in the American Museum of Natural History, misplaced: it should have been in the Metropolitan Museum of Art. This leaf insect has reproduced the appearance of a leaf down to such tiny details as serrated edges. The deception of enemies, or survival-value, has had nothing thinkable to do with some of the making of this remarkable likeness, because such minute particulars as serrations would be invisible to any bird, unless so close that the undisguisable insect-characteristics would be apparent.

I now have the case of what I consider a stigmatic bird. It is most unprotectively marked. Upon its breast it bears betrayal – or it is so conspicuously marked that one doubts that there is much for the theory of protective coloration to base upon, if conspicuously marked forms of life survive everywhere, and if many of them can not be explained away, as Darwin explained away some of them, in terms of warnings.

It is the story of sensitiveness of pigeons. I have told of the pigeons with whom I was acquainted. One day a boy shot one, and the body lay where the others saw it. They were so nervous that they flew, hearing trifling sounds that, before, they'd not have noticed. They were so suspicious that they kept away from the window sills. For a month they remembered.

The bleeding-heart pigeon of the Philippines – the spot of red on its breast – or that its breast remembered –

Or that once upon a time – back in plastic times when the forms and plumages of birds were not so fixed, or established, as they now are – an ancestral pigeon and her mate. The swoop of a hawk – a wound on his breast – and that sentiment in her plumage was so sympathetically moved that it stigmatised her, or reproduced on offsprings, and is to this day the recorded impression of an ancient little tragedy.

A simple red spot on the breast of a bird would not be conceived of, by me, as having any such significance. It is not a simple, red spot, only vaguely suggestive of a wound, on the breast of the bleeding-heart pigeon of the Philippines. The bordering red feathers are stiff, as if clotted. They have the appearance of coagulation.

Conceiving of the transmission of a pictorial representation, by heredity, is conceiving of external stigmatism, but of internal origin. If I could think that a human being's intense mental state, at the sight of a wound, had marked a pigeon, that would be more of a span over our gap. But I have noted an observation for thinking that the sight of a dead mutilated pigeon may intensely affect the imaginations of other pigeons. If anybody thinks that birds have not imagination, let him tell me with what a parrot of mine foresees what I am going to do to him, when I catch him up to some of his mischief, such as gouging furniture. The body of a dead and mutilated companion prints on the minds of other pigeons: but I have not a datum for thinking that the skeleton, or any part of the skeleton, of a pigeon, would be of any meaning to other pigeons. I have never heard of anything that indicates that in the mind of any other living thing is the mystic awe that human beings, or most human beings, have for bones –

Or a moth sat on a skull –

And that so rested, with no more concern than it would feel upon a stone. That a human being came suddenly upon the skull, and that, from him, a gush of mystic fright marked the moth –

The Death's Head Moth.

On the back of the thorax of this insect is a representation of a human skull that is as faithful a likeness as ever any pirate drew. In Borneo and many other places, there is not much abhorrence for a human skull, but the death's head moth is a native of England.

Or the death's heads that appeared upon the windowpanes, at Boulley – except that perhaps there were no such occurrences at Boulley. Suppose most of what I call data may be yarns. But the numbers of them – except, what does that mean? Oh, nothing, except that some of our opponents, if out in a storm long enough, might have it dawn on them that it was raining.

If I could say of any pictorial representation that has appeared on the wall of a church that it was probably not an interpretation of chance arrangements of lights and shades, but was a transference from somebody's mind, then from a case like this, of the pretty, the artistic, or of what would be thought of by some persons as the spiritual, and a subject to be treated reverently, would flow into probability a flood of everything that is bizarre, malicious, depraved, and terrifying in witchcraft – and of course jostles of suggestions of uses.

In this subject I have had much experience. Long ago, I experimented. I covered sheets of paper with scrawls, to see what I could visualise out of them; tacked a sheet of wrapping paper to a ceiling, and smudged it with a candle flame; made what I called a "visualising curtain", which was a white window shade, covered with scrawls and smudges; went on into three dimensions, with boards veneered with clay. It was long ago – about 1907. I visualised much, but the thought never occurred to me that I marked anything. It was my theory that, with a visualising device, I could make my imaginary characters perform for me more vividly than in my mind, and that I could write a novel about their doings. Out of this idea I developed nothing, anyway at the time. I have had much experience with visualisations that were, according to my beliefs, at the time, only my own imaginings, and I have had not one experience – so recognised by me – of ever having imaginatively marked anything. Not that I mean anything by anything.

There is one of these appearances that many readers of this book may investigate. Upon Feb. 23rd, 1932, New York newspapers reported a clearly discernible figure of Christ, in the variegations of the sepia-toned marble of the sanctuary wall, of St. Bartholomew's Church, Park Avenue and Fiftieth Street, New York City.

In the *New York Times* (Feb. 24, 1932), the rector of the church, the Rev. Dr. Robert Norwood, is quoted:

"One day, at the conclusion of my talk, I happened to glance at the sanctuary wall and was amazed to see this lovely figure of Christ in the marble. I had never noticed it before. As it seemed to me to be an actual expression on the face of the marble of what I was preaching, 'His Glorious Body', I consider it a curious and beautiful happening. I have a weird theory that the force of thought, a dominant thought, may be strong enough to be somehow transferred to stone in its receptive state."

In 1920, a censor stopped a show; but, in 1930, the *Ladies' Home Journal* (Dec. 1930; 117) published William Seabrook's story – clipping sent to me by Mr. Charles McDaniel, East Liberty P.O., Pittsburgh, Pennsylvania.

There was a performance in the village of Doa, in the Bin-Hounien territory (Bin Houyé) of the French West African Colony (Ivory Coast).

It is a story of sorceries practised by magicians, not upon their own bodies, but upon the bodies of others.

"There were the two living children, close to me. I touched them with my hands. They were three-dimensional warm flesh. And there equally close to be touched and seen were the two men with their swords. The swords were iron, three-dimensional, metal, cold and hard. And this is what I now *saw* with my eyes, but you will understand why I am reluctant to tell of it, and that I do not know what *seeing* means:

"Each man, holding his sword stiffly upward with his left hand, tossed a child high in the air with his right, then caught it full upon the point, impaling it like a butterfly on a pin. No blood flowed, but the two children were there, held aloft, pierced through and through, impaled upon swords.

"The crowd screamed now, falling to its knees. Many veiled their eyes with their hands, and others fell prostrate. Through the crowd the jugglers marched, each bearing a child aloft, impaled upon his sword, and disappeared into the witch doctor's inclosure."

Later Seabrook saw the children, and touched them, and had the impression that he would have, looking at a dynamo, or at a storm at sea, at something falling from a table, or at a baby crawling – that he was in the presence of the unknown.

CHAPTER 27

The twitch of the legs of a frog – and Emma Piggot swiped a powder puff.

The mysterious twitchings of electrified legs – and unutterable flutterings in the mind of Galvani. His travail on mental miscarriages – or ideas that could not be born properly. The twitch of trivialities that were faint and fantastic germinations in the mind of Galvani – the uninterpretable meanings of far-distant hums of motors – these pre-natal stirrings of aeroplanes and transportation systems and the lighting operations of cities –

Twitch of the legs of a frog –

A woman, from Brewster, N.Y., annoyed a hotel clerk.

My general expression is that all human beings who can do anything, and dogs that track unseen quarry, and homing pigeons, and bird-charming snakes, and caterpillars who transform into butterflies, are magicians. In the lower – or quite as truly higher, considering them the more aristocratic and established – forms of being, the miracles are standardised and limited: but human affairs are still developing, and "sports", as the biologists call them, are of far more frequent occurrence among humans. But their development depends very much upon a sense of sureness of reward for the pains, travail, and discouragements of the long, little-paid period of apprenticeship, which makes questionable whether it is ever worth while to learn anything. Reward depends upon harmonisation with the dominant spirit of an era.

Considering modern data, it is likely that many of the fakirs of the past, who are now known as saints, did, or to some degree did, perform the miracles that have been attributed to them. Miracles, or stunts, that were in accord with the dominant power of the period were fostered, and miracles that conflicted with, or that did not contribute to, the glory of the Church, were discouraged, or were savagely suppressed. There could be no development of mechanical, chemical, or electric miracles –

And that, in the succeeding age of Materialism – or call it the Industrial Era – there is the same state of subservience to a dominant, so that young men are trained to the glory of the job, and dream and invent in fields that are likely to interest stockholders, and are schooled into thinking that all magics, except their own industrial magics, are fakes, superstitions, or newspaper yarns.

I am of the Industrial Era, myself; and, even though I can see only advantages-disadvantages in all uses, I am very largely only a practical thinker –

Or the trail of a working witchcraft – and we're on the scent of utilities –

Or that, if a girl, in the town of Derby, set a house afire, by a process that is now somewhat understandable, a fireman could, if he had a still better understanding, have put out that fire without moving from his office. If the mechanism of a motor can invisibly be stopped, all the motors of the world may, without the dirt, crime, misery, and exploitation of coal-mining, be started and operated. If Ambrose Small was wished so far away that he never got back – though that there is magic in a mere wish, or in a mere hope, or hate, I do not think – the present snails of the wheels and planes may be replaced by instantaneous teleportations. If we can think that quacks and cranks and scientists of highest repute, who have announced successes, which were in opposition to supposed medical, physical, chemical, or biological principles – which are now considered impostures, or errors, or "premature announcements" – may not in all cases have altogether deceived themselves, or tried to deceive others, we – or maybe only I – extend this suspicion into mechanical fields.

Now it is my expression that all perpetual motion cranks may not have been dupes, or rascals – that they may have been right, occasionally – that their wheels may sometimes have turned, their marbles rolled, their various gimmicks twirled, in an excess of reaction over action, either because sometimes will occur exceptions to any such supposed law as "the conservation of energy", or because motivating "rays"emanated from the inventors –

That sometimes engines have run, fuelled with zeals – but have, by such incipient, or undeveloped, witchcraft, operated only transiently, or only momentarily – but that they may be forerunners to such a revolution of the affairs of this earth, as once upon a time were flutters of the little lids of tea kettles –

A new era of new happiness and new hells to pay; ambitions somewhat realised, and hopes dashed to nothing; new crimes, pastimes, products, employments, unemployments; labour troubles, or strikes that would be world-wide; new delights, new diseases, disasters such as had never before been heard of –

In this existence of the desirable-undesirable.

Wild carrots in a field – and to me came a dissatisfaction with ham and cabbage. That was too bad: there isn't much that is better. My notion was that probably all around were roots and shoots and foliages that might be, but that never had been, developed eatably – but that most unlikely would be the cultivation of something new to go with ham, in place of cabbage, because of the conventionalised requirements of markets. But once upon a time there were wild cabbages and wild beets and wild onions, and they were poor, little incipiencies until they were called for by markets. I think so. I don't know. At any

167

rate, this applies to wild fruits.

There are sword swallowers and fire eaters, fire breathers, fire walkers; basket tricksters, table tilters, handcuff escapers. There is no knowing what development could do with these wild talents: but *Help Wanted* if for –

Reasonable and confidential accntnts; comptometer oprs., fire re-ins., exp., Christian; sec'ys, credit exp., advance, Chris.; P & S expr.; fast sandwich men; reception men, 35-45, good educ., ap. tall, Chris. –

But I do think that one hundred years ago an advertisement for a fast sandwich man would have looked as strange as today would look an advertisement for "polt. grls."

Against all opposition in the world, I make this statement – that once I knew a magician. I was a witness of a performance that may some day be considered understandable, but that, in these primitive times, so transcends what is said to be the known that it is what I mean by magic.

When the magician and I were first acquainted, he gave no sign of occult abilities. He was one of the friendliest of fellows, but that was not likely to endear him to anybody, because he was about equally effusive to everybody. He had frenzies. Once he tore down the landlord's curtains. He bit holes into a book of mine, and chewed the landlord's slippers.

The landlord got rid of him. This was in London. The landlord took him about ten miles away, and left him, probably leaping upon somebody, writhing joy for anybody who would notice him. He was young.

It was about two weeks later. Looking out a front window, I saw the magician coming along, on the other side of the street. He was sniffing his way along, but went right past our house, without recognising it. He came to a point where he stopped and smelled. He smelled and he smelled. He crossed the street, and came back, and lay down in front of the house. The landlord took him in and gave him a bone.

But I can not accept that the magician smelled his way home, or picked up a trail, taking about two weeks on his way. The smelling played a part, and was useful in a final recognition; but smelling indiscriminately, he could have nosed his way, for years, through the streets of London, before coming to the right scent.

New York Sun (April 24, 1931) – an account, by Adolph Pezaldt, of Allentown, Pa., of a large, mongrel magician, who had been taken in a baggage car, a distance of 340 miles, and had found his way back home, in a week or so. *New York Herald Tribune* (July 4, 1931) – a curly magician, who, in Canada, had found his way back home, over a distance of 400 miles.

New York Herald Tribune (Aug. 13, 1931) – *The Man They Could Not Drown* –

"Hartford, Conn., Aug. 12 – Angelo Faticoni, known as 'the Human Cork', because he could stay afloat in water for fifteen hours with twenty pounds of lead tied to his ankles, died on August 2 in Jacksonville, Fla., it became known here today. He was seventy-two years old.

"Faticoni could sleep in water, roll up into a ball, lie on his side or assume any position asked of him. Once he was sewed into a bag and then thrown head foremost into the water, with a twenty-pound cannonball lashed to his legs. His head reappeared on the surface soon afterward, and he remained motionless in that position for eight hours. Another time he swam across the Hudson tied to a chair weighted with lead.

"Some years ago he went to Harvard to perform for the students and faculty. He had been examined by medical authorities, who failed to find support for their theories that he was able to float at such great length by the nature of his internal organs, which they believed were different from those of other men.

"Faticoni often had promised to reveal the secret of how he became 'the Human Cork', but he never did."

There are many accounts of poltergeist-phenomena that are so obscured by the preconceptions of witnesses that one can't tell whether they are stories of girls who had occult powers, or of invisible beings, who, in the presence of girl-mediums, manifested. But the story of Angelique Cottin is an account of a girl, who, by an unknown influence of her own, acted upon objects in ways like those that have been attributed to spirits. The phenomena of Angelique Cottin, of the town of La Perriere, France, began upon January 15, 1846, and lasted ten weeks. Anybody who would like to read an account of this wild, or undeveloped, talent, that is free from interpretations by spiritualists and anti-spiritualists, should go to the contemporaneous story, published in the *Journal des Debats* (Paris; February 18, 1846). Here are accounts by M. Arago and other scientists. When Angelique Cottin went near objects, they bounded away. She could have made a perpetual motion machine whiz. She was known as the *Electric Girl,* so called, because nobody knew what to call her. When she tried to sit in a chair, there was low comedy. The chair was pulled away, or, rather, was invisibly pushed away. There was such force here that a strong man could not hold the chair. A table, weighing 60 pounds, rose from the floor, when she touched it. When she went to bed, the bed rocked –

And I suppose that, in the early times of magnetic investigations, people who heard of objects that moved in the presence of a magnet, said –

"But what of it?"

Faraday showed them.

A table, weighing 60 pounds, rises a few feet from the floor – well, then, it's some time, far ahead, in the Witchcraft Era – and a multi-cellular formation of poltergeist girls is assembled in the presence of building materials. Stone blocks and steel girders rise a mile or so into their assigned positions in the latest sky-prodder. Maybe. Tall buildings will have their day, but first there will have to be a show-off of what could be done.

I now have a theory that the Pyramids were built by poltergeist-girls. The Chinese Wall is no longer mysterious. Every now and then I reconstruct a science. I may take up neo-archaeology sometime. Old archaeology, with its fakes and guesses, and conflicting pedantries, holds out an invitation for a ferocious and joyous holiday.

Human hopes, wishes, ambitions, prayers and hates – and the futility of them – the waste of millions of trickles of vibrations, today – unorganised forces that are doing nothing. But put them to work together, or concentrate mental ripples into torrents, and gather these torrents into Niagara Falls of emotions – and, if there isn't any happiness, except in being of use, I am conceiving of cataractuous happiness –

Or sometime in the Witchcraft Era – and every morning, promptly at nine o'clock, crowds of human wishers, dignified under the name of *transmediumisers,* arrive at their wishing stations, or mental power-houses, and in an organisation of what are now only scattered and wasted hopes and hates concentrate upon the running of all motors of all cities. Just as they're all nicely organised and pretty nearly satisfied, it will be learned that motors aren't necessary.

In one way, witchcraft has been put to work: that is that wild talents have been exhibited, and so have been sources of incomes. But here is only the incipiency of the stunt. In August, 1883, in the home of Lulu Hurst, aged 15, at Cedarville, Georgia, there were poltergeist disturbances. Pebbles moved in the presence of the girl: things vanished, crockery was smashed, and, if the girl thought of a tune, it would be heard, rapping at the head of her bed. In February, 1884, Lulu was giving public performances. In New York City, she appeared in Wallack's Theatre. It could be that a girl, aged 15, if competently managed, was able to deceive everybody who went up on the stage. She at least made all witnesses think that, when a man weighing 200 pounds, sat in a chair, she, by touching the chair, made it rise and throw him to the floor –

And I am very much like an Indian, of long ago: an Indian thinking of the force of a waterfall, unable to conceive of a waterwheel, simply thinking of all this force that was making only a little spectacle –

Or in the state of melancholy into which I am perhaps cast, thinking that a little poltergeist girl, if properly trained, could make all witnesses believe that she raised building materials forty or eighty stories, by simply touching them – thinking that nobody is doing anything about this –

Except that I am not clear that anything would be gained by it – or by anything else.

Lulu Hurst either had powers that far transcended muscular powers, or she had talents of deception far superior to the abilities of ordinary deceivers. Sometimes she tossed about 200- pound men, or made it look as if she did; and sometimes she placed her hands on a chair, and five men either could not move that chair, or were good actors, and earned whatever the confederates of stage magicians were paid, at that time.

In November, 1891, Mrs. Annie Abbott, called the *Little Georgia Magnet,* put on a show, in the Alhambra Music Hall, London. She weighed about 98 pounds, and, if she so willed it, a man could easily lift her. The next moment, six men, three on each side of her, grasping her by her elbows, could not lift her. When she stood on a chair, the six men could not, when the chair was removed, prevent her from descending to the floor. If anybody suggests that, when volunteers were called for from the audience, it was the same six who responded, at every performance, I think that that is a pretty good suggestion. Because of many other data, it hasn't much force with me; but, in these early times of us primitives, almost any suggestion has value. I take these accounts from A. Campbell Holms' *The Facts of Psychic Science and Philosophy* (278). I have them from other sources, also.

In September, 1921, Mary Richardson gave performances, at the Olympic Music Hall, Liverpool. Easily lifted one moment – the next moment, six men – same six, maybe – could not move her. By touching a man, she knocked him flat. It is either that she travelled with a staff of thirteen comedians, whose stunt it was to form in a line, pretending their utmost to push her, but seeming to fail comically, considering the size of her, or that she was a magician.

It is impossible to get anywhere by reasoning. This is because – as can be shown, monistically – there isn't anywhere. Or it is impossible to get anywhere, because one can get everywhere. I can find equally good reasons for laughing, or for being serious, about all this. Holms tells us that he was one of those in the audience, who, though not taking part, went up on the stage; and that he put his hand between Mrs. Richardson and the leader of the string of thirteen men, who were almost dislocating one another's shoulder blades, pushing their hardest against her, and that he felt no pressure. So he was convinced not that she resisted pressure, but that pressure could not touch her.

Suppose it was that pressure could not touch her. Could blows harm her? Could bullets touch her? Did Robert Houdin have this power, when he faced an Arab firing squad, and is the story of the substituted blanks for bullets only just more of what Taboo is telling everywhere? One untouchable man could own the world – except that he'd have a weakness somewhere, or, in general, could be no more than the untouchable-touchable. But he could add to our bewilderments by making much history before being touched. Well, then, if there are magicians, why haven't magicians seized upon political powers? I don't know why they haven't.

It may be the secret of fire-walking – or that wizards walk over red-hot stones, unharmed, because they do not touch the stones. However, for some readers, it is more comfortable to disbelieve that anybody ever has been a fire-walker. For an uncomfortable moment, read an account, in *Current Literature* (32, 98) – exhibition by a Tahitian fire-walker, at Honolulu, Jan. 19, 1901. The story is that this wizard walked on stones of "a fierce, red glow," with flames spouting from burning wood, underneath; walking back and forth four times.

There is a muscular strength of men, and it may be that sometimes appears a strength to which would apply the description "occult", or "psychic." In the *New York Herald Tribune* (Jan. 24, 1932) was reported the death of Mrs. Betsy Anna Talks, of 149-39 Fourteenth Road, Whitestone, Queens, N.Y. – who had often performed such feats as carrying a barrel of sugar, weighing 400 pounds – had carried, under each arm, a sack of potatoes, whereas, in fields, usually two men lug one sack – had impatiently watched two men, clumsily moving a 550-pound barrel of salt, in a cart, and had taken it down for them.

There are "gospel truths", and "irrefutable principles", and "whatever goes up must come down", and "men are strong and women are weak" – but somewhere there's a woman who takes a barrel of salt away from two men. But we think in generalisations, and enact laws in generalisations, and "women are weak", and, if I should look it up, I'd be not at all surprised to learn that Mrs. Talks was receiving alimony.

I now recall another series of my own experiences with what may be my own very wild talents. I took no notes upon the occurrences, because I had decided that note-taking would make me self-conscious. I do not now take this view. I was walking along West Forty-second Street, N.Y.C., when the notion came to me that I could "see" what was in a show window, which, some distance ahead, was invisible to me. I said to myself: "Turkey tracks in red snow." I should have noted that "red snow" was one of the phenomena of my interests, at this time. I came to the window, and saw track-like lines of black fountain pens, grouped in fours, one behind, and the three others trifurcating from it, on a background of pink cardboard.

At last I was a wizard!

Another time, picking out a distant window, invisible to me – or ocularly invisible to me – I said, "Ripple marks on a sandy beach." It was a show window. Several men were removing exhibits from it, and there was virtually nothing left except a yellow plush floor covering. Decoratively, this covering had been ruffled, or given a wavy appearance.

Another time – "Robinson Crusoe and Friday's footprints." When I came to the place, I saw that it was a cobbler's shop, and that, hanging in the window, was a string of shoe soles.

I'm sorry.

I should like to hear of somebody, who would manfully declare himself a wizard, and say – "Take it or leave it!" I can't do this, because I too well remember other circumstances. Maybe it's my timidity, but I now save myself from the resentment, or the mean envy, of readers, who say, of a distant store window, "popular novels", and its pumpkins. My experiments kept up about a month. Say that I experimented about a thousand times. Out of a thousand attempts, I can record only three seemingly striking successes, though I recall some minor ones. Throughout this book, I have taken the stand that nobody can be always wrong, but it does seem to me that I approximated so highly that I am nothing short of a negative genius. Nevertheless, the first of these experiences impresses me. It came to me when, so far as I know, I was not thinking of anything of the kind, though sub-consciously I was carrying much lore upon various psychic subjects.

These things may be done, but everybody who is interested has noticed the triviality and the casualness of them. They – such as telepathic experiences – come and go, and then when one tries to develop an ability, the successes aren't enough to encourage anybody, except somebody who is determined to be encouraged.

Well, then, if wild talents come and go, and can't be developed, or can't be depended upon, even people who are disposed to accept that they exist, can't see the good of them.

But accept that there are adepts; probably they had to go through long periods of apprenticeship, in which, though they deceived themselves by hugely over-emphasising successes, and forgetting failures, they could not impress any parlour, or speakeasy, audience. I have told of my experiments of about a month. It takes five years to learn the rudiments of writing a book, selling gents' hosiery, or panhandling.

Everybody who can do anything got from the gods, or whatever, nothing but a wild thing. Read a book, or look at a picture. The composer has taken a wild talent that nobody else in the world believed in: a thing that came and went and flouted and deceived him, maybe starved him, almost ruined him – and has put that damn thing to work.

Upon Nov. 29, 1931, died a wild talent. It was wild of origin, but was of considerable development. See the *New York Herald Tribune* (Nov. 30, 1931). John D. Reese had died, in his home, in Youngstown, Ohio. Mr. Reese was a "healer." He was not a "divine healer." He means much to my expression that the religionists have been permitted to take unto themselves much that is not theirs exclusively. Once we heard only of "divine healers." It is something of a start of a divorcement that may develop enormously. Sometime I am going to loot the records of saints, for suggestions that may be of value to bright atheists, willing to study and experiment. "He never studied medicine. The only instruction he ever received was from an aged healer in the mountains in Wales when he was a boy. Physicians could not explain his art and after satisfying themselves that he was not a charlatan, would shrug and say simply that he had 'divine power.'" But Reese never described himself as a "divine healer," and, though by methods no less divine than those of the Salvation Army and other religious organisations, he made a fortune out of his practices, he was associated with no church. He was about thirty years old when he became aware of his talent. One day, in the year 1887, a man in a rolling mill fell from a ladder, and was injured. It was "a severe spinal strain", according to a physician. "Mr. Reese stooped and ran his fingers up and down the man's back. The man smiled, and while the physician and the mill hands gaped in wonder, he rose to his feet and announced that he felt strong again, with not a trace of pain. He went back to work, and Mr. Reese's reputation as a healer was spread abroad."

Then there were thousands of cases of successful treatments. Hans Wagner, shortstop of the Pittsburgh Pirates, was carried from the baseball field, one day: something in his back had snapped, and it seemed that his career had ended. He was treated by Reese, and within a few days was back shortstopping. When Lloyd George visited the United States, after the War, he shook hands so many times that his hand was twisted out of shape. Winston Churchill, in a later visit, had what was said to be an automobile accident, and said that he was compelled to hold his arm in a sling. But Lloyd George was so cordially greeted that he was maimed. "Doctors said that only months of rest and massage would restore the cramped muscles." "Reese shook hands with the statesman, pressed gently, and then harder, disengaged their hands with a wrench, and Lloyd George's hand was strong again."

One of the most important particulars in this story of a talent, or of witchcraft, that was put to work, is that probably it was a case of a magician who was taught. Reese, when a boy, received instructions in therapeutic magic, and then, in the stresses of making a living, forgot, so far as went the knowledge of his active consciousness. But it seems that sub-consciously a development was going on, and suddenly, when the man was thirty- two years of age, manifested.

My notion is that wild talents exist in the profusion of weeds of the fields. Also my notion is that, were it not for the conventions of markets, many weeds could be developed into valuable, edible vegetables. The one great ambition of my life, for which I would abandon my typewriter at any time – well, not if I were joyously setting down some particularly nasty swipe at priests or scientists – is to say to chairs and tables "Fall in! forward! march!" and have them obey me. I have tried this, as I don't mind recording, because one can't be of an enquiring and experimental nature, and also be very sensible. But a more unmilitary lot of furniture than mine, nobody has. Most likely, for these attempts, I'll be hounded by pacifists. I should very much like to be a wizard, and be of great negative benefit to my fellow beings, by doing nothing for anybody. And I have had many experiences that lead me to think that almost everybody else not only would like to be a wizard, but at times thinks he is one. I think that he is right. It is monism that if anybody's a wizard, everybody is, to some degree, a wizard.

One time – spring of 1931 – my landlord received some chicks from the country, and put them in an enclosure at the end of the yard. They grew, and later I thought it interesting, listening to the first, uncertain attempts of two of them to crow. It was as interesting as is watching young, human males trying to take on grown-up ways. But then I thought of what was ahead, at four o'clock, or thereabouts, mornings. I'm a crank about sleeping, because at times I have put in much disagreeable time with insomnia. I worried about this, and I spoke about it.

There was not another sound from the two, little roosters.

At last!

Months went by. Confirmation. I was a wizard.

One day in October, the landlord's son-in-law said to me: "There hasn't been a sound from them since."

I tried not to look self-conscious.

Said he: "Last May, one day, I was looking at them, and I said, in my own mind: 'If we lost tenants on account of you, I'll wring your necks.' They never crowed again."

Again it's the Principle of Uncertainty, by which the path of a particle cannot be foretold, and by which there's no knowing who stopped the roosters. Well, we're both – or one of us is – very inferior in matters of magic, according to a story that is told of Madame Blavatsky. The little bird of a cuckoo clock annoyed her. Said she: "Damn that bird! shut up!" The cuckoo never spoke again.

By the cultivation of wild talents, I do not mean only the learning of the secret of the man they could not drown, and having the advantage of that ability, at times of shipwreck – of the man they could not confine, so that enormous would be the relief from the messiahs of the legislatures, if nobody could be locked up for failure to keep track of all their laws – of the woman they could not touch, so that there could be no more automobile accidents – of myself and the roosters – though just here my landlord's son-in-law will read scornfully – so that all radios can be stopped immediately after breakfast, and all tenors and sopranos forever –

Only the secret of burning mansions in England; appearances of wounds on bodies, or of pictures on hailstones; bodies on benches of a Harlem park; strange explosions, and forced landings of aeroplanes, and the case of Lizzie Borden –

Those are only specialisations. If all are only different manifestations of one force, or radio-activity, transmediumisation, or whatever, that is the subject for research and experiment that may develop –

New triumphs and new disasters; happiness and miseries – a new era, in which people will think back, with contempt, or with horror, at our times, unless they start to think a little more keenly of their own affairs.

In the presence of a poltergeist girl, who, so far as is now knowable, exerts no force, objects move.

But this is a book of no marvels.

In the presence of certain substances, which so far as is now knowable, exert no force, other substances move, or transmute into very different substances.

This is a common phenomenon, to which the chemists have given the name *catalysis.*

All around are wild talents, and it occurs to nobody to try to cultivate them, except as expressions of personal feelings, or as freaks for which to charge admission. I conceive of powers and the uses of human powers that will some day transcend the stunts of music halls and séances and sideshows, as public utilities have passed beyond the toy-stages of their origins. Sometimes I tend to thinking constructively – or batteries of witches teleported to Nicaragua, where speedily they cut a canal by dissolving trees and rocks – the tumults of floods, and then magic by which they can not touch houses – cyclones that smash villages, and then can not push feathers. But I also think that there is nothing in this subject that is more reasonable than is the Taboo that is preventing, or delaying, development. I mean that semi-enlightenment that so earnestly, and with such keen, one-sided foresight fought to suppress gunpowder and the printing press and the discovery of America. With the advantages of practical witchcraft would come criminal enormities. Of course they would be somewhat adapted to. But I'd not like to have it thought that I am only an altruist, or of the humble mental development of a Utopian, who advocates something, as a blessing, without awareness of it as also a curse. Every folly, futility, and source of corruption of today, if a change from affairs primordial, was at one time preached as cure and salvation by some messiah or another. One reason why I never pray for anything is that I'm afraid I might get it.

Or the uses of witchcraft in warfare –

But that, without the sanction of hypocrisy, superintendence by hypocrisy, the blessing by hypocrisy, nothing ever does come about –

Or military demonstrations of the overwhelming effects of trained hates – scientific uses of destructive bolts of a million hate-power – the blasting of enemies by disciplined ferocities –

And the reduction of cannons to the importance of fire crackers – a battleship at sea, a toy boat in a bathtub –

The palpitations of hypocrisy – the brass bands of hypocrisy – the peace on earth and good will to man, of hypocrisy – or much celebration, because of the solemn agreements of nations to scrap their battleships and armed aeroplanes – outlawry of poison gases, and the melting of cannon – once it is recognised that these things aren't worth a damn in the Era of Witchcraft –

But of course that witchcraft would be practised in warfare. Oh, no; witchcraft would make war too terrible. Really, the Christian thing to do would be to develop the uses of the new magic, so that in the future a war could not even be contemplated.

Later: A squad of poltergeists-girls – and they pick a fleet out of the sea, or out of the sky – if, as far back as the year 1923, something picked French aeroplanes out of the sky – arguing that some nations that renounced fleets, as obsolete, would go on building them, just the same.

Girls at the front – and they are discussing their usual not very profound subjects. The alarm – the enemy is advancing. Command to the poltergeist girls to concentrate – and under their chairs they stick their wads of chewing gum.

A regiment bursts into flames, and the soldiers are torches, Horses snort smoke from the combustion of their entrails. Re-enforcements are smashed under cliffs that are teleported from the Rocky Mountains. The snatch of Niagara Falls – it pours upon the battle field. The little poltergeist girls reach for their wads of chewing gum.

Chapter 28

That everything that is desirable is not worth having – that happiness and unhappiness are emotional rhythms that are so nearly independent of one's circumstances that good news or bad news only stimulate the amplitude of these waves, without affecting the ratio of ups to downs – or that one might as well try to make, in a pond, waves that are altitudes only, as to try to be happy, without suffering equal and corresponding unhappiness.

But, so severely stated, this is mechanistic philosophy.

And I am a mechanist-immechanist.

Sometimes something that is desirable is not only not worth having, but is a damn sight worse than that.

Is life worth living? Like everybody else, I have many times asked that question, usually deciding negatively, because I am most likely to ask myself whether life is worth living, at times when I am convinced it isn't. One day, in one of my frequent, and probably incurable, scientific moments, it occurred to me to find out. For a month, at the end of each day, I set down a plus sign, or a minus sign, indicating that, in my opinion, life had, or had not, been worth living, that day. At the end of the month, I totted up, and I can't say that I was altogether pleased to learn that the pluses had won the game. It is not dignified to be optimistic.

I had no units by which to make my alleged determinations. Some of the plus days may have been only faintly positive, and, here and there, one of the minus days may have been so ferociously negative as to balance a dozen faintly positive days. Of course I did attempt gradations of notation, but they were only cutting pseudo-units into smaller pseudo-units. Also, out of a highly negative, or very distressing, experience, one may learn something that will mean a row of pluses in the future. Also, some pluses simply mean that one has misinterpreted events of a day, and is in for much minus –

Or that nothing – a joy or a sorrow, the planet Jupiter, or an electron – can be picked out of its environment, so as finally to be labelled either plus or minus, because as a finally identifiable thing it does not exist – or that such attempted isolations and determinations are only scientific.

I have picked out witchcraft, as if there were witchcraft, as an identifiable thing, state, or activity. But, if by witchcraft, I mean phenomena as diverse as the mimicry of a leaf by a leaf-insect, and illness in a house where "Typhoid Mary" was cooking, and the harmless impalement, on spears, of children, I mean, by witchcraft in general, nothing that can be picked out of one commonality of phenomena. All phenomena are rhythmic, somewhere between the metrical and the frenzied, with final extremes unreachable in an existence of the metrical-unmetrical. The mechanical theory of existence is as narrowly lopsided as would be a theory that all things are good, large, or hot. It is Puritanism. It is the text-book science that tells of the clock-work revolutions of the planet Jupiter and omits mention of Jupiter's little, vagabond moons, which would be fired from any job, in human affairs, because of their unpunctualities – and omits mention that there's a good deal the matter with the clock-work of most clocks. Mechanistic philosophy is a dream of a finality of exact responses to stimuli, and of absolute equivalences. Inasmuch as the advantages and disadvantages of anything can be no more picked out, isolated, identified, and quantitatively determined, than can the rise of a wave be clipped from its fall, it is only scientific dreamery to say what anything is equal and opposite to.

And, at the same time, in the midst of a submergence in commonality, there is a permeation of all phenomena by an individuality that is so marked that, just as truly as all things merge indistinguishably into all other things, all things represent the unmergeable. So then there is something pervasive of every action and every advantage that makes it alone, incommensurable, and incomparable with a reaction, or a disadvantage.

Our state of the hyphen is the state of the gamble. Go to no den of a mathematician for enlightenment. Try Monte Carlo. Out of science is fading certainty as fast as ever it departed from theology. In its place we have adventure. Accepting that there is witchcraft, in the sense in which we accept that there is electricity, magnetism, or life, the acceptance is that there is no absolute poise between advantages and disadvantages –

Or that practical witchcraft, or the development of wild talents, might be of such benefits as to draw in future records of human affairs the new dividing line of *A.W.* and *B.W.* – or might be a catastrophe that would drive all human life back into Indians, or Zulus, or things furrier –

If by any chance the evils of witchcraft could compare with, or beat to an issue, the demoralisations of law, justice, business, sex, literature, education, pacifism, militarism, idealism, materialism, which at present, are incomprehensibly not yet equal and opposite to stabilisations that are saving us from, or are denying us, the jungles –

Or let all persons of foresight, if of sedentary habits, shift positions occasionally, so as not to suppress too much of their vertebral stubs that their descendants may need as bases of more graceful appendages.

But my own expression is that any state of being that can so survive its altruists and its egoists, its benefactors and its exploiters, its artists, gunmen, bankers, lawyers, and doctors would be almost immune to the eviler magics of witchcraft, because it is itself a miracle.

CHAPTER 29

Stunts of sideshows, and the miracles of pietists, and the phenomena of spiritualistic medium –

Or that the knack that tips a table may tilt an epoch.

Or much of the "parlour magic" of times gone by, and now it is industrial chemistry. And Taboo, by which earlier experimenters in the trained forces of today were under suspicion as traffickers with demons.

I take for a pseudo-principle, by which I mean a standard of judgment that sometimes works out, and sometimes doesn't work out – which is as near to wisdom as I can arrive, in an existence of truth-nonsense – that, someday to be considered right, is first to be unholy. It is out of blasphemy that new religions arise. It is by thinking things that schoolboys know better than to think that discoveries are made. It is because our visions are not delirious enough, or degraded, or nonsensical enough, that all of us are not prophets. Let any thoughtful, properly trained man, who has had all the benefits of an academic education, predict – at least, then, we know what won't be. We have, then, at our command, a kind of negative clairvoyance – if we know just where to go for an insight into what won't be.

The trail of a working witchcraft – but, if we are traffickers with demons, the traffic isn't much congested, at present. Someday almost every particular in this book may look quaint, but it may be that the principle of putting the witches to work will seem as sound as now seems the employment of steam and electric demons. Our instances of practical witchcraft have been practical enough, so long as they were paying attractions at exhibitions, but the exhibition implies the marvel, or what people regard as the marvel, and the spirit of this book is of commonplaceness, or of coming commonplaceness – or that there isn't anything in it, except of course its vagaries of theories and minor interpretations, that won't someday be considered as unsensational as the subject-matters of text books upon chemistry and mechanics. My interest is in magic, as the daily grind – the miracle as a job – sorceries as public utilities.

There is one manifestation of witchcraft that has been put to work. It is a miracle with a job.

Dowsing.

It is commonly known as water-divining. It is witchcraft. One can not say that, because of some unknown chemical, or bio-chemical, affinity, a wand bends in a hand, in the presence of underground water. The wand bends only in the hand of a magician.

It is witchcraft. So, though there are scientists who are giving in to its existence, there are others, or hosts of others, who never will give in. Something about both kinds of scientists was published in *Time* (New York, Feb. 9, 1931). It was said that Oscar E. Meinzer, of the U.S. Geological Survey, having investigated dowsers, had published his findings which were that "further tests ... of so-called 'witching' for water, oil, or other minerals, would be a misuse of public funds." Also it was shown that conclusions by Dr. Charles Albert Browne, of the U.S. Department of Agriculture, disagreed with Mr. Meinzer's findings. "On a large sugar-beet estate, near Magdeburg, Dr. Browne saw one of Germany's most famed dowsers at work. Covering his chest with a padded leather jacket, the dowser took in his hands a looped steel divining rod, and began to pace the ground. Suddenly the loop shot upward, hit him a hard blow on the chest. Continuing, he charted the outlines of the underground stream. Then using an aluminum rod, which he said was much more sensitive, he estimated the depth of the stream. A rod of still another metal indicated by a chest blow that the water was good for drinking. When Dr. Browne tried to use the rod himself, he could get no chest blows unless the dowser was holding one end." "Dr. Browne then questioned German scientists. The majority answered that, with all humbuggery discounted, a large number of successes remained which could not be accounted for by luck or chance." For queer places – or for places in which scientists of not so far back would have predicted that such yokelry as dowsing would never be admitted – see *Science* (n.s., 73, 84) or the *Annual Report of the Smithsonian Institute* (1928, 325). Here full particulars of Dr. Browne's investigations are published.

The Department of Public Works, of Brisbane, Queensland, Australia, has employed a dowser, since the year 1916 (*Notes and Queries,* 150, 235; *Cornhill Magazine,* 60, 346). *New York Times,* (July 26, 1931) – two Australian states were employing dowsers.

I don't know that I mean much by that. The freaks and faddists who get themselves employed by governments make me think that I am not very convincing here. But I have no record of a dowser with a political job before the year 1916; and, whenever I got all this respectfulness of mine for the job, it is the entrance of magic into the job that I am bent upon showing.

In the London *Observer* (May 2, 1926), it is said that the Government of Bombay was employing an official water diviner, who, in one district of scarcity of water, had indicated about fifty sources of supply, at forty-seven of which water had been found. The writer of this account says that members of one of the biggest firms of well-boring engineers had informed him that they had successfully employed dowsers in Wales, Oxfordshire, and Surrey.

In *Nature,* Sept. 8, 1928 (122, 348), there is an account, by Dr. A.E.M. Geddes, of experiments with dowsers. Geddes' conclusion is that the faculty of water-divining is possessed by some persons, who respond to at present unknown, external stimuli.

It is not that I am maintaining that out of the mouths of babes, and from the vapourings of yokels, we shall receive wisdom – but that sometimes we may. Peasants have believed in dowsing, and scientists used to believe that dowsing was only a belief of peasants. Now there are so many scientists who believe in dowsing that the suspicion comes to me that it may only be a myth, after all.

In the matter of dowsing, the opposition that Mr. Meinzer represents is as understandable as is the opposition that once was waged by priestcraft against the system that he now represents. Let in, against the former dominant, data of raised beaches, or of deposits of fossils, and each intruder would make a way for other iniquities. Now, relatively to the Taboo of today, let in any of the occurrences told of in this book, and by its suggestions and affiliations, or linkages, it would make an opening for an irruption.

Very largely, dowsing, or witchcraft put to work, has been let in.

CHAPTER 30

It has been my expression that, for instance, African fakirs achieved the harmless impalement of children by a process that would ordinarily be called imposing the imaginary upon the physical, but that is called by me imposing the imaginary-physical upon the physical-imaginary. I think that this is the conscious power and method of adepts; but I think that in the great majority of our stories, effects have been wrought unconsciously, so far as went active awareness, by witches and wizards. I am impressed more with an experience of my own than with any record of other doings. I looked, or stared, at a picture on a wall. Somewhere in my mind were many impressions of falling pictures. But I was not actively thinking of falling pictures. The picture fell from the wall.

See back to the Blackman case – the four judges, who "died suddenly." It was Blackman, who called attention to these deaths. Why? Vanity of the magician? I think that more likely these victims were removed by a wizardry of Blackman's of which he was unconscious. I think that if a man so earnestly objected to paying alimony that, instead, he went to jail four times, he'd over-look his judges and take a shorter cut, on behalf of his income, if he consciously reasoned about it.

It would seem that visualisations have had nothing to do with many occurrences told of in this book. Still, by a wild talent I mean something that comes and goes, and is under no control, but that may be caught and trained. Also there are cases that look very much like controlled uses of visualisations upon physical affairs. In this view, I have noted an aspect of doings that is a support for our expression upon *transmediumisation.*

The *real,* as it is called, or the objective, the external, the material, cannot be absolutely set apart from the subjective, or the imaginary; but there are quasi-attitudes of the imaginary. There have been occurrences that I think were *transmediumisations,* because I think that they were marked by indications of having carried over, from an imaginative origin, into physical being, or into what is called "real life," the quasi-attributes of their origin.

A peculiarity of fires that are called – or that used to be called – "spontaneous combustions of human bodies", is that fires do not communicate to surrounding objects and fabrics, or that they extend only to a small degree around. There are stories of other such fires, which can not be "real fires", as compared with fires called "real." In the *St. Louis Globe-Democrat* (about Oct. 2, 1889), there is a story of restricted fires, said to have occurred in the home of Samuel Miller, upon a farm, six miles west of Findlay, Ohio. A bed had burst into flames, burning down to a heap of ashes, but setting nothing else afire, not even scorching the floor underneath. The next day, "about the same time in the afternoon", a chest of clothes flamed, and was consumed, without setting anything else afire. The third day, at the same time, another bed, and nothing but the bed burned. See back to the fires in the house in Bladenboro, N.C., Feb., 1932. A long account of these fires, from a San Diego (Cal.) newspaper, was sent to me by Margaret M. Page, of San Diego. In it one of the phenomena considered most remarkable was that fires broke out close to inflammable materials that were unaffected by the flames. Names of several witnesses – Mayor J.A. Bridger, of Bladenboro, J.B. Edwards, a Wilmington health officer, and Dr. S.S. Hutchinson, of Bladenboro.

It is as if somebody had vengefully imagined fires, and in special places had localised fires, according to his visualisations. Such localising, or focusing, omitting surroundings, is a quasi-attribute of all visualisations. One vividly visualises a face, and a body is ignored by the imagination. Let somebody visualize a bed afire, and exhaust his imaginative powers in this specialisation: I conceive of the bed burning, as imagined, and nothing else burning, because nothing else was included in the mental picture that transmediumised, it having been taken for granted, by the visualiser, that, like a fire of physical origin, this fire would extend. It seems to me to be only ordinarily impossible to understand the burning of a woman on an unscorched bed as the "realisation" of an imagined scene in which the burning body was pictured, with neglect of anything else consuming.

See back to the unsatisfactory attempts to attribute punctures of window panes and automobile shields, to a missile-less weapon. The invisible bullets stopped short, after penetrating glass. If we can think of an intent, more mischievous than malicious, that was only upon shooting through glass, and that gave no consideration to subsequent courses of bullets, we can think of occurrences that took place, as visualised, and as restricted by visualisations.

Doings in closed rooms – but my monism, by which I accept that all psychical magic links somewhere with more or less commonplace physical magic –

New York Times (June 18, 1880) – Rochester, N.Y. – a woman dead in her bed, and the bed post hacked as if with a hatchet. It was known that nobody had entered this room. But something had killed this woman, leaving no sign of either entrance or exit.

It was during a thunderstorm, and the woman had been killed by lightning.

The man of one of our stories – J. Temple Johnson – alone in his room –

and that a pictorial representation of his death by fire was enacting in a distant mind – and that into the phase of existence that is called "real" stole the imaginary – scorching his body, but not his clothes, because so was pictured the burning of him – and that, hours later, there came into the mind of the sorcerer a fear that his imposition of what is called the imaginary upon what is called the physical bore quasi-attributes of its origin, or was not realistic, or would be, in physical terms, unaccountable, and would attract attention – and that the fire in the house was visualised, and was "realised", but by a visualisation that in turn left some particulars unaccounted for.

Lavinia Farrar was a woman of "independent means." Hosts of men and women have been shot, or stabbed, or poisoned, because of their "independent means." But that Mrs. Farrar was thought to death – or that upon her, too, out of the imaginary world in somebody's mind, stole a story – that it made of her, too, so fictional a being that of her death there is no explanation in ordinary, realistic terms –

That here, too, there was an after-thought, or an after-picturisation, which, by way of attempted explanation, "realised" a knife and blood on the floor, but overlooked other details that made this occurrence inexplicable in terms of ordinary murders – or that this woman had been stabbed in the heart, through unpunctured clothes, because it was, with the neglect of everything else, the wound in the heart that had been visualised.

The germ of this expression is in anybody's acceptance that a stigmatic girl can transfer a wound, as pictured in her mind, into appearance upon her body. The expression requires that there may be external, as well as personal, stigmatism.

It seems to me to be as nearly unquestionable as anything in human affairs goes, that there have been stigmatic girls. There may have been cases of different kinds of personal stigmatism. There are emotions that are as intense as religious excitation. One of them is terror.

The story of Isidore Fink is a story of a fear that preceded a murder. It could be that Fink's was a specific fear, of somebody whom he had harmed, and not a general fear of the hold-ups that, at the time, were so prevalent in New York City. According to Police Commissioner Mulrooney, it was impossible, in terms of ordinary human experience, to explain this closed-room murder –

Or Isidore Fink, at work in his laundry – and his mind upon somebody whom he had injured – and that his fears of revenge were picturing an assassination of which he was the victim – that his physical body was seized upon by his own picturisation of himself, as shot by an enemy.

CHAPTER 31

In February, 1885, in an English prison, there was one of the dream-like occurrences that the materialists think are real. But every character concerned in it was fading away, so that now there is probably no survivor. From time to time repairs had to be made, because the walls of the prison were dissolving. By way of rusts, the iron bars were disappearing.

Upon February 23rd, 1885 – as we say, in terms of our fanciful demarcations – just as if a 23rd of February, which is only relative to rhythms of sunshine, could be a real day – just as if one could say really where a January stops and a February begins – just as if one could really pick a period out of time, and say that there ever was really a year 1885 –

Early in what is called a morning of what is so arbitrarily and fancifully called the 23rd of February, 1885, John Lee, in his cell, in the penitentiary, at Exeter, England, was waiting to be hanged.

In the yard of a prison of stone, with bars of iron, John Lee led past a group of hard and motionless witnesses, to the scaffold. There were newspaper men present. Though they probably considered it professional to look as expressionless as stones, or bars of iron, there was nothing in Lee's case to be sentimental about. His crime had been commonplace and sordid. He was a labourer, who had lived with an old woman, who had a little property, and, hoping to get that, he had killed her. John Lee was led past a group, almost of minerals. It was a scene of the mechanism and solidity of legal procedure, as nearly real as mechanism and solidity can be.

Noose on his neck, and up on the scaffold they stood him on a trap door. The door was held in position by a bolt. When this bolt was drawn, the door fell –

John Lee, who hadn't a friend, and hadn't a dollar –

The Sheriff of Exeter, behind whom was Great Britain.

The Sheriff waved his hand. It represented Justice and Great Britain.

The bolt was drawn, but the trap door did not fall. John Lee stood with the noose around his neck.

It was embarrassing. He should have been strangling. There is something of an etiquette in all things, and this was indecorum. They tinkered with the bolt. There was no difficulty, whatsoever, with the bolt; but when it was drawn, with John Lee standing on the trap door, the door would not fall.

Something unreasonable was happening. Just what is the procedure, in the case of somebody, who is standing erect, when he should be dangling? The Sheriff ordered John Lee back to his cell.

The people in the prison yard were not so stolid. They fluttered, and groups of them were talking it over. But there was no talk that could do John Lee any good. This was what is called stern reality. The Sheriff did not flutter. I have a note upon him, twenty years later: he was in trouble with a religious sect of which he was a member, because he ordered his beer by the barrel. He was as solid as beer and beef and the British government.

The warders looked into the matter thoroughly – except that there wasn't anything to look into. Everytime they drew back the bolt, with John Lee out of the way, the door fell, as it should fall. One of the warders stood in Lee's place, where, instead of placing the noose around his neck, he clung to the rope. The bolt was drawn, the door fell, as it should fall, and down dropped the warder, as he should drop.

There was a woman they could not push. A man they could not crucify. The man they could not drown. There was the man they could not imprison. The dog they could not lose.

John Lee was led back to the scaffold. The witnesses did not know whether to be awed or not. But, after all, it was just one of those things that nobody could explain, but that could not happen again –

Or that to a college professor it could not – to anybody educated in the principles of mechanics and physics it could not – that, to anybody, not an untutored labouring man, but committed to unquestioning belief in everything that a professor of physics would say in maintaining that the trap door would have to fall –

The bolt was drawn.

The trap door would not fall.

John Lee stood unhangable.

That when, the first time, John Lee was led past these newspaper men, and town officials, and others who had been invited to the ceremony, any one of them could have overstepped any line that all were told to toe would have been little short of inconceivable. But a doctor, whose professional appearance was much faded, interceded. Others were shaky. The Sheriff said that John Lee had been sentenced to be hanged, and that John Lee would be hanged.

They had done everything thinkable. Any suggestions? Somebody suggested that rains might have swollen the wooden door, causing friction. There had been, in all tests, no friction; but, by way of taking every possible precaution, a warder planed the edges of the door. They experimented, and, every time, the door fell, as it should fall.

They stood him on the scaffold again.

The door would not fall.

This scene of an attempted execution dissolved, like a dream-picture. The newspaper men faded away, or burst away. The newspaper men ran out into the streets of Exeter. In the streets, they ran, shouting the news of the man who could not be hanged. The Sheriff, who had tried hard to be a real Sheriff, went to pieces. He'd do this about it, and then he'd do that about it, and then – "Take him away!" He communicated with the Home Secretary. There was something about all this that so shook the Home Secretary that he authorised a delay.

The matter was debated in the House of Commons, where some of the members denounced a proposed defeat of justice by superstition. Nevertheless the execution was not attempted again. Lee's sentence was commuted to life-imprisonment, but he was released in December, 1907. His story was re-told in the newspapers of that time. I take from *Lloyd's Weekly News* (Jan. 5, 1908).

I have tried to think of a conventional explanation, in the case of John Lee. All attempts fail. He hadn't a dollar.

There may be some commonplace explanation that I have not thought of; but my notion is that the explanation that I have thought of will some day be considered as commonplace as are now regarded the impenetrable mysteries of electricity and radio-activity.

CHAPTER 32

It's the old controversy – the action of mind upon matter. But, in the philosophy of the hyphen, an uncrossable gap is disposed of, and the problem is rendered into thinkable terms, by asking whether mind-matter can act upon matter-mind.

I am beginning to see whence all my specialisation, not much short of hypnotisation, upon magic, as the job. Just why am I so bent upon cooping people into multicellular formations, and setting batteries of disciplined sorcerers at work, bewitching into useful revolutions all the motors of the world?

As to the job, and anything that is supposed to be not a job, there is only the state of job-recreation, or recreation-job. I have cut out of my own affairs very much of so-called recreation, simply because I feel that I can not give to so-called enjoyments the labours that they exact. I'd often like to be happy, but I don't want to go through the equivalence of digging a ditch, or of breaking of stones, to enjoy myself. I have seen, by other persons, very laboured and painful efforts to be happy. So then I am so much concerned with the job, because, though it hyphenates, there isn't anything else.

Probably it will be some time before any college professor, of whatever we think we mean by *importance,* will admit that, by witchcraft, or by the development of what are now only wild talents, all the motors of this earth may be set going and kept at work. But "highest authority" no longer unitedly opposes the more or less remote possibility of such operations. See an interview, with Dr. Arthur H. Compton, Professor of Physics, at the University of Chicago, published in the *New York Times* (Jan. 3, 1932). Said Dr. Compton: "The new physics does not suggest a solution of the old question of how mind acts on matter. It does definitely, however, admit the possibility of such an action, and suggests where the action may take effect."

I don't know that I am much more of a heretic, myself. In my stories, I have admitted possibilities, and I have made suggestions.

But the difference is that the professors will not be concrete, and I give instances. Dr. Compton's views are ripe with the interpretation that transportation systems, and the lighting of cities, and the operation of factories may someday be the outcome of what he calls the "action of mind on matter", or what I'd call *mechanical witchcraft.* But toyers with abstractions falter, the moment one says – "For instance?"

The fuel-less motor, which is by most persons considered a dream, or a swindle, associates most with the name John Worrell Keely, though there have been other experimenters, or impostors, or magicians. The earliest fuel-less motor "crank" of whom I have record is John Murray Spear, back in the period 1855, though of course various "cranks" of all ages can be linked with this swindle, dream, or most practical project. The latest, at this writing, is a young man, Lester J. Hendershot, of Pittsburgh, Pa. I take data from the *New York Herald Tribune* (Feb. 27, March 1, 2, 8, 10, 1928). It was Hendershot's statement that he had invented a motor that operated by deriving force from "this earth's magnetic field." Nobody knows what that means. But Hendershot was backed by Major Thomas Lanphier, U.S. Army, commandant of Selfridge Field, Detroit. It was said that at tests of Selfridge Field, a model of the "miracle motor" had invisibly generated power enough to light two 110-volt lamps, and that another had run a small sewing machine. Major Lanphier stated that he had helped to make one of these models, which were of simple construction, and that he was sure that there was nothing fraudulent about it.

This espousal by Major Lanphier may, considering that to orthodox scientists it was the equivalence of belief in miracles, seem extraordinary; but it seems to me that the attacks that were made upon Hendershot were more extraordinary – or significant. It would seem that, if a simple, little contrivance, weighing less than ten pounds, were a fraud, the mechanics of Selfridge Field, or anywhere else, could determine that in about a minute, especially if they had themselves made it, under directions. If the thing were a fraud, it would seem that it would have to be obviously a fraud. Who'd bother? But Dr. Frederick Hochstetter, head of the Hochstetter Research Laboratories, of Pittsburgh, went to New York about it. He hired a lecture room, or a "salon", of a New York hotel, telling reporters that he had come to expose a fraud, which would be capable of destroying faith in science for 1,000 years. If so, even to me this would not be desirable. I should like to see faith in science destroyed for 20 years, and then be restored for a while, and then be knocked flat again, and then revive – and so on, in a healthy alternation. Dr. Hochstetter exhibited models of the motor. They couldn't generate the light of a 1-volt firefly. They couldn't stitch a fairy's breeches. Dr. Hochstetter lectured upon what he called a fraud. But the motive for all this? Dr. Hochstetter explained that his only motive was that "pure science might shine forth untarnished."

It was travelling far, going to trouble and expense to maintain the shine of a purity, the polish of which was threatened by no more than a youngster, of whom most of the world had never heard before. What I pick up is that there must have been an alarm that was no ordinary alarm, somewhere. I pick up that at tests, in Detroit, in Hendershot's presence, his motors worked; that, in

New York, not in his presence, his motors did not work.

Then came the denouement, by which most stories of exposed impostors end up, or are said to end up. Said Dr. Hochstetter – dramatically, I suppose, inasmuch as he was much worked up over all this – he had discovered that concealed in one of the motors was a carbon pencil battery.

Just about so, in the literature of Taboo, end almost all stories of doings that are "alarming." There is no chance of a come-back from the "exposed impostor." He is shown sneaking off-stage, in confusion and defeat. But some readers are having a glimmer of what I mean by taking so much material from the newspapers. They get statements from "exposed impostors." They ridicule and belittle, and publish much that is one-sided, but they do not give the chance for the come-back.

Came back Hendershot:

That Dr. Hochstetter was quite right in his accusation, but only insofar as it applied to an incident of several years before. In his early experiments Hendershot, having no assurance of the good faith of visitors, had stuck into his motor various devices "to lead them away from the real idea I was working on." But, in the tests at Selfridge Field there had been no such "leads," and there had been no means of concealments in motors that mechanics employed by Major Lanphier had made.

Two weeks later, Hendershot dropped out of the newspapers. Perhaps a manufacturer of ordinary motors bought him off. But he dropped out by way of a strange story. It is strange to me, because I recall the small claims that were made for the motor – alleged power not sufficient to harm anybody – only enough to run a sewing machine, or to light lamps with 220 volts. *New York Herald Tribune* (March 10, 1928) – that Lester J. Hendershot, the Pittsburgh inventor of the "miracle motor," was a patient in the Emergency Hospital, Washington, D.C. It is said that, in the office of a patent attorney, he was demonstrating his "fuel-less motor," when a bolt estimated at 2,000 volts shot from it, and temporarily paralysed him.

It was Hendershot's statement that his motor derived force from "this earth's magnetic field." It is probable that, if the motor was driven by his own magic, he would, even if he knew this, attribute it to something else. It is likely that spiritualistic mediums – or a few of them – have occult powers of their own; but they attribute them to spirits. Probably some stage magicians have occult powers; but, in a traditional fear of prosecutions of witchcraft, they feel that it is safer to say that the hand is quicker than the eye. "Divine healers" and founders of religions have been careful to explain that their talents were

193

not their own.

In November, 1874, John Worrell Keely exhibited, to a dozen well-known Philadelphians, his motor. They were hard-headed business men – as far as hard heads go – which isn't very far – but they were not dupes and gulls of the most plastic degree. They saw, or thought they saw, this motor operate, though connected in no way with any conventionally recognized source of power. Some of these witnesses considered the motor worth backing. Keely, too, explained that something outside himself was the moving force, but nobody has ever been able to explain his explanations. Unlike Hendershot's simple contrivance, Keely's motor was a large and complicated structure. The name of it was formidable. When spoken of familiarly, it was a *vibratory generator,* but the full name of the monster was the *Hydro-pneumatic-pulsating-vacuo-engine.* A company was organised, and, after that, everything was very unsatisfactory, except to Keely. There was something human about this engine – just as any monist, of course thinks there is to everything – such as rats and trees and people. It was like so many promising young men, who arrive at middle age, still promising, and go to their graves, having, just before dying, promised something or another. It can't be said that the engine worked. The human-like thing had talents, and was capable of sensational stunts, but it couldn't earn a dollar. That is, at an honest day's toil, it could not, but with its promises it brought ten of thousands of dollars to Keely. It is said that, though he lived well, he spent much of this money in experiments.

Here, too, just what I suspect – though don't have it that I think I'm the only one who has had this idea – was just what was not asserted. That his motor moved responsively to a wizardry of his own, was just what Keely never said. It could be that it was a motivation of his own, but that he did not know it. Mesmer, in his earlier phases, believed that he wrought cures with magnets, and he elaborated very terminological theories, in terms of magnets, until he either conceived, or admitted, that his effects were wrought by his own magic.

I should like to have an opinion upon fuel-less engines, from an official of General Motors, to compare with what the doctors of Vienna and Paris thought of Mesmer.

For eight years there was faith: but then (December, 1882), there was a meeting of disappointed stockholders of the Keely Motor Co. In the midst of protests and accusations, Keely announced that, though he would not publicly divulge the secret of his motor, he would tell everything to any representative of the dissatisfied ones. A stockholder named Boekel was agreed upon. Boekel's report was that it would be improper to describe the principle of the mechanism, but that "Mr. Keely had discovered all that he had claimed." There is no way of inquiring into how Mr. Boekel was convinced. Considering the billions of human beings who have been "convinced" by bombardments of words and phrases beyond their comprehension, I think that Mr. Boekel was reduced to a state of mental helplessness by flows of a *hydro-pneumatic-pulsating-vacuo* terminology; and that faithfully he kept his promise not to explain, because he had not more than the slightest comprehension of what it was that had convinced him.

But I do not think that any character of Mr. Keely's general abilities has ever practised successfully without the aid of religion. Be good for a little while, and you shall have everlasting reward. Keely was religious in preaching his doctrine of goodness: benefits to mankind, releases from enslavement, spare time for the cultivation of the best that is in everybody, promised by his motor – and in six months the stock will be quoted at several times its present value. I haven't a notion that John Worrell Keely, with a need for business, and a throb for suffering humanity, was any less sincere than was General Booth, for instance.

In November, 1898, Keely died. Clarence B. Moore, son of his patron, Mrs. Bloomfield Moore – short tens of thousands of dollars in his inheritance, because of Keely and his promises – rented Keely's house, and investigated. According to his findings, Keely was "an unadulterated rascal."

This is too definite to suit my notions of us phenomena. The unadulterated, whether of food we eat, or the air we breathe, or of idealism, or of villainy, is unfindable. Even adultery is adulterated. There are qualms and other mixtures.

Moore said that he had found the evidences of rascality. The motor was not the isolated mechanism that, according to him, the stockholders of the Keely Motor Co. had been deceived into thinking it was: he had found an iron pipe and other tubes, and wires that led from the motor to the cellar. Here was a large, spherical, metallic object. There were ashes.

Imposture exposed – the motor had been run by a compressed air engine, in the cellar (*New York Times,* Jan. 20, 1899).

Anybody who has ever tried to keep a secret twenty-four hours, will marvel at this story of an impostor who, against all the forces of revelation, such as gas men, and coal men, and other persons who get into cellars – against inquisitive neighbours, and, if possible, even more inquisitive newspaper men – against disappointed stockholders and outraged conventionalists – kept secret, for twenty-four years, his engine in the cellar.

It made no difference what else came out. Taboo had, or pretended it had, something to base on. Almost all people of all eras are hypnotics. Their beliefs are induced beliefs. The proper authorities saw to it that the proper belief should be induced, and people believed properly.

Stockholders said that they knew of the spherical object, or the alleged compressed air engine in the cellar, because Keely had made no secret of it. Nobody demonstrated that by means of this object, the motor could be run. But beliefs can run. So meaningless, in any sense of organisation, were the wires and tubes, that I think of Hendershot's statement that he had complicated his motor with "leads", as he called them.

Stones that have fallen in houses where people were dying – the rambles of a pan of soft soap – chairs that have moved about in the presence of poltergeist girls –

But, in the presence of John Worrell Keely, there were disciplined motions of a motor. For twenty-four years there were demonstrations, and though there was much of a stir-up of accusations, never was Keely caught helping out a little. There was no red light, nor semi-darkness. The motor stood in no cabinet. Keely's stockholders were of a superior intelligence, as stockholders go, inasmuch as many of them investigated, somewhat, before speculating. They saw this solemn, big contrivance go around and around. Sometimes they saw sensational stunts. The thing tore thick ropes apart, broke iron bars, and shot bullets through a twelve-inch plank. I conceive that the motivation of this thing was a wild talent – an uncultivated, rude, and unreliable power, such as is all genius in its infancy –

That Keely operated his motor by a development of mere "willing", or visualising, whether consciously, or not knowing how he got his effects – succeeding spasmodically sometimes, failing often, according to the experience of all pioneers – impostor and messiah –

Justifying himself, in the midst of promises that came to nothing, because he could say to himself something that Galileo should have said, but did not say – "Nevertheless it does move!"

INDEX

This index had to be trimmed to essentials to fit the available space. The major omissions were dates, which will be restored if the opportunity arises for a companion volume of combined indexes to all four of Fort's books.

199

138

London Underground Railway - 39

Long Island, NY, U.S. - 55

Lorelhei, Mrs - 85

Lorentz - 99

Lourdes, France - 142

Low, Professor A.M. - 104

Lower East Side, New York, NY, U.S. - 135

Lowry, Flight Sergeant Frank - 105

Lumsden, William - 5

lycanthropy - 51

Lymm, Cheshire, England - 127

Lynch
Mr & Mrs - 29
Rena - 29, 145

Lyric Theatre, New York City - 38

M

M., Captain - 106

MacDonald
Alexander - 75
Mary Ellen - 75

Mack
Mary - 86
Mr - 86, 87

Madagascar - 52

Magdeburg, Germany - 183

magic - 56, 79, 129, 144, 165, 186
black - 26

Magicians' Club, London - 66

Maidstone, Kent, England - 127

Mail, Madras - 19, 79

Maloney, Mary - 38

Malthus - 98

Malverne, NY, U.S. - 54

Mancuso - 53

manimals, ape-like - 53, 54, 55

Manner, nr Dinapore, India - 79

Mansion House, London, England - 30

Marie Antoinette - 156

Markey, John - 134

markings, pre-natal - 111

Marrick, T. - 135

Marshall, J.H. - 66

Mary-le-bone, London, England - 77

Maspeth, Long Island, NY, U.S. - 65

mastoiditis, contagious? - 131

Mathers, Dr. E.R. - 52

Maxey, W. - 135

Mayfair, London, England - 22

Mayow, Gen. - 16

McDaniel, Charles - 165

McLean, Dinah - 27, 28

McQuade - 53

Medical Center Hospital, N.Y. - 142

Medium and Daybreak - 27

Meehan, James - 15

Meinzer, Oscar E. - 183, 184

Memphis, TN, U.S. - 76

Menomonie, WI, U.S. - 29

Mercury - 99
irregularities of - 100

Mercury
Bedford - 60
Bristol - 86
Dean Forest - 134
Derby - 2, 8

Mesmer, Franz Anton - 194

Mesopotamia - 102

meteor-radiants, stationary - 4

Metropolitan Museum of Art, New York - 162

Metz, France - 108

Mexico - 118, 143

Meyers
Jerry - 139
Mrs. - 139

Michigan Medical News - 76

Middletown, OH, U.S. - 139

Midland Bank - 21

Milan, OH, U.S. - 108

Mill, John Stuart - 71

Miller, Samuel - 185

Mills, Elinor - 140

Milne, Miss Jean - 39

Minder
Mrs. - 131
Valentine - 131

Mineola, Long Island, NY, U.S. - 53, 54, 55

Minster Thanet, Kent, England - 127

miracles - 112, 141, 142, 143, 166

Mirror, Port of Spain - 85

mist, mysterious - 94

Mitchell, Arthur B. - 59

Mitchum Park, London, England - 45

Monkton, (?), England - 127

Monte Carlo, Monaco - 180

Month, The - 160

Moore
Clarence B. - 195
Howard R. - 47
Mrs. Bloomfield - 195

Morand, Second-Lieut. - 103

Morgan - 34

Morningside Park, Harlem, New York, NY, U.S. - 152, 153

Morphey, Thomas W. - 78

Morton
Alfred - 61
Mrs. - 61

Moscowitz, Grover M. - 53

Moses - 81, 98

Moth, Death's Head - 164

motors, fuel-less - 191-196

Mount Vernon, OH, U.S. - 135

Mount Wilson Observatory - 116

Mountsorrel, Leics, England - 127

Mt. Etna, eruption of - 141

Mt. Morris Park, Harlem, N. Y., NY, U.S. - 6, 152, 153

Mulrooney, Police Commissioner - 68, 187

mumiai scare - 41

mummy, growth of hair on the bald head of - 4

Munich, Germany - 162

murder - 3-6, 27, 35, 39, 43, 65, 130, 131, 137, 139, 140, 152
in locked room - 68
poisoning - 84

Murphy - 5

Murray-Aaron, Dr. E. - 37

N

nails, bed of - 162

Nanking (Nanjing), China - 30

Naples, Italy - 143

Nappi, Angelo - 27

Narrative of a Journey to the Shores of a Polar Sea (Franklin) - 118

Nassau County Police Department - 54

National Academy of Sciences - 52, 53

National Asylum, Washington, DC, U.S. - 35

National Laboratory for Psychical Research - 112

Nature - 184

Nauen, Germany - 103, 104

Nebraska, U.S. - 52

nebulae, receding, rates of - 116

Nemko, Alexander - 44

Neumann, Theresa - 160

New Conceptions of Matter (Darwin) - 59

New England, U.S. - 117

New Haven, CT, U.S. - 53

New Jersey, U.S. - 46, 54

New Orleans, LA, U.S. - 19, 118

New York, U.S. - 13, 20, 27, 36, 38, 39, 42, 43, 48, 53, 59, 62, 67, 69, 77, 82, 83, 95, 98, 100, 116, 125, 127, 131, 140, 142, 150, 162, 164, 165, 170, 172, 183, 187, 192, 193

New York State Department of Health - 81

New York State Prison Service - 16

Newark, N.J. - 27, 46

News, Glasgow - 70

News and Courier, Charleston - 65

News and Wansbeck Telegraph,

202